*Psychoanalytic Studies
of the Personality*

PSYCHOANALYTIC STUDIES
OF THE PERSONALITY

by

W. RONALD D. FAIRBAIRN

M.A., M.D., Dipl. Psych. (Edin.)
F.R.S.E., F.R.A.I., F.B.Ps.S.

With a Preface by
Ernest Jones

Tavistock/Routledge/
London and New York

First published in 1952
by Tavistock Publications Limited
in collaboration with
Routledge & Kegan Paul Limited
Reprinted in 1990 by
Routledge
11 New Fetter Lane
London EC4P 4EE

Simultaneously published in the USA and Canada
by Routledge
a division of Routledge, Chapman and Hall Inc.
29 West 35th Street, New York, NY 10001

Printed in Great Britain
Second impression 1962
Third impression 1966
Fourth impression 1972
Fifth impression 1976
Sixth impression 1978
Seventh impression 1981
Eighth impression 1984
Reprinted 1986

ISBN 0-415-05174-6

Preface

D R. FAIRBAIRN'S position in the field of psycho-analysis is a special one and one of great interest. Living hundreds of miles from his nearest colleagues, whom he seldom meets, has great advantages, and also some disadvantages. The main advantage is that, being subject to no distraction or interference, he has been able to concentrate entirely on his own ideas as they develop from his daily working experience. This is a situation that conduces to originality, and Dr. Fairbairn's originality is indisputable. On the other hand, it requires very special powers of self-criticism to dispense with the value of discussion with co-workers, who in the nature of things must be able to point out considerations overlooked by a lonely worker or to modify the risk of any one-sided train of thought. It is not for me to forestall the judgement that will be passed on the contents of the book, but I may be allowed to express the firm opinion that it will surely prove extremely stimulating to thought.

If it were possible to condense Dr. Fairbairn's new ideas into one sentence, it might run somewhat as follows. Instead of starting, as Freud did, from stimulation of the nervous system proceeding from excitation of various erotogenous zones and internal tension arising from gonadic activity, Dr. Fairbairn starts at the centre of the personality, the ego, and depicts its strivings and difficulties in its endeavour to reach an object where it may find support. Dr. Fairbairn has elaborated this theme in the pages that follow, and he has worked out its implications both biologically in regard to the problems of instinct and psychologically in the baffling interchange of external and internal objects. All this constitutes a fresh approach in psycho-analysis which should lead to much fruitful discussion.

ERNEST JONES

Contents

PART ONE

An Object-Relations Theory of the Personality

Contents

PART TWO
Clinical Papers

PART THREE
Miscellaneous Papers

Introduction

THIS book is a collection of various contributions which I have
made from time to time during the course of almost a quarter
of a century in furtherance of the psychoanalytical standpoint
as it has presented itself to me. Most of these contributions have
already been published in the form of articles in scientific journals,
whether medical, psychological or strictly psychoanalytical. A few,
however, have not been previously published. It may be added that
many of the contributions included in the collection were orally presented in the first instance; but in such cases the orally presented
version was commonly an abbreviation of the written version, which
must therefore be regarded as the original. As now presented in the
form of collected papers, the contributions consist in the original
written versions, subjected to such revision as has subsequently
seemed necessary or desirable.

Like Julius Caesar's Gaul, this book is divided into three parts.
Part I comprises a series of papers representing the evolution of a
point of view which derives its distinctive features from the explicit
formulation of (a) an object-relations theory of the personality, and
(b) a psychology of dynamic structure. This particular series of
papers has been entitled 'An Object-Relations Theory of the Personality' in order to indicate its principal theme; and the title of the
book itself has been selected with a special orientation towards the
papers comprised in this series, since I consider them to be the most
important in the whole collection. Part II, entitled 'Clinical Papers',
contains three clinical studies. No special comment is required here
except in the case of the paper entitled 'Features in the Analysis of a
Patient with a Physical Genital Abnormality'. This paper is of some
special interest in that, although actually written as early as in 1931, it
can now be seen to have adumbrated some of the views formulated
in the recent series of papers contained in Part I. Part III, entitled

Introduction

'Miscellaneous Papers', comprises four papers which have little in common apart from their general psychoanalytical orientation. They were addressed to audiences of a varying nature; and the nature of all these audiences required that they should be less technical than the papers comprised in the other parts of this book.

It will be observed by the reader that the papers as a whole are not arranged in chronological order, but that within each part the arrangement is chronological. This method of arrangement commended itself to me on the grounds that both community of subject-matter (as in Part I) and mode of treatment (as in Part II) should be accorded precedence over exclusively chronological considerations, since otherwise continuity of interest would be sacrificed and the general effect would be that of an unsolved jig-saw puzzle. The arrangement adopted seems to me to have special advantages where the papers contained in Part I are concerned. These papers constitute a series; and I feel it very necessary to draw attention to the fact that this series of papers represents, *not the elaboration of an already established point of view, but the progressive development of a line of thought*. In other words, the series embodies the actual working out of a point of view, step by step. One of the inevitable consequences of this fact is that certain of the views expressed at later stages in the series will be found to conflict with views expressed at earlier stages; and this is certainly a disadvantage. Once the evolutionary nature of the series has been recognized, however, very few of the contradictions which have arisen will be regarded as of serious moment, since in most cases the reasons for the replacement of one view by another are clearly stated in the argument in favour of the later view. Unfortunately this does not hold true in every case; and, when I addressed myself to the task of revising these papers for publication, I found one or two serious contradictions which had remained unresolved. I have attempted to remedy this state of affairs both in the 'Addendum' to 'Endopsychic Structure considered in terms of Object-Relationships' and in the final paragraph of 'A Synopsis of the Development of the Author's Views regarding the Structure of the Personality'; and I hope that I have been successful in my attempt. Another unfortunate, albeit less serious, consequence of the fact that this series of papers represents the actual working out of a point of view is that a certain amount of repetition has occurred. In some cases such repetition is, of course, necessitated by the nature of the paper in which it occurs—as in the case of the 'Synopsis' to which reference has just

Introduction

been made, and in the case of 'Steps in the Development of an Object-Relations Theory of the Personality'. In other cases, however, the repetition is relatively incidental and arises out of the occasional nature of the papers as originally written (and only now collected in a series). At first sight it might seem an easy task to eliminate such repetition; but attempts to undertake this task soon proved to me that it would destroy the balance of the papers in which such an attempt seemed indicated—even when the repetition was not so inextricably bound up with the argument as to render its elimination impossible. It was soon borne home to me that the occurrence of both contradictions and repetitions could only be avoided if I jettisoned the whole series of papers in their present form and embodied their content systematically in a fresh work. This would have involved a major task which circumstances rendered it quite impossible for me to undertake in the foreseeable future. I accordingly decided to content myself with subjecting the papers to minor revision; and I was influenced in this decision by the beneficent pressure of requests from many quarters that my papers should be rendered more readily accessible than has hitherto been the case. I feel to some extent reconciled to this 'Hobson's choice' of the easier course by the reflection that, where the development of a special line of thought is concerned, study of the various steps by which it is gradually evolved is not just a matter of historical interest, but actually an aid to the understanding of the conclusions reached, and to the assessment of their value.

Finally I desire to acknowledge my indebtedness to the proprietors and editors of the following journals for permission to incorporate in this volume articles which have appeared in the journals concerned: *The International Journal of Psycho-Analysis*, *The British Journal of Medical Psychology*, the *British Medical Journal*, and the *Edinburgh Medical Journal*. I should also like to make grateful acknowledgement of the part played by the agencies of the Tavistock Institute of Human Relations in promoting the publication of this book.

PART ONE

An Object-Relations Theory of the Personality

CHAPTER I

Schizoid Factors in the Personality (1940)[1]

MENTAL processes of a schizoid nature have latterly come to occupy my attention to an increasing degree; and cases in which such processes are sufficiently marked to impart a recognizably schizoid complexion to the personality now seem to me to provide the most interesting and fruitful material in the whole field of psychopathology. Amongst various considerations supporting this point of view, the following may be selected for special mention: (1) Since schizoid conditions constitute the most deep-seated of all psychopathological states, they provide an unrivalled opportunity for the study not only of the foundations of the personality, but also of the most basic mental processes. (2) The therapeutic analysis of the schizoid case provides an opportunity for the study of the widest range of psychopathological processes in a single individual; for in such cases it is usual for the final state to be reached only after all available methods of defending the personality have been exploited. (3) Contrary to common belief, schizoid individuals who have not regressed too far are capable of greater psychological insight than any other class of person, normal or abnormal—a fact due, in part at least, to their being so introverted (i.e. preoccupied with inner reality) and so familiar with their own deeper psychological processes (processes which, although not absent in individuals who would ordinarily be classified as simply 'psychoneurotic', are nevertheless excluded from the consciousness of such individuals by the most obstinate defences and stubborn resistances). (4) Again contrary to common belief, schizoid individuals show themselves capable of transference to a remarkable degree, and present unexpectedly favourable therapeutic possibilities.

[1] An abbreviated version of this paper was read before the Scottish Branch of the British Psychological Society on 9th November 1940.

3

So far as overtly schizoid conditions are concerned, the following groups may be differentiated:

(1) Schizophrenia proper.

(2) The Psychopathic Personality of a Schizoid Type—a group which may well comprise the majority of cases of psychopathic personality (not excluding epileptic personalities).

(3) The Schizoid Character—a large group comprising individuals whose personalities embody definitely schizoid traits, but who could not reasonably be regarded as psychopathic.

(4) The Schizoid State or transient schizoid episode—a category under which, in my opinion, a considerable proportion of adolescent 'nervous breakdowns' fall.

Apart from these overtly schizoid conditions, however, it is common to find features of a basically schizoid nature displayed by patients whose presenting symptoms are essentially psychoneurotic (e.g. hysterical, phobic, obsessional, or simply anxious). Such features, when present, are, of course, specially liable to emerge when the psychoneurotic defences by which the personality has been protected become weakened in the course of (and through the agency of) analytical treatment; but increasing familiarity with the underlying schizoid background renders it increasingly possible for the analyst to detect the presence of schizoid features in the initial interview. In this connection it is interesting to note the incidence of hysterical and obsessional symptoms in the previous history of thirty-two schizophrenics included in a series of 100 psychiatric cases studied by Masserman and Carmichael (*Journal of Mental Science*, Vol. LXXXIV, pp. 893–946). These authors found that 'in no less than fifteen of the thirty-two patients there was a definite history of hysterical symptoms which preceded the development of the more frankly schizophrenic syndrome'; and regarding the incidence of obsessions and compulsions they remark, 'These also occurred with the greatest frequency in the schizophrenics'—obsessions being found to be present in eighteen, and compulsions in twenty of the thirty-two cases. It may be of interest to add that, in a series of military cases which has come under my own observation, 50 per cent of those finally diagnosed as 'Schizophrenia' or 'Schizoid Personality' were submitted for investigation with a provisional diagnosis of either 'anxiety neurosis' or 'hysteria'. Whilst such figures are suggestive as an indication of the extent to which psychoneurotic defences are employed by the frankly schizoid patient in a vain attempt to defend his personality, they give no indication of the extent to which an under-lying schizoid trend may be masked by the success of such defences.

Once the prevalence of essentially schizoid features has come to be recognized in cases in which the presenting symptoms are ostensibly psychoneurotic, it becomes possible in the course of analytical treat-ment to detect the presence of similar features in a number of individuals who seek analytical aid on account of difficulties to which it is difficult to attach any definite psychopathological labels. To be included in this group are many of those who consult the analyst on account of such disabilities as social inhibitions, inability to concen-trate on work, problems of character, perverse sexual tendencies, and psychosexual difficulties such as impotence and compulsive mastur-bation. The group also includes most of those who complain of apparently isolated symptoms (e.g. fear of insanity or exhibitionistic anxiety), or who display a desire for analytical treatment on appar-ently inadequate grounds (e.g. 'because I feel it would do me good' or 'because it would be interesting'). It likewise includes all those who enter the consulting-room with a mysterious or mystified air, and who open the conversation either with a quotation from Freud or with such a remark as 'I don't really know why I have come'.

On the basis of an analytical study of cases belonging to the various categories which have now been mentioned, it becomes possible to recognize as essentially schizoid not only such phenomena as full-fledged depersonalization and derealization, but also relatively minor or transient disturbances of the reality-sense, e.g. feelings of 'artifi-ciality' (whether referred to the self or the environment), experi-ences such as 'the plate-glass feeling', feelings of unfamiliarity with familiar persons or environmental settings, and feelings of familiarity with the unfamiliar. Allied to the sense of familiarity with the un-familiar is the experience of 'déjà vu'—an interesting phenomenon which must likewise be regarded as involving a schizoid process. A similar view must be taken of such dissociative phenomena as somnambulism, the fugue, dual personality, and multiple person-ality. So far as the manifestations of dual and multiple personality are concerned, their essentially schizoid nature may be inferred from a discreet study of the numerous cases described by Janet, William James, and Morton Prince. And here it is apposite to remark that many of the cases described by Janet as manifesting the dissociative phenomena on the basis of which he formulated his classic concept of 'Hysteria' behaved suspiciously like schizophrenics—a fact which I interpret in support of the conclusion, which I have already reached on the basis of my own observations, that the personality of the hysteric invariably contains a schizoid factor in greater or lesser degree, however deeply this may be buried.

When the connotation of the term 'schizoid' is extended through an enlargement of our conception of schizoid phenomena in the manner indicated, the denotation of the term inevitably undergoes a corresponding extension; and the resulting schizoid group is then seen to become a very comprehensive one. It is found, for example, to include a high percentage of fanatics, agitators, criminals, revolutionaries, and other disruptive elements in every community. Schizoid characteristics, usually in a less pronounced form, are also common among members of the intelligentsia. Thus the disdain of the highbrow for the bourgeoisie and the scorn of the esoteric artist for the philistine may be regarded as minor manifestations of a schizoid nature. It is further to be noted that intellectual pursuits as such, whether literary, artistic, scientific, or otherwise, appear to exercise a special attraction for individuals possessing schizoid characteristics to one degree or another. Where scientific pursuits are concerned, the attraction would appear to depend upon the schizoid individual's attitude of detachment no less than upon his overvaluation of the thought-processes; for these are both characteristics which readily lend themselves to capitalization within the field of science. The obsessional appeal of science, based as this is upon the presence of a compulsive need for orderly arrangement and meticulous accuracy, has, of course, long been recognized; but the schizoid appeal is no less definite and demands at least equal recognition. Finally the statement may be hazarded that a number of outstanding historical figures lend themselves to the interpretation that they were either schizoid personalities or schizoid characters; and indeed it would appear as if it were often such who leave a mark upon the page of history.

Among the various characteristics common to the apparently conglomerate group of individuals who fall under the schizoid category as now envisaged three are of sufficient prominence to deserve special mention. These are (1) an attitude of omnipotence, (2) an attitude of isolation and detachment, and (3) a preoccupation with inner reality. It is important, however, to bear in mind that these characteristics are by no means necessarily overt. Thus the attitude of omnipotence may be conscious or unconscious in any degree. It may

6

also be localized within certain spheres of operation. It may be over-compensated and concealed under a superficial attitude of inferiority or humility; and it may be consciously cherished as a precious secret. Similarly the attitude of isolation and detachment may be masked by a façade of sociability or by the adoption of specific roles; and it may be accompanied by considerable emotionality in certain contexts. So far as the preoccupation with inner reality is concerned, this is un-doubtedly the most important of all schizoid characteristics; and it is none the less present whether inner reality be substituted for outer reality, identified with outer reality or superimposed upon outer reality.

It will not escape notice that the concept of 'Schizoid' which emerges from the preceding considerations corresponds remarkably closely, particularly where its denotation is concerned, to the concept of the 'Introvert' type as formulated by Jung; and it is significant that in one of his earlier writings (*Collected Papers on Analytical Psychology* (1917), p. 347) Jung expressed the view that the incidence of schizo-phrenia ('dementia praecox') was confined to the introvert type, thus indicating recognition on his part of an association between intro-version and schizoid developments. The correspondence between Jung's concept of 'Introvert' and the concept of 'Schizoid' as now envisaged is not without interest in so far as it provides confirmation of the actual existence of the group described, particularly since the two concepts were reached by completely independent paths. Recognition of such a correspondence does not, of course, imply any acceptance on my part of Jung's theory of fundamental psychological types. Indeed, on the contrary, my conception of the schizoid group is based upon a consideration, not of temperamental, but of strictly psychopathological factors. At the same time it may appear to some that, for purposes of describing the group in question, the term 'introvert' would be preferable to that of 'schizoid' in view of the somewhat sinister associations which have become attached to the latter term as the result of its original use. Yet, of the two terms, 'schizoid' has the inestimable advantage that, unlike the term 'intro-vert', it is not simply descriptive, but is explanatory in a psycho-genetic sense.

The criticism for which I must now prepare myself is that, accord-ing to my way of thinking, everybody without exception must be regarded as schizoid. Actually I am quite prepared to accept this criticism, but only with a very important qualification—one in the absence of which my concept of 'Schizoid' would be so comprehensive as to become almost meaningless. The qualification which confers meaning on the concept is that everything depends upon the mental level which is being considered. The fundamental schizoid phenomenon is the presence of splits in the ego; and it would take a bold man to claim that his ego was so perfectly integrated as to be incapable of revealing any evidence of splitting at the deepest levels, or that such evidence of splitting of the ego could in no circumstances declare itself at more superficial levels, even under conditions of extreme suffering or hardship or deprivation (e.g. under conditions of grave illness, or of Arctic exploration, or of exposure in an open boat in mid-Pacific, or of relentless persecution, or of prolonged subjection to the horrors of modern warfare). The all-important factor here is the mental depth which requires to be plumbed before evidence of splitting of the ego declares itself. In my opinion, at any rate, some measure of splitting of the ego is invariably present at the deepest mental level—or (to express the same thing in terms borrowed from Melanie Klein) *the basic position in the psyche is invariably a schizoid position*. This would not hold true, of course, in the case of a theoretically perfect person whose development had been optimum; but then there is really nobody who enjoys such a happy lot. Indeed it is difficult to imagine any person with an ego so unified and stable at its higher levels that in no circumstances whatever would any evidence of basic splitting come to the surface in recognizable form. There are probably few 'normal' people who have never at any time in their lives experienced an unnatural state of calm and detachment in face of some serious crisis, or a transient sense of 'looking on at oneself' in some embarrassing or paralysing situation; and probably most people have had some experience of that strange confusion of past and present, or of phantasy and reality, known as 'déjà vu'. And such phenomena, I venture to suggest, are essentially schizoid phenomena. There is one universal phenomenon, however, which proves quite conclusively that everyone without exception is schizoid at the deeper levels—viz. the dream; for, as Freud's researches have shown, the dreamer himself is commonly represented in the dream by two or more separate figures. Here I may say that the view which I myself have now come to adopt is to the effect that all figures appearing in dreams represent either (1) some part of the dreamer's personality, or (2) an object with whom some part of his personality has a relationship, commonly on a basis of identification, in inner reality. Be

8

that as it may, the fact that the dreamer is characteristically represented in the dream by more than one figure is capable of no other interpretation except that, at the level of the dreaming consciousness, the ego of the dreamer is split. The dream thus represents a universal schizoid phenomenon. The universal phenomenon of 'the super-ego' as described by Freud must also be interpreted as implying the presence of a split in the ego; for, in so far as 'the super-ego' is regarded as an ego-structure capable of distinction from 'the ego' as such, its very existence *ipso facto* provides evidence that a schizoid position has been established.

The conception of splitting of the ego, from which the term 'schizoid' derives its significance, can only be regarded as an illuminating conception when it is considered from a psychogenetic standpoint. It is, therefore, necessary to consider very briefly what is involved in the development of the ego. The function of the ego upon which Freud has laid most stress is its *adaptive* function—the function which it performs in relating primal instinctive activity to conditions prevailing in outer reality, and more particularly social conditions. It must be remembered, however, that the ego also performs *integrative* functions, among the most important of which are (1) the integration of perceptions of reality, and (2) the integration of behaviour. Another important function of the ego is discrimination between inner and outer reality. Splitting of the ego has the effect of compromising the progressive development of all these functions, although, of course, in varying degrees and varying proportions. Accordingly, we must recognize the possibility of development resulting in all degrees of integration of the ego; and we may conceive a theoretic scale of integration such that one end of the scale represents complete integration and the other end represents complete failure of integration, with all intermediate degrees. On such a scale schizophrenics would find a place towards the lower end, schizoid personalities a higher place, schizoid characters a still higher place, and so on; but a place at the very top of the scale, which would represent perfect integration and absence of splitting, must be regarded as only a theoretical possibility. If we keep such a scale in mind, it should help us to understand how it would be possible for any individual to display some schizoid feature under sufficiently extreme conditions, and how it comes about that some individuals manifest evidence of a split in the ego only in situations involving such readjustments as are involved in adolescence, marriage, or joining the army in wartime, whereas others again may manifest such evidence even under the most ordinary conditions of life. In actual practice, of course, the construction of a scale such as that just imagined would involve quite insuperable difficulties, of which only one is that arising out of the fact that quite a number of schizoid manifestations, as indeed Freud pointed out, are really defences against the splitting of the ego. However, it helps us to appreciate the general position as regards splitting of the ego if we envisage an imaginary scale of this sort.

Although, in conformity with the implications of Bleuler's classic conception of 'schizophrenia', we must regard splitting of the ego as the most characteristic schizoid phenomenon, psychoanalysts have always concerned themselves more with (and indeed have largely confined their attention to) the libidinal orientation involved in the schizoid attitude; and, under the influence of Abraham's psychogenetic theory of libidinal development, clinical manifestations of a schizoid order have come to be regarded as originating in a fixation in the early oral phase. It is presumably during this first phase of life, and under the influence of its vicissitudes upon the undeveloped and inexperienced infant, that splitting of the ego commences to occur; and there must thus be a very close association between splitting of the ego and a libidinal attitude of oral incorporation. In my opinion, the problems involved in splitting of the ego deserve much more attention than they have so far received; and some indication of the importance which I attach to these problems may be gathered from what has already been said so far. In what follows, however, I propose to consider some of the developments which appear to depend upon, or to be powerfully influenced by, a fixation in the early oral phase, and which thus play a prominent part in determining the pattern of the schizoid attitude.

The ego of the infant may be described as above all a 'mouth ego'; and, whilst this fact exercises a profound influence upon the subsequent development of every individual, the influence is particularly marked in the case of those who subsequently display schizoid characteristics. So far as the infant is concerned, the mouth is the chief organ of desire, the chief instrument of activity, the chief medium of satisfaction and frustration, the chief channel of love and hate, and, most important of all, the first means of intimate social contact. The first social relationship established by the individual is that between himself and his mother; and the focus of this relationship is the suckling situation, in which his mother's breast provides the focal point of his libidinal object, and his mouth the focal point of his own libidinal attitude. Accordingly, the nature of the relationship so established exercises a profound influence upon the subsequent relationships of the individual, and upon his subsequent social attitude in general. When circumstances are such as to give rise to a libidinal fixation in the early oral situation in question, the libidinal attitude appropriate to the early oral phase persists in an exaggerated form and gives rise to far-reaching effects; and the nature of these effects may perhaps best be considered in the light of the chief features which characterize the early oral attitude itself. These may be summarized as follows:

(1) Although the emotional relationship involved is essentially one between the child and his mother as a person, and although it must be recognized that his libidinal object is really his mother as a whole, nevertheless his libidinal interest is essentially focused upon her breast; and the result is that, in proportion as disturbances in the relationship occur, the breast itself tends to assume the role of libidinal object; i.e. the libidinal object tends to assume the form of a bodily organ or *partial object* (in contrast to that of a person or whole object).

(2) The libidinal attitude is essentially one in which the aspect of '*taking*' predominates over that of '*giving*'.

(3) The libidinal attitude is one characterized, not only by taking, but also by *incorporating and internalizing.*

(4) The libidinal situation is one which confers tremendous significance upon the states of *fullness and emptiness.* Thus, when the child is hungry, he is, and presumably feels, empty; and, when he has been fed to his satisfaction, he is, and presumably feels, full. On the other hand, his mother's breast, and presumably from the child's point of view his mother herself, is normally full before, and empty after suckling—maternal conditions which the child must be capable of appreciating in terms of his own experience of fullness and emptiness. In circumstances of deprivation, emptiness comes to assume quite special significance for the child. Not only does he feel empty himself, but he also interprets the situation in the sense that he has emptied his mother—particularly since deprivation has the effect not only of intensifying his oral need, but also of imparting an aggressive quality to it. Deprivation has the additional effect of enlarging the field of his incorporative need, so that it comes to include not simply the contents of the breast, but also the breast itself, and even his

mother as a whole. The anxiety which he experiences over emptying the breast thus gives rise to *anxiety over destroying his libidinal object*; and the fact that his mother customarily leaves him after suckling must have the effect of contributing to this impression. Consequently his libidinal attitude acquires for him the implication that it involves the disappearance and destruction of his libidinal object—an implication which tends to become confirmed at a later stage when he learns that food which is eaten disappears from the external world, and that he cannot both eat his cake and have it.

These various features of the libidinal attitude which characterizes the early oral phase become intensified and perpetuated in proportion as a fixation in this phase occurs; and they all operate as factors in determining schizoid characterology and symptomatology. In what follows consideration will be given to some of the developments to which each of these factors in turn would appear to give rise.

I. THE TENDENCY TO ORIENTATION TOWARDS A PARTIAL OBJECT (BODILY ORGAN)

Let us first consider the influence of this factor in the early oral attitude. Its effect is to promote the schizoid tendency to treat other people as less than persons with an inherent value of their own. Such a tendency may be illustrated in the case of a highly intelligent man of a schizoid type, who came to consult me because he felt that he could make no real emotional contact with his wife, was unduly critical towards her and was morose with her on occasions when a display of affection would have been more appropriate. After describing his very selfish attitude towards her, he added that his habits were unsociable in general, and that he treated other people more or less as if they were lower animals. From this last remark it was not difficult to detect one source of his difficulties. It will be recalled that animals commonly figure in dreams as symbols of bodily organs; and this only serves to confirm that his attitude towards his wife, as well as towards others, was that towards a partial object, and not towards a person. A similar attitude was revealed in a frankly schizophrenic patient, who described his attitude towards people whom he met as like that of an anthropologist among a tribe of savages. Somewhat analogous was the attitude displayed by a soldier whose history showed that he had always been a schizoid personality, and who passed into an acute schizoid state during the course of military service in wartime. His mother had died in his early childhood; and the only parent whom he could remember was his father. He had left home shortly after his schooling was finished; and he had never communicated with his father since. Indeed he did not know whether his father was alive or dead. For years he lived a roving and unsettled life; but eventually it occurred to him that it would do him good to settle down and marry. This he accordingly did. When I asked him whether he had been happy in his marriage, a look of surprise at my question spread over his face, followed by a rather scornful smile. 'That's what I married for', he replied in a superior tone, as if that provided a sufficient answer. Whilst this reply, of course, provides an illustration of the schizoid failure to discriminate adequately between inner and outer reality, it also serves to illustrate the tendency of those with schizoid characteristics to treat libidinal objects as means of satisfying their own requirements rather than as persons possessing inherent value; and this is a tendency which springs from the persistence of an early oral orientation towards the breast as a partial object.

Here it may be remarked that the orientation towards partial objects found in individuals displaying schizoid features is largely a regressive phenomenon determined by unsatisfactory emotional relationships with their parents, and particularly their mothers, at a stage in childhood subsequent to the early oral phase in which this orientation originates. The type of mother who is specially prone to provoke such a regression is the mother who fails to convince her child by spontaneous and genuine expressions of affection that she herself loves him as a person. Both possessive mothers and indifferent mothers fall under this category. Worst of all perhaps is the mother who conveys the impression of both possessiveness and indifference —e.g. the devoted mother who is determined at all costs not to spoil her only son. Failure on the part of the mother to convince the child that she really loves him as a person renders it difficult for him to sustain an emotional relationship with her on a personal basis; and the result is that, in order to simplify the situation, he tends regressively to restore the relationship to its earlier and simpler form and revive his relationship to his mother's breast as a partial object. A regression of this sort may be illustrated by the case of a schizophrenic youth who, whilst evincing the bitterest antagonism towards his actual mother, dreamed of lying in bed in a room from the ceiling of which there poured a stream of milk—the room in question being a room in his home just beneath his mother's bedroom. This type of regressive process may perhaps best be described as *Depersonalization of the Object*; and it is characteristically accompanied by a regression in the quality of the relationship desired. Here again the regressive movement is in the interests of a simplification of relationships; and it takes the form of a substitution of bodily for emotional contacts. It may perhaps be described as *De-emotionalization of the Object-relationship*.

2. PREDOMINANCE OF TAKING OVER GIVING IN THE LIBIDINAL ATTITUDE

In conformity with the predominance of taking over giving in the early oral attitude, individuals with a schizoid tendency experience considerable difficulty over giving in the emotional sense. In this connection it is interesting to recall that, if the oral incorporative tendency is the most fundamental of all tendencies, those next in importance for the organism are the excretory activities (defaecation and urination). The biological aim of the excretory activities is, of course, the elimination of useless and noxious substances from the body; but, although, in conformity with their biological aim, the child soon learns to regard them as the classic means of dealing with bad libidinal objects, their earliest psychological significance for him would appear to be that of creative activities. They represent the first creative activities of the individual; and their products are his first creations—the first internal contents that he externalizes, the first things belonging to himself that he gives. In this respect the excretory activities stand in contrast to oral activity, which essentially involves an attitude of taking. This particular contrast between the two groups of libidinal activity must not be taken to preclude the coexistence of another contrast between them in an opposite sense; for there is, of course, also a respect in which the oral incorporative attitude towards an object implies valuation of the object, whereas the excretory attitude towards an object implies its devaluation and rejection. What is relevant for the immediate purpose, however, is the fact that, at a deep mental level, taking is emotionally equivalent to amassing bodily contents, and giving is emotionally equivalent to parting with bodily contents. It is further relevant that, at a deep mental level, there is an emotional equivalence between mental and bodily contents, with the result that the individual's attitude towards the latter tends to be reflected in his attitude towards the former. In the case of the individual with a schizoid tendency, accordingly, there is an over-valuation of mental contents corresponding to the over-valuation of bodily contents implied in the oral incorporative attitude of early childhood. This over-valuation of mental contents shows itself, for example, in the difficulty experienced by the individual with a schizoid tendency over expressing emotion in a social context. For such an individual, that element of giving which is involved in expressing emotion towards others has the significance of losing contents; and it is for this reason that he so often finds social contacts exhausting. Thus, if he is long in company, he is liable to feel that 'virtue has gone out of him', and that he requires a period of quiet and solitude afterwards in order that the inner storehouse of emotion may have an opportunity to be replenished. Thus one of my patients felt unable to make dates with his prospective fiancée on consecutive days on the grounds that, when he met her too often, he felt his personality to be impoverished. In the case of those with whom the schizoid tendency is marked, defence against emotional loss gives rise to *repression of affect* and an attitude of detachment which leads others to regard them as remote—and, in more extreme cases, even as inhuman. Such individuals are commonly described as 'shut in personalities'; and, in view of the extent to which they keep their emotional contents shut in, the description is singularly apt. Anxiety over emotional loss sometimes manifests itself in curious ways. Take, for example, the case of a young man seeking analysis, in whom I detected at the first consultation that vaguely mysterious air which I have come to regard as pathognomonic of an underlying schizoid tendency, and which is so often accompanied by inability to describe any concrete symptoms. This patient was a university under-graduate; and in his case the objective problem consisted in repeated failure to pass examinations. Oral examinations presented a special difficulty for him; and a striking feature of this difficulty was that, even when he really knew the correct answer to a question, he was usually unable to *give* it. It will be obvious, of course, that problems over his relationship with his father were involved; but the form assumed by this particular difficulty derived its significance from the fact that, so far as he was concerned, giving the correct answer represented giving the examiner something which had only been acquired (i.e. internalized) with difficulty, and so parting with something too *precious* to be lost. In an attempt to overcome difficulties involved for them in emotional giving, individuals with a schizoid propensity avail themselves of various techniques, of which two may be mentioned here. These are: (*a*) the technique of playing roles, and (*b*) the technique of exhibitionism.

(*a*) *The Technique of Playing Roles*

By playing a role or acting an adopted part, the schizoid individual is often able to express quite a lot of feeling and to make what appear to be quite impressive social contacts; but, in doing so, he is really giving nothing and losing nothing, because, since he is only playing a part, his own personality is not involved. Secretly he disowns the part which he is playing; and he thus seeks to preserve his own personality intact and immune from compromise. It should be added, however, that, whilst in some cases parts are played quite consciously, in other cases the individual is quite unconscious of the fact that he is playing a part and only comes to realize this in the course of analytical treatment. Conscious playing of a part may be illustrated in the case of a markedly schizoid young man who entered my consulting-room for the first consultation with a quotation from Freud upon his lips. He thus sought from the start to establish himself in my eyes as a devotee of psychoanalysis; but my immediate suspicion that he was only playing a part was fully confirmed as soon as analytical treatment commenced. His adopted role was really a defence against genuine emotional contact with me, and against genuine emotional giving.

(*b*) *The Exhibitionistic Technique*

Exhibitionistic trends always play a prominent part in the schizoid mentality; and, of course, they are closely related to the tendency to adopt roles. They may be largely unconscious; and they are often masked by anxiety. Even so, however, they emerge quite clearly in the course of analytical treatment; and the attraction of literary and artistic activities for individuals with a schizoid propensity is partly due to the fact that these activities provide an exhibitionistic means of expression without involving direct social contact. The significance of the exploitation of exhibitionism as a defence lies in the fact that it represents a technique for giving without giving, by means of a substitution of 'showing' for 'giving'. This means of attempting to solve the problem of giving without losing is not without its attendant difficulties, however; for the anxiety originally attached to the act of giving is liable to become transferred to the act of showing, with the result that 'showing off' assumes the quality of 'showing up'. When this happens, exhibitionistic situations may become extremely painful; and 'being seen' at all may then give rise to acute self-consciousness. The connection between giving and showing may be illustrated by the reaction of an unmarried female patient with a schizoid component in her personality after reading in the paper one morning in 1940 that a German bomb had fallen in the vicinity of my house during the night. It was plain to her from the newspaper account that the bomb had fallen at a sufficient distance from my house to ensure that I would be safe; and she experienced a tremendous sense of thankfulness over this fact. Her emotional reserve was such, however, that she could not bring herself to give any direct expression to feelings about me which she nevertheless wanted to express. What she did, in an attempt to get round this difficulty, at the next session was to hand me a piece of paper on which she had written down, at the cost of considerable effort, some information about *herself*. Thus she did give me something; but what she gave me was a view of herself, so to speak, reflected on paper. Actually, what was registered in this instance was a certain advance from an attitude of showing in the direction of an attitude of giving; for after all, in an indirect fashion, she did give me mental contents, to which she attached great narcissistic value, and with which she found it an effort to part. There was also registered a certain advance from a narcissistic valuation of her own mental contents in the direction of a valuation of me as an external object and as a person. In the light of this incident it is not surprising that analysis revealed in this case a tremendous conflict over parting with bodily contents.

3. THE INCORPORATIVE FACTOR IN THE LIBIDINAL ATTITUDE

The early oral attitude is one characterized, not only by taking, but also by incorporating or internalizing. Regressive reinstatement of the early oral attitude would appear to be most readily brought about by a situation of emotional frustration in which the child comes to feel (*a*) that he is not really loved for himself as a person by his mother, and (*b*) that his own love for his mother is not really valued and accepted by her. This is a highly traumatic situation giving rise to a further situation characterized as follows:

(*a*) The child comes to regard his mother as a bad object in so far as she does not seem to love him.

(*b*) The child comes to regard outward expressions of his own love as bad, with the result that, in an attempt to keep his love as good as possible, he tends to retain his love inside himself.

(*c*) The child comes to feel that love relationships with external objects in general are bad, or at least precarious.

The net result is that the child tends to transfer his relationships with his objects to the realm of inner reality. This is a realm in which his mother and her breast have already been installed as internalized objects under the influence of situations of frustration during the early oral phase; and, under the influence of subsequent situations of frustration, internalization of objects is further exploited as a defensive technique. This process of internalization is promoted, if not actually instigated, by the very nature of the oral attitude itself; for the inherent aim of the oral impulse is incorporation. The incorporation in question is, of course, originally physical incorporation; but we must believe that the emotional mood accompanying incorporative strivings has itself an incorporative colouring. Hence, when a fixation in the early oral phase occurs, an incorporative attitude inevitably becomes woven into the structure of the ego. In the case of individuals with a schizoid component in their personality, accordingly, there is a great tendency for the outer world to derive its meaning too exclusively from the inner world. In actual schizophrenics this tendency may become so strong that the distinction between inner and outer reality is largely obscured. Such extreme cases apart, however, there is a general tendency on the part of individuals with a schizoid component to heap up their values in the inner world. Not only do their objects tend to belong to the inner rather than to the outer world, but they tend to identify themselves very strongly with their internal objects. This fact contributes materially to the difficulty which they experience in giving emotionally. In the case of individuals whose object-relationships are predominantly in the outer world, giving has the effect of creating and enhancing values, and of promoting self-respect; but, in the case of individuals whose object-relationships are predominantly in the inner world, giving has the effect of depreciating values, and of lowering self-respect. When such individuals give, they tend to feel impoverished, because, when they give, they give at the expense of their inner world. Where a woman of such a nature is concerned, this tendency may lead to tremendous anxiety over childbirth; for to such a woman childbirth signifies not so much the gain of a child, but loss of contents with resulting emptiness. Indeed I have had female patients of this type, in the case of whom deep unwillingness to part with contents has given rise to an extremely difficult labour. In these cases, of course, it is actually a case of parting with bodily contents; but an analogous phenomenon within a more mental sphere may be illustrated in the case of an artist who, after completing a picture, used to feel, not that he had created or gained something as a result, but that virtue had gone out of him. Such a phenomenon goes a long way to explain the periods of sterility and discontent which follow periods of creative activity in the case of certain artists, and which did so in the case of the artist to whom I have referred.

To mitigate a sense of impoverishment following giving and creating, the individual with a schizoid component often employs an interesting defence. He adopts the attitude that what he has given or created is worthless. Thus the artist whose case has just been quoted lost all interest in his pictures once they had been painted; and the completed pictures were characteristically either just dumped in the corner of the studio or treated simply as commodities for sale. In the same way women of a similar mentality sometimes lose all interest in their children after they are born. On the other hand, a totally opposite form of defence against loss of contents may be adopted by individuals with schizoid attributes; for they may attempt to safeguard themselves against a sense of loss by treating what they have produced as if it were still part of their own contents. Thus, so far from being indifferent to her child once he is born, a mother may continue to regard him in the light of her own contents and to overvalue him accordingly. Such mothers are unduly possessive of their children and are unable to accord them the status of separate persons —with grievous consequences for the unfortunate children. Similarly, although with less grievous results, an artist may defend himself against a sense of loss of contents by continuing to regard his pictures as his own possessions, in an unrealistic sense, even after they have been acquired by others. In this connection reference may be made again to that form of defence which consists in a substitution of showing for giving. The artist 'shows' or exhibits his pictures, of course; and, in so doing, he reveals himself indirectly. Similarly, the author reveals himself to the world from a distance through the medium of his books. The various arts thus provide very favourable channels of expression for individuals with a schizoid tendency. For by means of artistic activity they are able both to substitute showing for giving and, at the same time, to produce something which they can still regard as part of themselves even after it has passed from the inner into the outer world.

Another important manifestation of preoccupation with the inner world is a tendency to *intellectualization*; and this is a very characteristic schizoid feature. It constitutes an extremely powerful defensive technique; and it operates as a very formidable resistance in psychoanalytical therapy. Intellectualization implies an over-valuation of the thought processes; and this over-valuation of thought is related to the difficulty which the individual with a schizoid tendency experiences in making emotional contacts with other people. Owing to preoccupation with the inner world and the repression of affect which follows in its train, he has difficulty in expressing his feelings naturally towards others, and in acting naturally and spontaneously in his relations with them. This leads him to make an effort to work out his emotional problems intellectually in the inner world. It would appear that, so far as conscious intention is concerned, his attempts to solve his emotional problems intellectually are meant in the first instance to pave the way for adaptive behaviour in relation to external objects; but, since emotional conflicts springing from deep sources in the unconscious defy solution in this way, he tends increasingly to substitute intellectual solutions of his emotional problems for attempts to achieve a practical solution of them within the emotional sphere in his relationships with others in the outer world. This tendency is, of course, strongly reinforced by the libidinal cathexis of internalized objects. The search for intellectual solutions of what are properly emotional problems thus gives rise to two important developments: (1) The thought processes become highly libidinized; and the world of thought tends to become the predominant sphere of creative activity and self-expression; and (2) ideas tend to become substituted for feelings, and intellectual values for emotional values.

Where actual schizophrenics are concerned, the substitution of ideas for feelings is carried to extreme lengths. When feelings do assert themselves in such cases, they are usually quite out of keeping with ideational content, and quite inappropriate to the occasion; or alternatively, as in catatonic cases, emotional expression assumes the form of sudden and violent outbursts. The adoption of the term 'schizophrenia' was, of course, based in the first instance upon observation of this divorce between thought and feeling, suggestive as it is of a split within the mind. It must now be recognized, however, that the split in question is fundamentally a split in the ego. What manifests itself on the surface as a divorce between thought and feeling must accordingly be construed as the reflection of a split between (1) a more superficial part of the ego representing its higher levels and including the conscious, and (2) a deeper part of the ego representing its lower levels and including those elements which are most highly endowed with libido and are hence the source of affect. From the dynamic psychoanalytical standpoint, such a split can only be explained in terms of repression; and, on this assumption, we can only conclude that it is a case of the deeper and more highly libidinal part of the ego being repressed by the more superficial part of the ego, in which thought processes are more highly developed.

In the case of individuals in whom schizoid features are only present to a lesser degree, the divorce between thought and feeling is, of course, less marked. Nevertheless, there is a characteristic tendency not only towards a substitution of intellectual for emotional values, but also towards a high libidinization of the thought processes. Such individuals are often more inclined to construct intellectual systems of an elaborate kind than to develop emotional relationships with others on a human basis. There is a further tendency on their part to make libidinal objects of the systems which they have created. 'Being in love with love' would appear to be a phenomenon of this nature; and schizoid infatuations often have just such an element in them. Infatuations of this kind may lead to unpleasant enough consequences for the ostensible love-object; but, when we find a really schizoid personality in love with some extreme political philosophy, the consequences become more serious, because the toll of victims may then run into millions. Such a personality, when he is in love with an intellectual system which he interprets rigidly and applies universally, has all the makings of a fanatic—which indeed is what he really is. When, further, such a fanatic has both the inclination and the capacity to take steps to impose his system ruthlessly upon others, the situation may become catastrophic—although at times it may admittedly be potent for good as well as for evil. However, not all those who are in love with an intellectual system have either the desire or the capacity thus to impose their system upon the outer world. Indeed it is far commoner for them to stand aside, in some measure at least, from the life of the everyday world, and to look down from their intellectual retreats upon common humanity with a superior attitude (the attitude adopted, for example, by members of the intelligentsia towards the bourgeoisie).

At this point it is appropriate to draw attention to the fact that, where individuals with a schizoid tendency are concerned, a sense of inner superiority is always present in some degree, even when, as is commonly the case, this is largely unconscious. Quite commonly a considerable resistance has to be overcome before its presence is revealed in the course of analytical treatment; and an even more formidable resistance is encountered when efforts are made to analyse the sources from which it springs. When its sources are uncovered, however, this sense of superiority is found to be based upon: (1) a general *secret* over-valuation of personal contents, mental as well as physical; and (2) a narcissistic inflation of the ego arising out of *secret* possession of, and considerable identification with, internalized libidinal objects (e.g. the maternal breast and the paternal penis). Here it would be difficult to exaggerate the importance of the element of *secrecy*. It is this that accounts for the secretive and mysterious air so commonly displayed by markedly schizoid individuals; but, even in the case of those in whom the schizoid component plays a relatively minor part, it still remains an important factor in the unconscious situation. The inner necessity for secrecy is, of course, partly determined by guilt over the possession of internalized objects which are in a sense 'stolen'; but it is also in no small measure determined by fear of the loss of internalized objects which appear infinitely precious (even precious as life itself), and the internalization of which is a measure of their importance and the extent of dependence upon them. The secret possession of such internalized objects has the effect of leading the individual to feel that he is 'different' from other people —even if not, as often happens, actually exceptional or unique. When this sense of difference from others is investigated, however, it is found to be closely associated with a sense of being 'the odd man out'; and, with individuals in whom it is present, dreams embodying the theme of being left out are a common occurrence. Such an individual is only too frequently found to have been the boy who, although apparently his mother's boy at home, was anything but a boys' boy at school, and who devoted to personal achievement in study the energy which more ordinary boys devoted to participation in school games. Sometimes, it is true, personal achievement may have been sought within the realm of sport. Even so, however, there is usually evidence to show that there has been difficulty over emotional relationships within the group; and, in any case, it remains true that it is towards attainment within the intellectual sphere that attempts to circumvent such difficulties are more commonly directed. Here we can already detect evidence of the operation of the intellectual defence; and it is remarkable how often the previous history of an actual schizophrenic reveals that he (or she) was regarded as a promising scholar during some part at least of his (or her) school career. If we look still further into the sources of that sense of difference from others which characterizes individuals with a schizoid element in their personality, we find evidence of the following among other features: (1) that in early life they gained the conviction, whether through apparent indifference or through apparent possessiveness on the part of their mother, that their mother did not really love and value them as persons in their own right; (2) that, influenced by a resultant sense of deprivation and inferiority, they remained profoundly fixated upon their mother; (3) that the libidinal attitude accompanying this fixation was one not only characterized by extreme dependence, but also rendered highly self-preservative and narcissistic by anxiety over a situation which presented itself as involving a threat to the ego; (4) that, through a regression to the attitude of the early oral phase, not only did the libidinal cathexis of an already internalized 'breast-mother' become intensified, but also the process of internalization itself became unduly extended to relationships with other objects; and (5) that there resulted a general over-valuation of the internal at the expense of the external world.

4. EMPTYING OF THE OBJECT AS AN IMPLICATION OF THE LIBIDINAL ATTITUDE

Emptying of the object is an implication of the incorporative quality of the early oral attitude; and, when attention was drawn to this feature earlier (pp. 11–12), some account was given of its psychological consequences for the child. Thus it was pointed out how, in circumstances of deprivation, the anxiety which arises in the child's mind over his own emptiness gives rise to anxiety over emptiness affecting his mother's breast. It was also pointed out how he comes to interpret any apparent or actual emptiness of his mother's breast as due to his own incorporative strivings, and how he thus comes to entertain anxiety over being responsible for the disappearance and destruction, not simply of his mother's breast, but of his mother herself—anxiety considerably increased by the effect of deprivation in imparting an aggressive quality to his libidinal need. Such anxiety finds a classic expression in the fairy tale of 'Little Red Riding Hood'. In the story, it will be remembered, the little girl finds to her horror that the grandmother whom she loves has disappeared, and that she is left alone with her own incorporative need in the form of a devouring wolf. The tragedy of Little Red Riding Hood is the tragedy of the child in the early oral phase. Of course, the fairy tale has a happy ending, as fairy tales do. And, of course, the infant does discover that the mother, whom he fears he has eaten up, does eventually reappear again. Nevertheless, in their infancy children, although they do not lack intelligence, yet lack the organized experience from which they might otherwise derive reassurance against their anxiety. In due course they acquire sufficient conscious knowledge to realize that in actual fact their mothers do not disappear in consequence of the apparent destructiveness of their incorporative needs; and the whole experience of the traumatic situation arising out of deprivation during the early oral phase becomes subjected to repression. At the same time the anxiety attached to this situation persists in the unconscious, ready to be reactivated by any subsequent experience of an analogous kind. In the presence of a marked fixation in the early oral phase, the traumatic situation is particularly liable to be reactivated if the child later comes to feel that he is not really loved and valued as a person by his mother, and that she does not really appreciate and accept his love as good.

It is important to bear in mind the distinction between the situation which arises in the early oral phase and that which arises during the late oral phase, when the biting tendency emerges and takes its place side by side with the sucking tendency. In the late oral phase there occurs a differentiation between oral love, associated with sucking, and oral hate, associated with biting; and the development of ambivalence is a consequence of this. The early oral phase is pre-ambivalent; and this fact is specially important in the light of the further fact that the oral behaviour of the child during this pre-ambivalent phase represents the individual's first way of expressing love. The child's oral relationship with his mother in the situation of suckling represents his first experience of a love relationship, and is, therefore, the foundation upon which all his future relationships with love objects are based. It also represents his first experience of a social

24

relationship; and it therefore forms the basis of his subsequent attitude to society. Bearing these considerations in mind, let us return to the situation which arises when the child who is fixated in the early oral phase comes to feel that he is not really loved and valued as a person by his mother, and that she does not really appreciate and accept his love as good. What happens in these circumstances is that the original traumatic situation of the early oral phase becomes emotionally reactivated and reinstated; and the child then feels that the reason for his mother's apparent lack of love towards him is that he has destroyed her affection and made it disappear. At the same time he feels that the reason for her apparent refusal to accept his love is that his own love is destructive and bad. This is, of course, an infinitely more intolerable situation than the comparable situation which arises in the case of a child fixated in the late oral phase. In the latter case the child, being essentially ambivalent, interprets the situation in the sense that it is his hate, and not his love, that has destroyed his mother's affection. It is then in his hate that his badness seems to him to reside; and his love is thus able to remain good in his eyes. This is the position which would appear to underlie the manic-depressive psychosis, and to constitute the depressive position. By contrast the position underlying schizoid developments would appear to be one arising in the pre-ambivalent early oral phase—the position in which the individual feels that his love is bad because it appears destructive towards his libidinal objects; and this may be appropriately described as *the schizoid position*. It represents an essentially tragic situation; and it provides the theme of many of the great tragedies of literature, as well as providing a favourite theme for poetry (as in the case of the 'Lucy' poems of Wordsworth). It is small wonder then that individuals with any considerable schizoid tendency experience such difficulty in showing love; for they always entertain the deep anxiety expressed by Oscar Wilde in *The Ballad of Reading Gaol* when he wrote, 'Each man kills the thing he loves'. It is small wonder too that they experience difficulty in emotional giving; for they can never entirely escape the fear that their gifts are deadly, like the gifts of a Borgia. Hence the remark of a patient of mine, who, after bringing me a present of some fruit, opened the next day's session with the question, 'Have you been poisoned?'

We are now in a position to appreciate that the individual with a schizoid tendency has another motive for keeping his love inside himself besides that arising from the feeling that it is too precious to part with. He also keeps his love shut in because he feels that it is too dangerous to release upon his objects. Thus he not only keeps his love in a safe, but also keeps it in a cage. The matter does not end there, however. Since he feels that his own love is bad, he is liable to interpret the love of others in similar terms. Such an interpretation does not necessarily imply projection on his part; but, of course, he is always liable to have recourse to this defensive technique. It is illustrated, for example, in the fairy tale of 'Little Red Riding Hood', to which reference has already been made; for although, as we have seen, the wolf does represent her own incorporative oral love, the story also tells us that the wolf takes her grandmother's place in the bed—which means, of course, that she attributes her own incorporative attitude to her libidinal object, who then seems to turn into a devouring wolf. So it comes about that the individual with schizoid characteristics is liable to feel driven to erect defences, not only against his love for others, but also against their love for him; and it was on this account that a rather schizoid young woman, who was a patient of mine, used sometimes to say to me, 'Whatever you do, you must never like me'.

When, accordingly, an individual with a schizoid tendency makes a renunciation of social contacts, it is above all because he feels that he must neither love nor be loved. He does not always rest content with a mere passive aloofness, however. On the contrary, he often takes active measures to drive his libidinal objects away from him. For this purpose he has an instrument ready to hand inside himself in the form of his own differentiated aggression. He mobilizes the resources of his hate, and directs his aggression against others—and more particularly against his libidinal objects. Thus he may quarrel with people, be objectionable, be rude. In so doing, he not only substitutes hate for love in his relationships with his objects, but also induces them to hate, instead of loving, him; and he does all this in order to keep his libidinal objects at a distance. Like the Troubadours (and perhaps also the dictators), he can only permit himself to love and be loved from afar off. This is the second great tragedy to which individuals with a schizoid tendency are liable. The first is, as we have seen, that he feels his love to be destructive of those he loves. The second arises when he becomes subject to a compulsion to hate and be hated, while all the time he longs deep down to love and to be loved.

There are two further motives, however, by which an individual with a schizoid tendency may be actuated in substituting hating for loving—curiously enough one an immoral, and the other a moral motive; and incidentally these would appear to be specially powerful motives in the case of the revolutionary and the Quisling. The immoral motive is determined by the consideration that, since the joy of loving seems hopelessly barred to him, he may as well deliver himself over to the joy of hating and obtain what satisfaction he can out of that. He thus makes a pact with the Devil and says, 'Evil be thou my good'. The moral motive is determined by the consideration that, if loving involves destroying, it is better to destroy by hate, which is overtly destructive and bad, than to destroy by love, which is by rights creative and good. When these two motives come into play, therefore, we are confronted with an amazing reversal of moral values. It becomes a case, not only of 'Evil be thou my good', but also of 'Good be thou my evil'. This is a reversal of values, it must be added, which is rarely consciously accepted; but it is none the less one which often plays an extremely important part in the unconscious—and that this should be so is the third great tragedy to which individuals with a schizoid tendency are liable.

CHAPTER II

A Revised Psychopathology of the Psychoses and Psychoneuroses (1941)[1]

INTRODUCTION

WITHIN recent years I have become increasingly interested in the problems presented by patients displaying schizoid tendencies to one degree or another; and I have devoted special attention to these problems.[2] The result has been the emergence of a point of view which, if it proves to be well-founded, must necessarily have far-reaching implications both for psychiatry in general and for psychoanalysis in particular. My various findings and the conclusions to which they lead involve not only a considerable revision of prevailing ideas regarding the nature and ætiology of schizoid conditions, but also a considerable revision of ideas regarding the prevalence of schizoid processes and a corresponding change in current clinical conceptions of the various psychoneuroses and psychoses. My findings and conclusions also involve a recasting and reorientation of the libido theory together with a modification of various classical psychoanalytical concepts.

For various reasons the present survey will be for the most part restricted to a consideration of the more general aspects of the point of view to which I have been led by the study of schizoid tendencies; but it may be stated at the outset that much of the argument which follows depends upon the conclusion, to which my own analytical findings have led me, to the effect that the schizoid group is much more comprehensive than has hitherto been generally recognized, and that a high percentage of anxiety states and of paranoid, phobic, hysteri-

[1] Originally published in *The International Journal of Psycho-Analysis*, Vol. XXII, Pts. 3 and 4, and now republished with minor amendments.

[2] A previous paper entitled 'Schizoid Factors in the Personality' is devoted to this subject, and is included in the present volume.

cal, and obsessional symptoms have a definitely schizoid background. The comprehensive meaning which I have come to attach to the concept of 'Schizoid' may perhaps best be indicated by the statement that, according to my findings, the schizoid group corresponds to the group to which the Jungian concept of 'Introvert' would apply. The fundamental feature of an overtly schizoid state (as indeed the term implies) is a splitting of the ego; and it is the commonest thing for a deep analysis to reveal splits in the ego not only in individuals suffering from frankly psychopathological conditions, but also in individuals who present themselves for analysis on account of difficulties to which no definite psychopathological labels have been attached. The significance of splitting of the ego can only be fully appreciated when it is considered from a developmental standpoint.

THE INHERENT LIMITATIONS OF THE LIBIDO THEORY

Current psychoanalytical conceptions regarding ego–development have been considerably influenced by Freud's original formulation of the libido theory to the effect that libido is initially distributed over a number of bodily zones, some of which are specially significant and are themselves erotogenic. In accordance with this conception, the success of libidinal development depends upon the integration of the various libidinal distributions under the mastery of the genital impulse. Nevertheless, as will shortly appear, the libido theory contains an inherent weakness which is best appreciated when we consider it in the form in which it emerged from Abraham's revision. Abraham, of course, allotted to each of the more significant libidinal zones a special place in psychogenetic development and postulated a series of phases of development, each characterized by the dominance of a specific zone; and, in accordance with this scheme, each of the classical psychoses and psychoneuroses came to be attributed to a fixation at a specific phase. There can be no question of the correctness of relating schizoid conditions to a fixation in the earlier oral phase characterized by the dominance of sucking. Nor, for that matter, can there be any doubt about the correctness of attributing manic-depressive conditions to a fixation in the later oral phase characterized by the emergence of biting. It is not such plain sailing, however, where the two anal phases and the earlier genital or phallic phase are concerned. There can be no doubt that, as Abraham pointed out so clearly, the paranoiac employs a primitive anal technique for the rejection of his objects, the obsessional employs a more developed anal technique for gaining control of his objects, and the hysteric attempts to improve his relationship with his objects by a technique involving a renunciation of the genital organs. Nevertheless, my own findings leave me in equally little doubt that the *paranoid, obsessional,* and *hysterical* states—to which may be added the *phobic* state—essentially represent, not the products of fixations at specific libidinal phases, but simply *a variety of techniques employed to defend the ego against the effects of conflicts of an oral origin.* The conviction that this is so is supported by two facts: (*a*) that the analysis of paranoid, obsessional, hysterical, and phobic symptoms invariably reveals the presence of an underlying oral conflict, and (*b*) that paranoid, obsessional, hysterical, and phobic symptoms are such common accompaniments and precursors of schizoid and depressive states. By contrast, it is quite impossible to regard as a defence either the schizoid or the depressive state in itself—each a state for which an orally based ætiology has been found. On the contrary, these states have all the character of conditions against which the ego requires to be defended.[1]

Further consideration of Abraham's modification of the libido theory raises the question whether the 'anal phases' are not in a sense an artefact; and the same question arises in the case of the 'phallic phase'. Abraham's phases were, of course, intended to represent not only stages in libidinal organization, but also stages in the development of object-love. Nevertheless, it is not without significance that the nomenclature employed to describe the various phases is based upon the nature of the libidinal aim, and not upon the nature of the object. Thus, instead of speaking of 'breast' phases, Abraham speaks of 'oral' phases; and, instead of speaking of 'fæces' phases, he speaks of 'anal' phases. It is when we substitute 'fæces phase' for 'anal phase' that the limitation in Abraham's scheme of libidinal development is

---

[1] It must be recognized, of course, that associated with both the schizoid and the depressive state there may exist certain more or less *specific defences,* which are called into operation by the state itself rather than by the conflicts underlying it; and, where the depressive state is concerned, the *manic defence* may be cited as an outstanding example. Such specific defences appear to be called into operation when the *non-specific techniques* just mentioned (viz. the paranoid, obsessional, hysterical, and phobic techniques) have failed to achieve their purpose of defending the ego against the onset of a schizoid or depressive state. Nevertheless, these specific defences must be distinguished from the basic schizoid and depressive states which instigate them.

seen to declare itself; for, whilst the breast and the genital organs are natural and biological objects of libido, fæces certainly is not. On the contrary it is only a symbolic object. It is only, so to speak, the clay out of which a model of the object is moulded.[1]

The historical importance of the libido theory and the extent to which it has contributed to the advance of psychoanalytical know-ledge requires no elaboration; and the merit of the theory has been proved by its heuristic value alone. Nevertheless, it would appear as if the point had now been reached at which, in the interests of pro-gress, the classic libido theory would have to be transformed into *a theory of development based essentially upon object-relationships*. The great limitation of the present libido theory as an explanatory system resides in the fact that it confers the status of libidinal attitudes upon various manifestations which turn out to be merely *techniques for regulating the object-relationships of the ego*. The libido theory is based, of course, upon the conception of erotogenic zones. It must be recog-nized, however, that in the first instance erotogenic zones are simply channels through which libido flows, and that a zone only becomes erotogenic when libido flows through it. *The ultimate goal of libido is the object*; and in its search for the object libido is determined by similar laws to those which determine the flow of electrical energy, i.e. it seeks the path of least resistance. The erotogenic zone should, therefore, be regarded simply as a path of least resistance; and its actual erotogenicity may be likened to the magnetic field established by the flow of an electrical current. The position is then as follows.

[1] Here it is of interest to note that the nomenclature adopted by Abraham to describe the various phases in his scheme of libidinal development differs from that already employed to describe stages of libidinal development in the scheme which prevailed previous to his revision of the libido theory. In the earlier scheme three stages of development were recognized; and these were described respectively as (1) 'the autoerotic', (2) 'the narcissistic', and (3) 'the alloerotic'. This nomenclature in itself implied that the earlier scheme was based essentially upon an object-refer-ence (and not upon a reference to the nature of the libidinal aim). Questions of terminology apart, Abraham's account of libidinal development was, of course, essentially a modification of the earlier scheme—a modification characterized particularly by the interpolation of two 'anal phases' between the narcissistic ('later oral') and the alloerotic ('genital') phases. The special purpose of this inter-polation was to enable a stage of 'partial love' to be introduced into the scheme of libidinal development; but, whatever value may be attached to such a purpose, it is significant that Abraham's interpolation of the 'anal phases' should have been accompanied by a change in nomenclature which eliminated all reference to the object from the terms used to describe every phase in the revised scheme.

In infancy, owing to the constitution of the human organism, the path of least resistance to the object happens to lie almost exclusively through the mouth; and the mouth accordingly becomes the dominant libidinal organ. In the mature individual on the other hand (and again owing to the constitution of the human organism) the genital organs provide a path of least resistance to the object—but, in this case, only in parallel with a number of other paths. The real point about the mature individual is not that the libidinal attitude is essentially genital, but that the genital attitude is essentially libidinal. There is thus an inherent difference between the infantile and the mature libidinal attitude arising out of the fact that, whereas in the case of the infant the libidinal attitude must be of necessity predominantly oral, in the case of the emotionally mature adult libido seeks the object through a number of channels, among which the genital channel plays an essential, but by no means exclusive, part. Whilst, therefore, it is correct to describe the libidinal attitude of the infant as characteristically oral, it is not correct to describe the libidinal attitude of the adult as characteristically genital. It should properly be described as 'mature'. This term must, however, be understood to imply that the genital channels are available for a satisfactory libidinal relationship with the object. At the same time, it must be stressed that it is not in virtue of the fact that the genital level has been reached that object-relationships are satisfactory. On the contrary, it is in virtue of the fact that satisfactory object-relationships have been established that true genital sexuality is attained.[1]

From what precedes it will be seen that (as it happens) Abraham's 'oral phases' are amply justified by the facts. It is otherwise, however, with his 'earlier genital or phallic phase'. His 'final genital' phase is justified in the sense that the genital organs constitute a natural channel for mature libido; but, like the 'anal phases', his 'phallic phase' is an artefact. It is an artefact introduced under the influence of the misleading conception of fundamental erotogenic zones. A deep

---

[1] It should be explained that it is not any part of my intention to depreciate the significance of the 'genital' stage in comparison with the oral stage. My intention is rather to point out that the real significance of the 'genital' stage lies in a *maturity of object-relationships*, and that a genital attitude is but an element in that maturity. It would be equally true to say that the real significance of the oral stage lies in an immaturity of object-relationships, and that the oral attitude is but an element in that immaturity; but at the oral stage the importance of the physical, as against the psychical, element in relationships is more marked than at the 'genital' stage owing to the physical dependence of the infant.

analysis of the phallic attitude invariably reveals the presence of an underlying oral fixation associated with phantasies of a fellatio order. The phallic attitude is thus dependent upon an identification of the object's genital organs with the breast as the original part-object of the oral attitude—an identification which is characteristically accompanied by an identification of the subject's genital organs with the mouth as a libidinal organ. The phallic attitude must, accordingly, be regarded, not as representing a libidinal phase, but as constituting a technique; and the same holds true of the anal attitudes.

The conception of fundamental erotogenic zones constitutes an unsatisfactory basis for any theory of libidinal development because it is based upon a failure to recognize that the function of libidinal pleasure is essentially to provide a sign-post to the object. According to the conception of erotogenic zones the object is regarded as a sign-post to libidinal pleasure; and the cart is thus placed before the horse. Such a reversal of the real position must be attributed to the fact that, in the earlier stages of psychoanalytical thought, the paramount importance of the object-relationship had not yet been sufficiently realized. Here again we have an example of the misunderstandings which arise when a technique is mistaken for a primary libidinal manifestation. In every case there is a critical instance; and in this case thumb-sucking may be taken as such. Why does a baby suck his thumb? Upon the answer to this simple question depends the whole validity of the conception of erotogenic zones and the form of libido theory based upon it. If we answer that the baby sucks his thumb because his mouth is an erotogenic zone and sucking provides him with erotic pleasure, it may sound convincing enough; but we are really missing the point. To bring out the point, we must ask ourselves the further question—'Why his thumb?' And the answer to this question is—'Because there is no breast to suck'. Even the baby must have a libidinal object; and, if he is deprived of his natural object (the breast), he is driven to provide an object for himself. Thumb-sucking thus represents a technique for dealing with an unsatisfactory object-relationship; and the same may be said of masturbation. Here it will doubtless occur to the reader that thumb-sucking and masturbation should properly be described, not simply as 'erotic', but more specifically as 'autoerotic' activities. This, of course, is true. Nevertheless, it would also seem to be true that the conception of erotogenic zones is itself based upon the phenomenon of autoerotism and has arisen largely owing to a mistaken interpretation of the real significance of this phenomenon. Autoerotism is essentially a technique whereby the individual seeks not only to provide for himself what he cannot obtain from the object, but to provide for himself an object which he cannot obtain. The 'anal phases' and the 'phallic phase' largely represent attitudes based upon this technique. It is a technique which originates in an oral context, and which always retains the impress of its oral origin. It is thus intimately associated with incorporation of the object—which is, after all, only another aspect of the process whereby the individual attempts to deal with frustration in oral relationships. In view of this intimate association it will be seen that at the very outset thumb-sucking, as an auto-erotic (and erotic) activity, acquires the significance of a relationship with an internalized object. It is no exaggeration to say that *the whole course of libidinal development depends upon the extent to which objects are incorporated and the nature of the techniques which are employed to deal with incorporated objects*. These techniques are about to be discussed. Meanwhile, it is sufficient to point out that the significance of the anal and phallic attitudes lies in the fact that they represent the libidinal aspects of techniques for dealing with objects which have been incorporated. It must always be borne in mind, however, that it is not the libidinal attitude which determines the object–relationship, but the object–relationship which determines the libidinal attitude.

A THEORY OF THE DEVELOPMENT OF OBJECT–RELATIONSHIPS BASED ON THE QUALITY OF DEPENDENCE UPON THE OBJECT

It is one of the chief conclusions to which I have been led by the study of cases displaying schizoid features that the development of object-relationships is essentially *a process whereby infantile dependence upon the object gradually gives place to mature dependence upon the object*. This process of development is characterized (*a*) by the gradual abandonment of an original object-relationship based upon primary identification,[1] and (*b*) by the gradual adoption of an object-relationship based upon differentiation of the object. The gradual change

[1] I employ the term '*primary identification*' here to signify the cathexis of an object which has not yet been differentiated from the cathecting subject. The unqualified term 'identification' is, of course, sometimes used in this sense; but it is more commonly used to signify the establishment of a relationship based on non-differentiation with an object which has already been differentiated in some measure at least. This latter process represents a revival of the type of relationship involved in

from identification to differentiation

which thus occurs in the nature of the object-relationship is accompanied by a gradual change in libidinal aim, whereby an original oral, sucking, incorporating and predominantly 'taking' aim comes to be replaced by a mature, non-incorporating and predominantly 'giving' aim compatible with developed genital sexuality. The stage of infantile dependence contains within it two recognizable phases—the earlier and later oral phases; and the stage of mature dependence corresponds to Abraham's 'final genital phase'. Between these two stages of infantile and mature dependence is a transition stage characterized by an increasing tendency to abandon the attitude of infantile dependence and an increasing tendency to adopt the attitude of mature dependence. This transition stage corresponds to three of Abraham's phases—the two anal phases and the early genital (phallic) phase.

The transition stage only begins to dawn when the ambivalence of the later oral phase has already commenced to give way to an attitude based upon dichotomy of the object. *Dichotomy of the object* may be defined as a process whereby the original object, towards which both love and hate have come to be directed, is replaced by two objects— *an accepted object*, towards which love is directed, and *a rejected object*, towards which hate is directed. It should be added, however, that, in accordance with the developments which have occurred during the oral phases, both the accepted and the rejected objects tend to be treated largely as internalized objects. In so far as the transition stage is concerned with the abandonment of infantile dependence, it is now seen to be inevitable that rejection of the object will play an all-important part. Consequently, the operation of *rejective techniques* is a characteristic feature of the stage; and it is upon this feature that Abraham seems to have fastened when he introduced the conception of the anal phases. In its biological nature defæcation is, of course, essentially a rejective process; and in virtue of this fact it naturally lends itself to be exploited psychologically as a symbol of emotional rejection of the object, and readily forms the basis of rejective mental

primary identification, and should thus, strictly speaking, be described as '*secondary identification*'. The distinction is one which it is theoretically important to bear in mind; but, so long as it is not forgotten, the simple term 'identification' may be used for convenience without any specific reference to the primary or secondary nature of the process in question; and it is so used in what follows. The term is also used in another sense to describe the establishment of an emotional equivalence between objects which are essentially different (e.g. penis and breast).

techniques. At the same time it readily lends itself to acquire the psychological significance of an exercise of power over the object. What applies to defæcation also applies to urination; and there is reason to think that the importance of urination as a function of symbolic rejection has been underestimated in the past, especially since, for anatomical reasons, the urinary function provides a link between the excretory and genital functions.

In accordance with the point of view here adopted, paranoia and the obsessional neurosis are not to be regarded as expressions of a fixation at the earlier and later anal phases respectively. On the contrary, they are to be regarded as states resulting from the employment of special defensive techniques which derive their pattern from rejective excretory processes. The paranoid and obsessional techniques are not exclusively rejective techniques, however. Both of them combine acceptance of the good object with rejection of the bad object. The essential difference between them will be considered shortly. Meanwhile it may be noted that the paranoid technique represents a higher degree of rejection; for in externalizing the rejected internal object the paranoid individual treats it as unreservedly and actively bad—as a persecutor indeed. For the obsessional individual, on the other hand, excretory acts represent not only rejection of the object, but also parting with contents.[1] In the obsessional technique, accordingly, we find a compromise between the predominantly taking attitude of infantile dependence and the predominantly giving attitude of mature dependence. Such an attitude of compromise is completely alien to the paranoid individual— for whom excretory acts represent nothing but rejection.

Hysteria provides another example of a state resulting from the use of a special rejective technique, as against a state resulting from a fixation at a specific stage of libidinal development, viz. the phallic phase. According to Abraham's scheme, of course, the hysterical state is attributed to a rejection of the genital organs during the phallic phase in consequence of excessive guilt over the Œdipus situation. This view is not altogether in line with my recent findings, which suggest that it involves a certain misconception regarding the Œdipus situation as a psychological, in contrast to a sociological,

---

[1] This is in conformity with the fact that, although the excretory functions are inherently rejective by nature, they are also in a sense productive and thus readily acquire for the child the additional psychological significance of creative and 'giving' activities.

phenomenon. Psychologically speaking, the deeper significance of the situation would appear to reside in the fact that it represents a differentiation of the single object of the ambivalent (later oral) phase into two objects, one being an accepted object, identified with one of the parents, and the other being a rejected object, identified with the remaining parent. The guilt attached to the Œdipus situation, accordingly, is derived not so much from the fact that this situation is triangular as from the facts (1) that the incestuous wish represents a demand for parental love which does not seem freely bestowed, and (2) that there has arisen in the child a sense that his own love is rejected because it is bad. This was well borne out in the case of one of my female patients, who during childhood was placed in circumstances calculated to stimulate incestuous phantasies to the highest degree. Owing to disagreements between her parents they occupied separate bedrooms. Between these bedrooms lay an interconnecting dressing-room; and, to protect herself from her husband, my patient's mother made her sleep in this dressing-room. She obtained little display of affection from either parent. At a very early age she acquired a crippling infirmity, which made her much more dependent upon others in reality than is an average child. Her disability was treated as a sort of skeleton in the family cupboard by her mother, whose guiding principle in her upbringing was to force the pace in making her independent as quickly as possible. Her father was of a detached and unapproachable personality; and she experienced greater difficulty in making emotional contact with him than with her mother. After her mother's death, which occurred in her teens, she made desperate attempts to establish emotional contact with her father, but all in vain. It was then that the thought suddenly occurred to her one day: 'Surely it would appeal to him if I offered to go to bed with him!' Her incestuous wish thus represented a desperate attempt to make an emotional contact with her object— and, in so doing, both to elicit love and to prove that her own love was acceptable. Such a wish is not dependent upon any specific Œdipus context. In the case of my patient the incestuous wish was, of course, renounced; and, as might be expected, it was followed by an intense guilt-reaction. The guilt was no different, however, from the guilt which had arisen in relation to her demands upon her mother for expressions of love which were not forthcoming, and in default of which it seemed proved that her own love was bad. Her unsatisfactory emotional relationship with her mother had already given rise to a regression to the oral stage, in virtue of which the breast had been reinstated as an object, and in consequence of which one of her chief symptoms was inability to eat in the presence of others without feeling nausea. Her rejection of her father's penis thus had behind it a rejection of her mother's breast; and there was evidence of a definite identification of the penis with the breast.

This case serves to illustrate the fact that, whilst there is no occasion to deny a rejection of the genital organs on the part of the hysteric, this rejection is determined not so much by the specific nature of the Œdipus situation as by the fact that the hysteric identifies the genital organs as a part-object with the original part-object of the stage of infantile dependence, viz. the breast. The hysteric's rejection of the genital organs thus resolves itself into an unsuccessful attempt to abandon the attitude of infantile dependence. The same holds true of the rejection of the object embodied in the paranoid and obsessional techniques. It is no part of the hysterical technique, however, to externalize the rejected object. On the contrary, the rejected object remains incorporated. Hence the characteristic hysterical dissociation —the significance of which lies ultimately in the fact that it represents the rejection of an incorporated object. At the same time the hysterical technique, like the obsessional technique, embodies a partial acceptance of the giving attitude of mature dependence; for it is characteristic of the hysterical individual that he desires to surrender everything to his love-objects except his genital organs and what these organs represent to him—an attitude which is accompanied by an idealization of the love-object motivated, in part at least, by a wish to establish dependence upon a more reassuring basis.

The significance of paranoia, the obsessional neurosis and hysteria is now seen to lie in the fact that each represents a state resulting from the employment of a specific technique; and the phobic state must be regarded in a similar light. Each of the various techniques in question may now be interpreted as a specific method of attempting to deal with the characteristic conflict of the transition stage in so far as this conflict has remained unresolved. The conflict is one between (a) a developmental urge to advance to an attitude of mature dependence upon the object, and (b) a regressive reluctance to abandon the attitude of infantile dependence upon the object.

In accordance with what precedes, it is now submitted that the norm for the development of object-relationships conforms to the following scheme:

I. Stage of Infantile Dependence, characterized predominantly by
an Attitude of Taking.
   (1) Early Oral—Incorporating—Sucking or Rejecting (Pre-
   Ambivalent).
   (2) Late Oral—Incorporating—Sucking or Biting (Ambivalent).
II. Stage of Transition between Infantile Dependence and Mature
   Dependence, or Stage of Quasi-Independence—Dichotomy
   and Exteriorization of the Incorporated Object.
III. Stage of Mature Dependence, characterized predominantly by
   an Attitude of Giving—Accepted and Rejected Objects
   Exteriorized.

The distinctive feature of this scheme is that it is based upon the
nature of the object-relationship, and that the libidinal attitude is relegated to a secondary place. What has convinced me of the paramount
importance of the object-relationship is the analysis of patients displaying schizoid characteristics; for it is in such individuals that difficulties over relationships with objects present themselves most clearly.
During the course of analysis, such an individual provides the most
striking evidence of a conflict between an extreme reluctance to
abandon infantile dependence and a desperate longing to renounce it;
and it is at once fascinating and pathetic to watch the patient, like a
timid mouse, alternately creeping out of the shelter of his hole to
peep at the world of outer objects and then beating a hasty retreat. It
is also illuminating to observe how, in his indefatigable attempts to
emerge from a state of infantile dependence, he resorts by turns to
any or all four of the transitional techniques which have been described—the paranoid, obsessional, hysterical, and phobic. What
emerges as clearly as anything else from the analysis of such a case is
that the greatest need of a child is to obtain conclusive assurance
(*a*) that he is genuinely loved as a person by his parents, and (*b*) that
his parents genuinely accept his love. It is only in so far as such
assurance is forthcoming in a form sufficiently convincing to enable
him to depend safely upon his real objects that he is able gradually to
renounce infantile dependence without misgiving. In the absence of
such assurance his relationship to his objects is fraught with too much
anxiety over separation to enable him to renounce the attitude of
infantile dependence; for such a renunciation would be equivalent in
his eyes to forfeiting all hope of ever obtaining the satisfaction of his
unsatisfied emotional needs. Frustration of his desire to be loved as a

person and to have his love accepted is the greatest trauma that a child can experience; and it is this trauma above all that creates fixations in the various forms of infantile sexuality to which a child is driven to resort in an attempt to compensate by substitutive satisfactions for the failure of his emotional relationships with his outer objects. Fundamentally these substitutive satisfactions (e.g. masturbation and anal erotism) all represent *relationships with internalized objects, to which the individual is compelled to turn in default of a satisfactory relationship with objects in the outer world.* Where relationships with outer objects are unsatisfactory, we also encounter such phenomena as exhibitionism, homosexuality, sadism, and masochism; and these phenomena should be regarded as in no small measure attempts to salvage natural emotional relationships which have broken down. Valuable as it is to understand the nature of these 'relationships by default', such understanding is much less important than a knowledge of the factors which compromise spontaneous relationships. By far the most important of these factors is a situation in childhood which leads the individual to feel that his objects neither love him as a person nor accept his love. It is when such a situation arises that the inherent libidinal drive towards the object leads to the establishment of aberrant relationships and to the various libidinal attitudes which accompany them.

The scheme of development outlined in the preceding table has been based on the quality of dependence upon the object because there is reason to think that this is the most important factor in early relationships. It is desirable, however, to be clear as to the nature of the object appropriate to each stage of development. And here it is important to distinguish between the natural (biological) object and the incorporated object which is so largely substituted for it in psychopathological cases. Objects may, of course, be either part-objects or whole objects; and, when the biological history of early childhood is considered, it becomes plain that there is only one natural part-object, viz. the breast of the mother, and that the most significant whole object is the mother—with the father as rather a poor second. As has already been pointed out, fæces is not a natural object. It is a symbolic object; and the same may be said of the genital organs in so far as these are treated as phallic objects, viz. part-objects. Thus, whilst the most important immediate factor in male homosexuality is doubtless a search for the father's penis, this search involves the substitution of a part-object for a whole object and is a regressive

40

phenomenon representing a revival of the original (oral) relationship
with the original part-object (the breast). The homosexual's search
for his father's penis thus resolves itself, so to speak, into a search for
his father's breast. The persistence of the breast as a part-object is
well marked in the case of hysterics, for whom the genital organs
always retain an oral significance. This is well illustrated in the case of
a female hysterical patient, who, in describing her pelvic 'pain',
remarked: 'It feels as if something wanted feeding inside.' The frequency with which, as wartime experience has shown, hysterical
soldiers complain of gastric symptoms is similarly significant.

In the light of what has just been said, the natural objects appropriate to the various stages of development may be indicated as
follows:

I. Infantile Dependence.
   (1) Early Oral—Breast of the Mother—Part-Object.
   (2) Late Oral—Mother with the Breast—Whole Object treated
       characteristically as a Part-Object.
II. Quasi-Independence (Transitional).
    Whole Object treated characteristically as Contents.
III. Mature Dependence.
     Whole Object with Genital Organs.[1]

THE STAGE OF TRANSITION BETWEEN INFANTILE AND ADULT
DEPENDENCE, ITS TECHNIQUES AND ITS PSYCHOPATHOLOGY

It will be noticed that in the preceding tables the transition stage
has been described as a stage of 'Quasi-Independence'; and the reason
for the adoption of this description is of sufficient importance to
demand special attention. It emerges clearly from the study of
individuals with schizoid tendencies that the most characteristic fea-

[1] This table is intended to represent the norm of libidinal development, so far as
this can be assessed; but it is important to bear in mind the distinction between such
a norm and the actual process of development revealed by the analysis of a psychopathological case. Thus it must be explicitly recognized that the natural object
during the early oral phase remains the *actual* breast of the mother quite irrespective of any process whereby the breast is *mentally* incorporated and established as an
internal object, as also that during this phase the individual is in actual fact both
physically and emotionally dependent upon the breast as an external object quite
apart from any emotional dependence upon an internalized breast. It must also be
recognized that the breast may persist as an internal object during later libidinal
phases in which the natural object is other than the breast.

41

ture of the state of infantile dependence is *primary identification with the object*. Indeed, it would not be going too far to say that, psychologically speaking, identification with the object and infantile dependence are but two aspects of the same phenomenon. On the other hand, mature dependence involves a relationship between two independent individuals, who are completely *differentiated* from one another as mutual objects.[1] This distinction between the two kinds of dependence is identical with Freud's distinction between the narcissistic and the anaclitic choice of objects. The relationship involved in mature dependence is, of course, only theoretically possible. Nevertheless, it remains true that *the more mature a relationship is, the less it is characterized by primary identification*; for what such identification essentially represents is failure to differentiate the object. It is when identification persists at the expense of differentiation that a markedly compulsive element enters into the individual's attitude towards his objects. This is well seen in the infatuations of schizoid individuals. It may also be observed in the almost uncontrollable impulse so commonly experienced by schizoid and depressive soldiers in wartime to return to their wives or their homes, when separated from them owing to military necessities. *The abandonment of infantile dependence involves an abandonment of relationships based upon primary identification in favour of relationships with differentiated objects.* In dreams the process of differentiation is frequently reflected in the theme of trying to cross a gulf or chasm, albeit the crossing which is attempted may also occur in a regressive direction. The process itself is commonly attended by considerable anxiety; and this anxiety finds characteristic expression in dreams of falling, as also in such symptoms as acrophobia and agoraphobia. On the other hand, anxiety over failure of the process is reflected in nightmares about being imprisoned or confined underground or immersed in the sea, as well as in the symptom of claustrophobia.

The process of differentiation of the object derives particular significance from the fact that infantile dependence is characterized not only by identification, but also by an oral attitude of incorporation. In virtue of this fact the object with which the individual is identified becomes equivalent to an incorporated object, or, to put the matter in a more arresting fashion, the object in which the individual is incor-

[1] An important aspect of the difference between infantile dependence and mature dependence is that, whereas the former is a state which has not yet been abandoned, the latter is a state which has been already achieved.

42

porated is incorporated in the individual. This strange psychological anomaly may well prove the key to many metaphysical puzzles. Be that as it may, however, it is common to find in dreams a remarkable equivalence between being inside an object and having the object inside. I had a patient, for example, who had a dream about being in a tower; and his associations left no room for doubt that this theme represented for him not only an identification with his mother, but also the incorporation of his mother's breast—and, incidentally, his father's penis.

Such then being the situation, the task of differentiating the object tends to resolve itself into a problem of expelling an incorporated object, i.e. to become a problem of expelling contents. Herein lies much of the rationale of Abraham's 'anal phases'; and it is in this direction that we must look for much of the significance of the anal techniques which play such an important part during the transition stage. It is important here as elsewhere to ensure that the cart is not placed before the horse, and to recognize that it is not a case of the individual being preoccupied with the disposal of contents at this stage because he is anal, but of his being anal because he is pre-occupied at this stage with the disposal of contents.

The great conflict of the transition stage may now be formulated as a conflict between a progressive urge to surrender the infantile attitude of identification with the object and a regressive urge to maintain that attitude. During this period, accordingly, the behaviour of the individual is characterized both by desperate endeavours on his part to separate himself from the object and desperate endeavours to achieve reunion with the object—desperate attempts 'to escape from prison' and desperate attempts 'to return home'. Although one of these attitudes may come to preponderate, there is in the first instance a constant oscillation between them owing to the anxiety attending each. The anxiety attending separation manifests itself as a fear of isolation; and the anxiety attending identification manifests itself as a fear of being shut in, imprisoned or engulfed ('cribbed, cabined, and confined'). These anxieties, it will be noticed, are essentially phobic anxieties. It may accordingly be inferred that it is to the conflict between the progressive urge towards separation from the object and the regressive lure of identification with the object that we must look for the explanation of *the phobic state*.

Owing to the intimate connection existing between primary identification and oral incorporation, and consequently between

43

separation and excretory expulsion, the conflict of the transition period also presents itself as a conflict between an urge to expel and an urge to retain contents. Just as between separation and reunion, so here there tends to be a constant oscillation between expulsion and retention, although either of these attitudes may become dominant. Both attitudes are attended by anxiety—the attitude of expulsion being attended by a fear of being emptied or drained, and the attitude of retention by a fear of bursting (often accompanied or replaced by a fear of some internal disease like cancer). Such anxieties are essentially obsessional anxieties; and it is the conflict between an urge to expel the object as contents and an urge to retain the object as contents that underlies *the obsessional state*.

The phobic and obsessional techniques are thus seen to represent two differing methods of dealing with the same basic conflict; and these two differing methods correspond to two differing attitudes towards the object. From the phobic point of view the conflict presents itself as one between flight from and return to the object. From the obsessional point of view, on the other hand, the conflict presents itself as one between expulsion and retention of the object. It thus becomes obvious that the phobic technique corresponds in the main to a passive attitude, whereas the obsessional technique corresponds in the main to an active attitude. The obsessional technique also expresses a much higher degree of overt aggression towards the object; for, whether the object be expelled or retained, it is being subjected to forcible control. For the phobic individual, on the other hand, the choice lies between escaping from the power of the object and submitting to it. In other words, whilst the obsessional technique is predominantly sadistic in nature, the phobic technique is predominantly masochistic.

In the hysterical state we can recognize the operation of another technique for attempting to deal with the basic conflict of the transition period. In this case the conflict appears to be formulated as simply one between acceptance and rejection of the object. Acceptance of the object is clearly manifested in the intense love-relationships which are so typical of the hysteric; but the very exaggeration of these emotional relationships in itself raises a suspicion that a rejection is being over-compensated. This suspicion is confirmed by the propensity of the hysteric to dissociative phenomena. That these dissociative phenomena represent a rejection of the genitals need not be stressed; but, as was pointed out earlier, analysis can always unmask

44

an identification of the rejected genitals with the breast as the original libidinal object during the period of infantile dependence. This being so, it is noteworthy that what is characteristically dissociated by the hysteric is an organ or function in himself. This can only have one meaning—that the rejected object is an internalized object with which there is a considerable measure of identification. On the other hand, the hysteric's over-valuation of his real objects leaves little room for doubt that in his case the accepted object is an externalized object. *The hysterical state* is thus seen to be characterized by acceptance of the externalized object and rejection of the internalized object—or, alternatively, by externalization of the accepted object and internalization of the rejected object.

If the paranoid and the hysterical states are now compared, we are confronted with a significant contrast. Whereas the hysteric over-values objects in the outer world, the paranoid individual regards them as persecutors; and, whereas the hysterical dissociation is a form of self-depreciation, the attitude of the paranoid individual is one of extravagant grandiosity. *The paranoid state* must, accordingly, be regarded as representing rejection of the externalized object and acceptance of the internalized object—or, alternatively, externalization of the rejected object and internalization of the accepted object.

Having interpreted both the hysterical and paranoid techniques in terms of the acceptance and rejection of objects, we can now obtain interesting results by applying a similar interpretation to the phobic and obsessional techniques. The conflict underlying the phobic state may be concisely formulated as one between flight to the object and flight from the object. In the former case, of course, the object is accepted, whereas in the latter case the object is rejected. In both cases, however, the object is treated as external. In the obsessional state, on the other hand, the conflict presents itself as one between the expulsion and the retention of contents. In this case, accordingly, both the accepted and the rejected objects are treated as internal. If in the case of the phobic state both the accepted and the rejected objects are treated as external and in the obsessional state both are treated as internal, the situation as regards the hysterical and paranoid states is that one of these objects is treated as an externalized object and the other as an internalized object. In the hysterical state, it is the accepted object that is externalized, whereas, in the paranoid state, the object which is externalized is the rejected object. The nature of the object-relationships characteristic of the four techniques may be summarized in the following table:

Technique	Accepted Object	Rejected Object
Obsessional	Internalized	Internalized
Paranoid	Internalized	Externalized
Hysterical	Externalized	Internalized
Phobic	Externalized	Externalized

The chief features of the stage of transition between infantile and mature dependence may now be briefly summarized. The transition period is characterized by a process of development whereby object-relationships based upon identification gradually give place to relationships with a differentiated object. Satisfactory development during this period, therefore, depends upon the success which attends the process of differentiation of the object; and this in turn depends upon the issue of a conflict over separation from the object—a situation which is both desired and feared. The conflict in question may call into operation any or all of four characteristic techniques—the obsessional, the paranoid, the hysterical and the phobic; and, if object-relationships are unsatisfactory, these techniques are liable to form the basis of characteristic psychopathological developments in later life. The various techniques cannot be classified in any order corresponding to presumptive levels of libidinal development. On the contrary, they must be regarded as alternative techniques, all belonging to the same stage in the development of object-relationships. Which of the techniques is employed, or rather to what extent each is employed would appear to depend in large measure upon the nature of the object-relationships established during the preceding stage of infantile dependence. In particular it would seem to depend upon the degree to which objects have been incorporated, and upon the form assumed by relationships which have been established between the developing ego and its internalized objects.

THE STAGE OF INFANTILE DEPENDENCE AND ITS PSYCHOPATHOLOGY

Now that the nature of the transition period and the defences which characterize it have been considered at some length, it is time for us to turn our attention to the period of infantile dependence and to those psychopathological states which are germinated in this period.

The outstanding feature of infantile dependence is its unconditional character. The infant is completely dependent upon his object not only for his existence and physical well-being, but also for the satisfaction of his psychological needs. It is true, of course, that mature individuals are likewise dependent upon one another for the satisfaction of their psychological, no less than their physical, needs. Nevertheless, on the psychological side, the dependence of mature individuals is not unconditional. By contrast, the very helplessness of the child is sufficient to render him dependent in an unconditional sense. We also notice that, whereas in the case of the adult the object-relationship has a considerable spread, in the case of the infant it tends to be focused upon a single object. The loss of an object is thus very much more devastating in the case of an infant. If a mature individual loses an object, however important, he still has some objects remaining. His eggs are not all in one basket. Further, he has a choice of objects and can desert one for another. The infant, on the other hand, has no choice. He has no alternative but to accept or to reject his object—an alternative which is liable to present itself to him as a choice between life and death. His psychological dependence is further accentuated by the very nature of his object-relationship; for, as we have seen, this is based essentially upon identification. Dependence is exhibited in its most extreme form in the intra-uterine state; and we may legitimately infer that, on its psychological side, this state is characterized by an absolute degree of identification and absence of differentiation. Identification may thus be regarded as representing the persistence into extra-uterine life of a relationship existing before birth. In so far as identification persists after birth, the individual's object constitutes not only his world, but also himself; and it is to this fact, as has already been pointed out, that we must attribute the compulsive attitude of many schizoid and depressive individuals towards their objects.

Normal development is characterized by a process whereby progressive differentiation of the object is accompanied by a progressive decrease in identification. So long as infantile dependence persists, however, identification remains the most characteristic feature of the individual's emotional relationship with his object. Infantile dependence is equivalent to oral dependence—a fact which should be interpreted, not in the sense that the infant is inherently oral, but in the sense that the breast of the mother is his original object. During the oral phases, accordingly, identification remains the most characteristic feature of the individual's emotional relationship with his object. The tendency to identification, which is so characteristic of emotional relationships during these phases, also invades the cognitive sphere, with the result that certain orally fixated individuals have only to hear of someone else suffering from any given disease in order to believe that they are suffering from it themselves. In the conative sphere, on the other hand, identification has its counterpart in oral incorporation; and it is the merging of emotional identification with oral incorporation that confers upon the stage of infantile dependence its most distinctive features. These features are based upon the fundamental equivalence for the infant of being held in his mother's arms and incorporating the contents of her breast.

The phenomenon of narcissism, which is one of the most prominent characteristics of infantile dependence, is an attitude arising out of identification with the object. Indeed *primary narcissism* may be simply defined as just such *a state of identification with the object*, *secondary narcissism* being *a state of identification with an object which is internalized.* Whilst narcissism is a feature common to both the early and the late oral phases, the latter phase differs from the former in virtue of a change in the nature of the object. In the early oral phase the natural object is the breast of the mother; but in the late oral phase the natural object becomes the mother with the breast. The transition from one phase to the other is thus marked by the substitution of a whole object (or person) for a part-object; but it is also characterized by the emergence of the biting tendency. Thus, whereas in the early oral phase the libidinal attitude of sucking monopolizes the field, in the late oral phase it is in competition with an accompanying attitude of biting. Now biting must be regarded as being essentially destructive in aim, and indeed as constituting the very prototype of all differentiated aggression. Consequently the late oral phase is characterized by a high degree of emotional ambivalence. The early oral phase has been well described by Abraham as 'preambivalent'; but this does not preclude simple rejection or refusal of the object without any of that aggressive biting which characterizes the late oral phase. Such rejection does not imply ambivalence; and I consider that the early oral urge to incorporate is essentially a libidinal urge, to which differentiated and direct aggression makes no contribution. The recognition of this fact is of the greatest importance for an understanding of the essential problem underlying schizoid states. It is true that the incorporative urge is destructive in effect, in the sense that what is eaten disappears. Nevertheless the urge is not destructive in aim. When a child says that he 'loves' cake, it is certainly implied that the cake will vanish, and, *ipso facto*, be destroyed. At the same time the destruction of the cake is not the aim of the child's 'love'. On the contrary, the disappearance of the cake is, from the child's point of view, a most regrettable consequence of his 'love' for it. What he really desires is both to eat his cake and have it. If the cake proves to be 'bad', however, he either spits it out or is sick. In other words, he rejects it; but he does not bite it for being bad. This type of behaviour is specially characteristic of the early oral phase. What is characteristic is that, in so far as the object presents itself as good, its contents are incorporated, and, in so far as it presents itself as bad, it is rejected; but, even when it appears bad, no attempt is made to destroy it. At the same time, under conditions of deprivation anxiety arises lest the object itself should have been incorporated together with its contents and so destroyed, albeit not by intention.[1] In the late oral phase the situation is different; for in this phase the object may be bitten in so far as it presents itself as bad. This means that differentiated aggression, as well as libido, may be directed towards the object. Hence the appearance of the ambivalence which characterizes the late oral phase.

In accordance with what precedes, it becomes evident that the emotional conflict which arises in relation to object-relationships during the early oral phase takes the form of the alternative, 'to suck or not to suck', i.e. 'to love or not to love'. This is the conflict underlying the schizoid state. On the other hand, the conflict which characterizes the late oral phase resolves itself into the alternative, 'to suck or to bite', i.e. 'to love or to hate'. This is the conflict underlying the depressive state. It will be seen, accordingly, that the great problem of the schizoid individual is how to love without destroying by love, whereas the great problem of the depressive individual is how to love without destroying by hate. These are two very different problems.

The conflict underlying the schizoid state is, of course, much more devastating than the conflict underlying the depressive state; and, since the schizoid reaction has its roots in an earlier stage of development than the depressive reaction, the schizoid individual is less capable of dealing with conflict than is the depressive. It is owing to

[1] The situation involved is considered at greater length in my earlier paper entitled 'Schizoid Factors in the Personality' (included in the present volume).

49

these two facts that the disturbance of the personality found in schizophrenia is so much more profound than that found in depression. The devastating nature of the conflict associated with the early oral phase lies in the fact that, if it seems a terrible thing for an individual to destroy his object by hate, it seems a much more terrible thing for him to destroy his object by love. It is the great tragedy of the schizoid individual that his love seems to destroy; and it is because his love seems so destructive that he experiences such difficulty in directing libido towards objects in outer reality. He becomes afraid to love; and therefore he erects barriers between his objects and himself. He tends both to keep his objects at a distance and to make himself remote from them. He rejects his objects; and at the same time he withdraws libido from them. This withdrawal of libido may be carried to all lengths. It may be carried to a point at which all emotional and physical contacts with other persons are renounced; and it may even go so far that all libidinal links with outer reality are surrendered, all interest in the world around fades and everything becomes meaningless. In proportion as libido is withdrawn from outer objects it is directed towards internalized objects; and, in proportion as this happens, the individual becomes introverted. And incidentally it is the observation that this process of introversion is so characteristic of the onset of schizoid states that provides the basis for the conclusion that the 'introvert' is fundamentally schizoid. It is essentially in inner reality that the values of the schizoid individual are to be found. So far as he is concerned, the world of internalized objects is always liable to encroach upon the world of external objects; and in proportion as this happens his real objects become lost to him.

If loss of the real object were the only trauma of the schizoid state, the position of the schizoid individual would not be so precarious. It is necessary, however, to bear in mind the vicissitudes of the ego, which accompany loss of the object. Reference has already been made to the narcissism which results from an excessive libidinization of internalized objects; and such narcissism is specially characteristic of the schizoid individual. Accompanying it we invariably find an attitude of superiority which may manifest itself in consciousness to a varying degree as an actual sense of superiority. It should be noticed, however, that this attitude of superiority is based upon an orientation towards internalized objects, and that in relation to objects in the world of outer reality the basic attitude of the schizoid individual is essentially one of inferiority. It is true that the externally oriented inferiority may be masked by a façade of superiority based upon an identification of external with internalized objects. Nevertheless, it is invariably present; and it is evidence of a weakness in the ego. What chiefly compromises the integrity of the ego in the case of the schizoid individual is the apparently insoluble dilemma which attends the direction of libido towards objects. Failure to direct libido towards the object is, of course, equivalent to loss of the object; but, since, from the point of view of the schizoid individual, libido itself seems destructive, the object is equally lost when libido *is* directed towards it. It can thus readily be understood that, if the dilemma becomes sufficiently pronounced, the result is a complete *impasse*, which reduces the ego to a state of utter impotence. The ego becomes quite incapable of expressing itself; and, in so far as this is so, its very existence becomes compromised. This is well exemplified by the following remarks of a patient of mine during an analytical session: 'I can't say anything. I have nothing to say. I'm empty. There's nothing of me. . . . I feel quite useless; I haven't done anything. . . . I've gone quite cold and hard; I don't feel anything. . . . I can't express myself; I feel futile.' Such descriptions well illustrate not only the state of impotence to which the ego may be reduced, but also the extent to which the very existence of the ego may be compromised by the schizoid dilemma. The last quoted remark of this patient is perhaps particularly significant as drawing attention to the characteristic affect of the schizoid state; for *the characteristic affect of the schizoid state is undoubtedly a sense of futility*.

Amongst other schizoid phenomena which may be mentioned here are a sense of being wasted, a sense of unreality, intense self-consciousness and a sense of looking on at oneself. Taken together, these various phenomena clearly indicate that an actual splitting of the ego has occurred. This splitting of the ego must be regarded as more fundamental than the impotence and impoverishment of the ego already noted. It would seem, however, that withdrawal of libido from external objects has the result of intensifying not only the effects of the splitting process, but the actual extent of the splitting process itself. This fact is particularly significant as evidence of the extent to which the integrity of the ego depends upon object-relationships as contrasted with libidinal attitudes.

In acute schizoid states withdrawal of libido from object-relationships may proceed to such lengths that libido is withdrawn from the realm of the conscious (that part of the psyche which is, so to speak, nearest to objects) into the realm of the unconscious. When this happens, the effect is as if the ego itself had withdrawn into the unconscious; but the actual position would seem to be that, when libido is withdrawn from the field of the conscious part of the ego, the unconscious part of the ego is all that is left to behave as a functioning ego. In extreme cases libido would seem to be withdrawn, to some extent at least, even from the field of the unconscious part of the ego, leaving on the surface only the picture with which Kraepelin has familiarized us in his account of the last phase of dementia præcox. Whether such a mass-withdrawal of libido can properly be ascribed to repression is a debatable question, although where the process is restricted to a withdrawal from object-relationships it gives that impression. At any rate I am assured by a very intelligent patient in whom a fairly extensive withdrawal of libido has occurred that the effect 'feels quite different' from that of simple repression. There can be no doubt, however, that withdrawal of libido from the conscious part of the ego has the effect of relieving emotional tension and mitigating the danger of violent outbursts of precipitate action; and in the case of the patient just mentioned the withdrawal did occur just after a violent outburst. There can be equally little doubt that much of the schizoid individual's anxiety really represents fear of such outbursts occurring. This fear commonly manifests itself as a fear of going insane or as a fear of imminent disaster. It is possible, therefore, that massive withdrawal of libido has the significance of a desperate effort on the part of an ego threatened with disaster to avoid all emotional relationships with external objects by a repression of the basic libidinal tendencies which urge the individual on to make emotional contacts. In the case of the schizoid individual, of course, these tendencies are essentially oral. It is when this effort is within measurable distance of succeeding that the individual begins to tell us that he feels as if there were nothing of him, or as if he had lost his identity, or as if he were dead, or as if he had ceased to exist. The fact is that in renouncing libido the ego renounces the very form of energy which holds it together; and the ego thus becomes lost. *Loss of the ego* is the ultimate psychopathological disaster which the schizoid individual is constantly struggling, with more or with less success, to avert by exploiting all available techniques (including the transitional techniques) for the control of his libido. In essence, therefore, the schizoid state is not a defence, although evidence of the presence of defences may be detected in it. It represents the major disaster which may befall the individual who has failed to outgrow the early oral phase of dependence.

If the great problem which confronts the individual in the early oral phase is how to love the object without destroying it by love, the great problem which confronts the individual in the late oral phase is how to love the object without destroying it by hate. Accordingly, since the depressive reaction has its roots in the late oral phase, it is the disposal of his hate, rather than the disposal of his love, that constitutes the great difficulty of the depressive individual. Formidable as this difficulty is, the depressive is at any rate spared the devastating experience of feeling that his love is bad. Since his love at any rate seems good, he remains inherently capable of a libidinal relationship with outer objects in a sense in which the schizoid is not. His difficulty in maintaining such a relationship arises out of his ambivalence. This ambivalence in turn arises out of the fact that, during the late oral phase, he was more successful than the schizoid in substituting direct aggression (biting) for simple rejection of the object. Whilst his aggression has been differentiated, however, he has failed in some degree to achieve that further step in development which is represented by dichotomy of the object. This further step, had it been adequately achieved, would have enabled him to dispose of his hate by directing it, predominantly at least, towards the rejected object; and he would have been left free to direct towards his accepted object love which was relatively unaccompanied by hate. In so far as he has failed to take such a step, the depressive remains in that state which characterized his attitude towards his object during the late oral phase, viz. a state of ambivalence towards the incorporated object. The presence of such an inner situation is less disabling so far as outer adjustments are concerned than is the corresponding inner situation in the case of the schizoid; for in the case of the depressive there is no formidable barrier obstructing the outward flow of libido. Consequently the depressive individual readily establishes libidinal contacts with others; and, if his libidinal contacts are satisfactory to him, his progress through life may appear fairly smooth. Nevertheless the inner situation is always present; and it is readily reactivated if his libidinal relationships become disturbed. Any such disturbance immediately calls into operation the hating element in his ambivalent attitude; and, when his hate becomes directed towards the internalized object, a depressive reaction supervenes. Any frustration in

loss of object — trauma in depressive state

object-relationships is, of course, functionally equivalent to loss of the object, whether partial or complete; and, since severe depression is so common a sequel to actual loss of the object (whether by the death of a loved person or otherwise), *loss of the object* must be regarded as the essential trauma which provokes the depressive state.

What precedes may at first sight appear to leave unexplained the fact that a depressive reaction so commonly follows physical injury or illness. Physical injury or illness obviously represents loss. Yet what is actually lost is not the object, but part of the individual himself. To say that such a loss, e.g. the loss of an eye or a limb, represents symbolic castration takes us little further; for it still remains to be explained why a reaction which is characteristically provoked by loss of the object should also be provoked by loss of part of the body. The true explanation would appear to lie in the fact that the depressive individual still remains to a marked degree in a state of infantile identification with his object. To him, therefore, bodily loss is functionally equivalent to loss of the object; and this equivalence is reinforced by the presence of an internalized object, which, so to speak, suffuses the individual's body and imparts to it a narcissistic value.

There still remains to be explained the phenomenon of involutional melancholia. There are many psychiatrists, of course, who tend to regard the ætiology of this condition as entirely different from that of 'reactive depression'. Nevertheless, the two conditions have sufficient in common from a clinical standpoint to justify us in invoking the principle of *entia non sunt multiplicanda præter necessitatem*; and indeed it is not really difficult to explain both conditions on similar principles. Involutional melancholia is by definition closely associated with the climacteric; and the climacteric would seem to be in itself evidence of a definite waning of libidinal urges. It cannot be said, however, that there is any equivalent diminution of aggression. The balance between the libidinal and the aggressive urges is thus disturbed; and, further, it is disturbed in the same direction as when the hate of any ambivalent individual is activated by loss of the object. Accordingly, in an individual of the depressive type the climacteric has the effect of establishing the same situation as does actual loss of the object where object-relationships are concerned; and the result is a depressive reaction. If the prospect of recovery in the case of involutional melancholia is less hopeful than in the case of reactive depression, this is not difficult to explain; for, whereas in the latter case libido is still available for a restoration of the balance, in the former case it is not. Involutional melancholia is thus seen to conform to the general configuration of the depressive state; and it imposes upon us no necessity to modify the conclusion already envisaged—that loss of the object is the basic trauma underlying the depressive state. As in the case of the schizoid state, this state is not a defence. On the contrary, it is a state against which the individual seeks to defend himself by means of such techniques (including the transitional techniques) as are available for the control of his aggression. It represents the major disaster which may befall the individual who has failed to outgrow the late oral stage of infantile dependence.

In accordance with what precedes, we find ourselves confronted with two basic psychopathological conditions, each arising out of a failure on the part of the individual to establish a satisfactory object-relationship during the period of infantile dependence. The first of these conditions, viz. the schizoid state, is associated with an unsatisfactory object-relationship during the early oral phase; and the second of these conditions, viz. the depressive state, is associated with an unsatisfactory object-relationship during the late oral phase. It emerges quite clearly, however, from the analysis of both schizoid and depressive individuals that unsatisfactory object-relationships during the early and late oral phases are most likely to give rise to their characteristic psychopathological effects when object-relationships continue to be unsatisfactory during the succeeding years of early childhood. The schizoid and depressive states must, accordingly, be regarded as largely dependent upon a regressive reactivation, during subsequent childhood, of situations arising respectively during the early and late oral phases. The traumatic situation in either case is one in which the child feels that he is not really loved as a person, and that his own love is not accepted. If the phase in which infantile object-relationships have been pre-eminently unsatisfactory is the early oral phase, this trauma provokes in the child a reaction conforming to the idea that he is not loved because his own love is bad and destructive; and this reaction provides the basis for a subsequent schizoid tendency. If, on the other hand, the phase in which infantile object-relationships have been pre-eminently unsatisfactory is the late oral phase, the reaction provoked in the child conforms to the idea that he is not loved because of the badness and destructiveness of his hate; and this reaction provides the basis for a subsequent depressive tendency. Whether in any given case a schizoid or depressive tendency will eventually give rise to an actual schizoid or depressive state depends in part, of course, upon the circumstances which the individual is called upon to face in later life; but the most important determining factor is the degree to which objects have been incorporated during the oral phases. The various defensive techniques which characterize the transition period (i.e. the obsessional, paranoid, hysterical, and phobic techniques) all represent attempts to deal with difficulties and conflicts attending object-relationships in consequence of the persistence of incorporated objects. These defensive techniques may now also be seen to resolve themselves into differing methods of controlling an underlying schizoid or depressive tendency, and thus averting the onset of a schizoid or depressive state, as the case may be. Where a schizoid tendency is present, they represent methods designed to avert the ultimate psychopathological disaster which follows from loss of the ego; and, where a depressive tendency is present, they represent methods designed to avert the ultimate psychopathological disaster which follows from loss of the object.

It must be recognized, of course, that no individual born into this world is so fortunate as to enjoy a perfect object-relationship during the impressionable period of infantile dependence, or for that matter during the transition period which succeeds it. Consequently, no one ever becomes completely emancipated from the state of infantile dependence, or from some proportionate degree of oral fixation; and there is no one who has completely escaped the necessity of incorporating his early objects. It may consequently be inferred that there is present in every one either an underlying schizoid or an underlying depressive tendency, according as it was in the early or in the late oral phase that difficulties chiefly attended infantile object-relationships. We are thus introduced to the conception that every individual may be classified as falling into one of two basic psychological types—the schizoid and the depressive. It is not necessary to regard these two types as having more than phenomenological significance. Nevertheless, it is impossible to ignore the fact that in the determination of these two types some part may be played by a hereditary factor—viz. the relative strength of the inborn tendencies of sucking and biting.

Here we are reminded of Jung's dualistic theory of psychological types. According to Jung, of course, the 'introvert' and the 'extravert' represent fundamental types, into the constitution of which psychopathological factors do not primarily enter. My own conception of basic types differs from that of Jung not only in so far as I describe the two basic types as the 'schizoid' and the 'depressive' respectively, but also in so far as I consider that a psychopathological factor enters into the very constitution of the types envisaged. There is, however, another essentially dualistic conception of psychological types, with which my own conception is in much greater agreement than with that of Jung—the conception which is expounded by Kretschmer in his two works entitled *Physique and Character* and *The Psychology of Men of Genius*, and according to which the two basic psychological types are the 'schizothymic' and the 'cyclothymic'. As these terms themselves imply, he regards the schizothymic individual as predisposed to schizophrenia, and the cyclothymic individual to manic-depressive psychoses. There is thus a striking agreement between Kretschmer's conclusions and my own findings —an agreement all the more striking since my views, unlike his, have been reached by an essentially psychoanalytical approach. The only significant divergence between the two views arises out of the fact that Kretschmer regards the temperamental difference between the types as based essentially upon constitutional factors and attributes their psychopathological propensities to this temperamental difference, whereas my view is that psychopathological factors arising during the period of infantile dependence make at any rate a considerable contribution to the temperamental difference. There is, however, sufficient agreement between Kretschmer's views and those here advanced to provide some independent support for my conclusion that the schizoid and the depressive states represent two fundamental psychopathological conditions, in relation to which all other psychopathological developments are secondary. Kretschmer's views also provide some independent support for the conclusion that, so far as psychopathological propensities are concerned, individuals may be classified in terms of the relative strength of underlying schizoid and depressive tendencies.

Every theory of basic types is inevitably confronted with the problem of 'mixed types'. Kretschmer freely acknowledges the existence of mixed types; and he explains their occurrence on the grounds that the incidence of a type is governed by the balance of two antagonistic biological (and perhaps hormonic) groups of factors, which may be unusually evenly balanced. According to the views here presented, the occurrence of mixed types is to be explained not so much in terms of the balance of antagonistic elements as in terms of the relative strength of fixations in developmental phases. Where difficulties over object-relationships assert themselves pre-eminently during the early oral phase, a schizoid tendency is established; and, where difficulties over object-relationships assert themselves pre-eminently during the late oral phase, the establishment of a depressive tendency is the result. In so far, however, as such difficulties are fairly evenly distributed between the two phases, we may expect to find a fixation in the late oral phase superimposed upon one in the early oral phase; and in that case a deeper schizoid tendency will be found underlying a superimposed depressive tendency. That such a phenomenon may occur admits of no doubt whatsoever; and indeed even the most 'normal' person must be regarded as having schizoid potentialities at the deepest levels. It is open to equally little question that even the most 'normal' person may in certain circumstances become depressed. Similarly, schizoid individuals are not wholly immune to depression; and depressed individuals are sometimes found to display certain schizoid characteristics. Whether a depressive or a schizoid state will declare itself in any given case doubtless depends in part upon whether the precipitating circumstances take the form of loss of the real object or of difficulties in object-relationships assuming some other form; and, where there is a fairly even balance between fixations in the early and the late oral phases, this may be the determining factor. Nevertheless the most important factor must always remain the degree of regression which is provoked; and this is determined primarily by the relative strength of fixations. In the last instance the degree of regression must depend upon whether the chief problem of the individual lies in the disposal of his love or in the disposal of his hate; and there must be few individuals in whom the disposal of love and the disposal of hate are attended by equal difficulty.

CHAPTER III

The Repression and the Return of Bad Objects (with special reference to the 'War Neuroses,)[1] (1943)

I. THE IMPORTANCE OF OBJECT-RELATIONSHIPS

IN the earlier phases of his psychoanalytical thought Freud was chiefly concerned with the nature and the fate of impulse—a fact to which the formulation of his famous libido theory bears eloquent witness. Thus it came about that modern psychopathology was founded essentially upon a psychology of impulse; and Freud's libido theory has remained one of the corner-stones in the edifice of psychoanalytical thought, albeit this theory is now generally accepted only with such modifications as were introduced by Abraham in deference to developmental considerations. It was always foreign to Freud's intention, however, to convey the impression that all the problems of psychopathology could be solved in terms of the psychology of impulse; and in the later phases of his thought—from a time which may be conveniently dated by the publication of The Ego and the Id—his attention was predominantly directed to the growth and the vicissitudes of the ego. Thus a developing psychology of the ego came to be superimposed upon an already established psychology of impulse; and, whatever developments the psychology of the ego may have subsequently undergone in psychoanalytical thought, the underlying libido theory has remained relatively unquestioned. This is a situation which I have lately come to regard as most regrettable. Unfortunately, the present occasion does not permit of an examination of the grounds upon which I have reached this opinion; and it must suffice to say that I have been influenced by clinical and psychotherapeutic,

[1] Originally published in The British Journal of Medical Psychology, Vol. XIX, Pts. 3 and 4, and now republished with minor amendments.

no less than by theoretical, considerations. My point of view may, however, be stated in a word. In my opinion it is high time that psychopathological inquiry, which in the past has been successively focused, first upon impulse, and later upon the ego, should now be focused upon *the object* towards which impulse is directed. To put the matter more accurately if less pointedly, the time is now ripe for a psychology of *object-relationships*. The ground has already been prepared for such a development of thought by the work of Melanie Klein; and indeed it is only in the light of her conception of *internalized objects* that a study of object-relationships can be expected to yield any significant results for psychopathology. From the point of view which I have now come to adopt, psychology may be said to resolve itself into a study of the relationships of the individual to his objects, whilst, in similar terms, psychopathology may be said to resolve itself more specifically into a study of the relationships of the ego to its internalized objects. This point of view has received its initial formulation in my paper entitled 'A Revised Psychopathology of the Psychoses and Psychoneuroses'.

Amongst the conclusions formulated in the above-mentioned paper two of the most far-reaching are the following: (1) that libidinal 'aims' are of secondary importance in comparison with object-relationships, and (2) that a relationship with the object, and not gratification of impulse, is the ultimate aim of libidinal striving. These conclusions involve a complete recasting of the classic libido theory; and in the paper in question an attempt is made to perform this task. The task to which I shall now turn is that of considering what are the implications of the view that libido is essentially orientated towards objects for the classic theory of repression. The importance of this task would be difficult to exaggerate; for what Freud said in 1914 still remains true—that 'the doctrine of repression is the foundation-stone upon which the whole structure of psychoanalysis rests'[1] (albeit I should prefer to see 'theory' substituted for 'doctrine').

2. THE NATURE OF THE REPRESSED

It is to be noted that, in directing his attention predominantly to problems regarding the nature and fate of impulse in the earlier phases of his thought, Freud was concerning himself essentially with the repressed. On the other hand, when in *The Ego and the Id* he

[1] *Collected Papers* (1924), Vol. I, p. 297.

turned his attention to problems regarding the nature and growth of the ego, his concern was deliberately transferred from the repressed to the agency of repression. If, however, it is true to say that libido (and indeed 'impulse' in general) is directed essentially towards objects (and not towards pleasure), the moment is opportune for us to turn our attention once more to the nature of the repressed; for, if in 1923 Freud was justified in saying, 'Pathological research has centred our interest too exclusively on the repressed',[1] it may now be equally true to say that our interest is too exclusively centred upon the repressive functions of the ego.

In the course of his discussion upon the repressive functions of the ego in *The Ego and the Id* Freud makes the following statement: 'We know that as a rule the ego carries out repressions in the service and at the behest of the super-ego.'[2] This statement is of special significance if object-relationships are as overwhelmingly important as I have come to regard them; for, if, as Freud says, the super-ego represents 'a deposit left by the earliest object-choices of the id',[3] that endopsychic structure must be regarded as essentially an internalized object, with which the ego has a relationship. This relationship is based upon a process of identification, as Freud so justly points out. The identification of the ego with the super-ego is, of course, rarely, if ever, complete; but, in so far as it exists, repression must be regarded as a function of the relationship of the ego to an internalized object which is accepted as 'good'. At this point I feel driven to make the confession that my last quotation from Freud was a phrase deliberately torn from its sentence in order to enable me to make a point. Quotations torn from their context are notoriously misleading; and I therefore hasten to make amends, now that the mutilation for which I am responsible has served its purpose. The complete sentence reads: 'The super-ego is, however, *not merely* a deposit left by the earliest object-choices of the id; it also represents *an energetic reaction formation against those choices*' (present author's italics). In the light of the full quotation it now becomes doubtful whether the relationships of the ego to internalized objects can be exhaustively described in terms of a relationship between the ego and the super-ego. It will be noted that the super-ego remains a 'good' object to the ego, whether the identification is strong and the ego yields to the appeal of the super-ego, or whether the identification is weak and the appeal of the super-ego is defied by the ego. The question accord-

[1] *The Ego and the Id* (1927), p. 19.   [2] Ibid., p. 75.   [3] Ibid., p. 44.

ingly arises whether there are not also 'bad' internalized objects with which the ego may be identified in varying degrees. That such 'bad' objects are to be found within the psyche the work of Melanie Klein can leave us in no doubt. The demands of a psychology based upon object-relationships will, therefore, require us to infer that, if the clue to the agency of repression lies in the relationship of the ego to 'good' internalized objects, the clue to the nature of the repressed will lie in the relationship of the ego to 'bad' internalized objects.

It will be recalled that, in his original formulation of the concept of repression, Freud described the repressed as consisting of intolerable memories, against the unpleasantness of which repression provided the ego with a means of defence. The nuclear memories against which this defence was directed were, of course, found by Freud to be libidinal in nature; and, to explain why libidinal memories, which are inherently pleasant, should become painful, he had recourse to the conception that repressed memories were painful because they were guilty. To explain in turn why libidinal memories should be guilty, he fell back upon the conception of the Œdipus situation. When subsequently he formulated his conception of the super-ego, he described the super-ego as a means of effecting a repression of the Œdipus situation and attributed its origin to a need on the part of the ego for an internal defence against incestuous impulses. In accordance with this point of view, he came to speak of the repressed as consisting essentially of guilty impulses and explained the repression of memories as due to the guilt of impulses operative in the situations which such memories perpetuated. In the light of the considerations already advanced, however, it becomes a question whether Freud's earlier conception of the nature of the repressed was not nearer the mark, and whether the repression of impulses is not a more secondary phenomenon than the repression of memories. I now venture to formulate the view that *what are primarily repressed are neither intolerably guilty impulses nor intolerably unpleasant memories, but intolerably bad internalized objects.* If memories are repressed, accordingly, this is only because the objects involved in such memories are identified with bad internalized objects; and, if impulses are repressed, this is only because the objects with which such impulses impel the individual to have a relationship are bad objects from the standpoint of the ego. Actually, the position as regards the repression of impulses would appear to be as follows. Impulses become bad if they are directed towards bad objects. If such bad objects are internalized, then

Bad internalized objects are repressed

the impulses directed towards them are internalized; and the repression of internalized bad objects thus involves the repression of impulses as a concomitant phenomenon. It must be stressed, however, that what are primarily repressed are bad internalized objects.

3. REPRESSED OBJECTS

Once it has come to be recognized that repression is directed primarily against bad objects, this fact assumes the complexion of one of those obvious phenomena which are so frequently missed, and which are often the most difficult to discover. At one time I used frequently to have the experience of examining problem children; and I remember being particularly impressed by the reluctance of children who had been the *victims* of sexual assaults to give any account of the traumatic experiences to which they had been subjected. The point which puzzled me most was that, the more innocent the victim was, the greater was the resistance to anamnesis. By contrast, I never experienced any comparable difficulty in the examination of individuals who had *committed* sexual offences. At the time, I felt that these phenomena could only be explained on the assumption that, in resisting a revival of the traumatic memory, the victim of a sexual assault was actuated by guilt over the unexpected gratification of libidinal impulses which had been renounced by the ego and repressed, whereas in the case of the sexual offender there was no comparable degree of guilt and consequently no comparable degree of repression. I always felt rather suspicious of this explanation; but it seemed the best available at the time. From my present standpoint it seems inadequate. As I now see it, the position is that the victim of a sexual assault resists the revival of the traumatic memory primarily because this memory represents a record of a relationship with a bad object. It is difficult to see how the experience of being assaulted could afford any great measure of gratification except to the more masochistic of individuals. To the average individual such an experience is not so much guilty as simply 'bad'. It is intolerable in the main, not because it gratifies repressed impulses, but for the same reason that a child often flies panic-stricken from a stranger who enters the house. It is intolerable because a bad object is always intolerable, and a relationship with a bad object can never be contemplated with equanimity.

It is interesting to observe that a relationship with a bad object is felt by the child to be not only intolerable, but also shameful. It may accordingly be inferred that, if a child is ashamed of his parents (as is quite often the case), his parents are bad objects to him; and it is in the same direction that we must look for an explanation of the fact that the victim of a sexual assault should feel ashamed of being assaulted. That a relationship with a bad object should be shameful can only be satisfactorily explained on the assumption that in early childhood all object-relationships are based upon identification.[1] This being the case, it follows that, if the child's objects present themselves to him as bad, he himself feels bad; and indeed it may be stated with equal truth that, if a child feels bad, it implies that he has bad objects. If he behaves badly, the same consideration applies; and it is for this reason that a delinquent child is invariably found to have (from the child's point of view at any rate) bad parents. At this point we are confronted with another of those obvious phenomena which are so rarely noticed. At one time it fell to my lot to examine quite a large number of delinquent children from homes which the most casual observer could hardly fail to recognize as 'bad' in the crudest sense—homes, for example, in which drunkenness, quarrelling, and physical violence reigned supreme. It is only in the rarest instances, however, (and those only instances of utter demoralization and collapse of the ego) that I can recall such a child being induced to admit, far less volunteering, that his parents were bad objects. It is obvious, therefore, that in these cases the child's bad objects had been internalized and repressed. What applies to the delinquent child can be shown to apply also to the delinquent adult—and not only to the delinquent adult, but also to the psychoneurotic and psychotic. For that matter, it also applies to the ostensibly 'normal' person. It is impossible for anyone to pass through childhood without having bad objects which are internalized and repressed.[2] Hence internalized bad objects are present in the

[1] The fact that all object-relationships are originally based upon identification was recognized by Freud, as may be judged from his statement: 'At the very beginning, in the primitive oral phase of the individual's existence, object-cathexis and identification are hardly to be distinguished from each other' (*The Ego and the Id* (1927), p. 35). This theme is developed at some length in my paper entitled 'A Revised Psychopathology of the Psychoses and Psychoneuroses', and indeed forms the basis of the revised psychopathology which I envisage.

[2] This would appear to be the real explanation of the classic massive amnesia for events of early childhood, which is only found to be absent in individuals whose ego is disintegrating (e.g. in incipient schizophrenics, who so often display a most remarkable capacity for reviving traumatic incidents of early childhood, as is illustrated by a case to be quoted on page 77.

minds of all of us at the deeper levels. Whether any given individual becomes delinquent, psychoneurotic, psychotic or simply 'normal' would appear to depend in the main upon the operation of three factors: (1) the extent to which bad objects have been installed in the unconscious and the degree of badness by which they are characterized, (2) the extent to which the ego is identified with internalized bad objects, and (3) the nature and strength of the defences which protect the ego from these objects.

4. THE MORAL DEFENCE AGAINST BAD OBJECTS

If the delinquent child is reluctant to admit that his parents are bad objects, he by no means displays equal reluctance to admit that he himself is bad. It becomes obvious, therefore, that the child would rather be bad himself than have bad objects; and accordingly we have some justification for surmising that one of his motives in becoming bad is to make his objects 'good'. In becoming bad he is really taking upon himself the burden of badness which appears to reside in his objects. By this means he seeks to purge them of their badness; and, in proportion as he succeeds in doing so, he is rewarded by that sense of security which an environment of good objects so characteristically confers. To say that the child takes upon himself the burden of badness which appears to reside in his objects is, of course, the same thing as to say that he internalizes bad objects. The sense of outer security resulting from this process of internalization is, however, liable to be seriously compromised by the resulting presence within him of internalized bad objects. Outer security is thus purchased at the price of inner insecurity; and his ego is henceforth left at the mercy of a band of internal fifth columnists or persecutors, against which defences have to be, first hastily erected, and later laboriously consolidated.

The earliest form of defence resorted to by the developing ego in a desperate attempt to deal with internalized bad objects is necessarily the simplest and most readily available, viz. repression. The bad objects are simply banished to the unconscious.[1] It is only when repression fails to prove an adequate defence against the internalized bad objects and these begin to threaten the ego that the four classic

[1] Here I may say that, in explaining the process of repression to my patients, I find it useful to speak of the bad objects as being, as it were, buried in the cellar of the mind behind a locked door which the patient is afraid to open for fear either of revealing the skeletons in the cupboard, or of seeing the ghosts by which the cellar is haunted.

psychopathological defences are called into operation, viz. the phobic, the obsessional, the hysterical, and the paranoid defences.[1] There is, however, another form of defence by which the work of repression is invariably supported, and to which special attention must now be directed. I refer to what may be called 'the defence of the super-ego' or 'the defence of guilt' or 'the moral defence'.

I have already spoken of the child 'taking upon himself the burden of badness which appears to reside in his objects'; and, at the time, I spoke of this process as equivalent to the internalization of bad objects. At this point, however, a distinction must be drawn between two kinds of badness, which I propose to describe respectively as 'unconditional' and 'conditional' badness. Here I should explain that, when I speak of an object as 'unconditionally bad', I mean 'bad from a libidinal standpoint', and that, when I speak of an object as 'conditionally bad', I mean 'bad from a moral standpoint'. The bad objects which the child internalizes are unconditionally bad; for they are simply persecutors. In so far as the child is identified with such internal persecutors, or (since infantile relationships are based upon identification) in so far as his ego has a relationship with them, he too is unconditionally bad. To redress this state of unconditional badness he takes what is really a very obvious step. He internalizes his good objects, which thereupon assume a super-ego role. Once this situation has been established, we are confronted with the phenomena of conditional badness and conditional goodness. In so far as the child leans towards his internalized bad objects, he becomes conditionally (i.e. morally) bad *vis-à-vis* his internalized good objects (i.e. his super-ego); and, in so far as he resists the appeal of his internalized bad objects, he becomes conditionally (i.e. morally) good *vis-à-vis* his super-ego. It is obviously preferable to be conditionally good than conditionally bad; but, in default of conditional goodness, it is preferable to be conditionally bad than unconditionally bad. If it be asked how it comes about that conditional badness is preferred to unconditional badness, the cogency of the answer may best be appreciated if the answer is framed in religious terms; for such terms provide the best representation for the adult mind of the situation as it presents itself to the child. Framed in such terms the answer is that it is better to be a sinner in a world ruled by God than to live in a world ruled by

---

[1] The nature and significance of these defences, as also their relationship to one another, are described in my paper entitled 'A Revised Psychopathology of the Psychoses and Psychoneuroses'.

the Devil. A sinner in a world ruled by God may be bad; but there is always a certain sense of security to be derived from the fact that the world around is good—'God's in His heaven—All's right with the world!'; and in any case there is always a hope of redemption. In a world ruled by the Devil the individual may escape the badness of being a sinner; but he is bad because the world around him is bad. Further, he can have no sense of security and no hope of redemption. The only prospect is one of death and destruction.[1]

5. THE DYNAMICS OF THE INFLUENCE OF BAD OBJECTS

At this point it is worth considering whence bad objects derive their power over the individual. If the child's objects are bad, how does he ever come to internalize them? Why does he not simply reject them as he might reject 'bad' cornflour pudding or 'bad' castor oil? As a matter of fact, the child usually experiences considerable difficulty in rejecting castor oil, as some of us may know from personal experience. He would reject it if he could; but he is allowed no opportunity to do so. The same applies to his bad objects. However much he may want to reject them, he cannot get away from them. They force themselves upon him; and he cannot resist them because they have power over him. He is accordingly compelled to internalize them in an effort to control them. But, in attempting to control them in this way, he is internalizing objects which have wielded power over him in the external world; and these objects retain their prestige for power over him in the inner world. In a word, he is 'possessed' by them, as if by evil spirits. This is not all, however. The child not only internalizes his bad objects because they force themselves upon him and he seeks to control them, but also, and above all, because he *needs* them. If a child's parents are bad objects, he cannot reject them, even if they do not force themselves upon him; for he cannot do without them. Even if they **neglect** him, he cannot reject them; for, if they neglect him, his need for them is increased. One of my male patients had a dream which aptly illustrates the central dilemma of the child. In this dream he was standing beside his mother with a

[1] Here it is interesting to note how commonly in the course of a deep analysis patients speak of death when the resistance is weakening and they are faced with the prospect of a release of bad objects from the unconscious. It should always be borne in mind that, from the patient's point of view, the maintenance of the resistance presents itself (literally) as a matter of life and death.

bowl of chocolate pudding on a table before him. He was ravenously hungry; and he knew that the pudding contained deadly poison. He felt that, if he ate the pudding, he would die of poisoning and, if he did not eat the pudding, he would die of starvation. There is the problem stated. What was the dénouement? He ate the pudding. He incorporated the contents of the poisonous breast because his hunger was so great. In the light of this dream the reader will hardly be surprised to learn that among the symptoms from which this patient suffered was a fear that his system was being poisoned by intestinal toxins which had so affected his heart that he was threatened with heart failure. What was really wrong with his heart was, however, eloquently revealed in another dream—a dream in which he saw his heart lying upon a plate and his mother lifting it with a spoon (i.e. in the act of eating it). Thus it was because he had internalized his mother as a bad object that he felt his heart to be affected by a fatal disease; and he had internalized her, bad object though she was for him, because as a child he needed her. It is above all the need of the child for his parents, however bad they may appear to him, that compels him to internalize bad objects; and it is because this need remains attached to them in the unconscious that he cannot bring himself to part with them. It is also his need for them that confers upon them their actual power over him.

6. GUILT AS A DEFENCE AGAINST THE RELEASE OF BAD OBJECTS

After this digression it is time that we turned our attention once again to the moral defence. The essential feature, and indeed the essential aim, of this defence is the conversion of an original situation in which the child is surrounded by bad objects into a new situation in which his objects are good and he himself is bad. The moral situation which results belongs, of course, to a higher level of mental development than the original situation; and this level is characteristically a 'civilized' level. It is the level at which the super-ego operates, and to which the interplay between the ego and the super-ego belongs. It is the level at which analytical interpretations in terms of guilt and the Œdipus situation are alone applicable; and it would appear to be the level at which psychotherapy is often rather exclusively conducted. That psychotherapy should be exclusively conducted at this level is undesirable; for, as should be clear from the preceding argument, the phenomena of guilt must be regarded (from a strictly psychopathological standpoint, of course) as partaking of the nature of a defence. In a word, *guilt operates as a resistance in psychotherapy*. Interpretations in terms of guilt may thus actually play into the hands of the patient's resistance. That the more coercive and moralizing forms of psychotherapy must have this effect is obvious; for a coercive and moralizing psychotherapist inevitably becomes either a bad object or a super-ego figure to his patient. If he becomes simply a bad object to the patient, the latter leaves him, possibly with intensified symptoms. If, however, he becomes a super-ego figure to the patient, he may effect a temporary improvement in symptoms by supporting the patient's own super-ego and intensifying repression. On the other hand, most analytically minded psychotherapists may be expected to make it their aim to mitigate the harshness of the patient's super-ego and thus to reduce guilt and anxiety. Such an endeavour is frequently rewarded with excellent therapeutic results. Nevertheless, I cannot help feeling that such results must be attributed, in part at least, to the fact that in the transference situation the patient is provided in reality with an unwontedly good object, and is thereby placed in a position to risk a release of his internalized bad objects from the unconscious and so to provide conditions for the libidinal cathexis of these objects to be dissolved—albeit he is also under a temptation to exploit a 'good' relationship with the analyst as a defence against taking this risk. An analysis conducted too exclusively at the guilt or super-ego level may, however, easily have the effect of producing a negative therapeutic reaction; for the removal of a patient's defence of guilt may be accompanied by a compensatory access of repression which renders the resistance impenetrable. There is now little doubt in my mind that, in conjunction with another factor to be mentioned later, the deepest source of resistance is fear of the release of bad objects from the unconscious; for, when such bad objects are released, the world around the patient becomes peopled with devils which are too terrifying for him to face. It is largely owing to this fact that the patient undergoing analysis is so sensitive, and that his reactions are so extreme. It is also to this fact that we must look in no small measure for an explanation of the 'transference neurosis'. At the same time there is now little doubt in my mind that the release of bad objects from the unconscious is one of the chief aims which the psychotherapist should set himself out to achieve, even at the expense of a severe 'transference neurosis'; for it is only when the internalized bad objects are released from the un-conscious that there is any hope of their cathexis being dissolved. The bad objects can only be safely released, however, if the analyst has become established as a sufficiently good object for the patient. Otherwise the resulting insecurity may prove insupportable. Given a satisfactory transference situation, a therapeutically optimal release of bad objects can, in my opinion, only be promoted if caution is exer-cised over interpretations at the guilt or super-ego level. Whilst such interpretations may relieve guilt, they may actually have the effect of intensifying the repression of internalized bad objects and thus leav-ing the cathexis of these objects unresolved.[1] It is to the realm of these bad objects, I feel convinced, rather than to the realm of the super-ego that the ultimate origin of all psychopathological develop-ments is to be traced; for it may be said of all psychoneurotic and psychotic patients that, if a True Mass is being celebrated in the chancel, a Black Mass is being celebrated in the crypt. It becomes evident, accordingly, that the psychotherapist is the true successor to the exorcist, and that he is concerned, not only with 'the forgiveness of sins', but also with 'the casting out of devils'.

7. A SATANIC PACT

At this point I must resist the temptation to embark upon a study of the mysteries of demoniacal possession and exorcism. Such a study could not fail to prove as profitable as it would be interesting, if I am justified in my view that it is in the realm of internalized bad objects rather than in the realm of internalized good objects (i.e. the realm of the super-ego) that we must lay the foundations of psychopathology. Unfortunately, the present occasion does not permit of such a divert-ing excursion; but I cannot refrain from directing the attention of the reader in search of a good bed-time story to Freud's fascinating paper entitled 'A Neurosis of Demoniacal Possession in the Seventeenth Century'.[2] Here we find recorded, with a pertinent psychoanalytical commentary, the story of a destitute artist, one Christoph Haitz-

---

[1] The fact that relief of guilt may be accompanied by an intensification of repression can only be satisfactorily explained in terms of the conclusion already recorded to the effect that *the defence of the super-ego and repression are separate defences.*

[2] *Collected Papers*, Vol. IV, pp. 436–72.

mann, who made a pact with the Devil while in a melancholic state precipitated by the death of his father. From the point of view of a psychopathology based upon object-relationships, the signing of the pact admirably illustrates the difficulty encountered by the psycho-neurotic or psychotic in parting with his bad objects; for, as Freud leaves us in no doubt, the Devil with whom the pact was signed was intimately associated with the deceased father of Christoph. It is interesting to note too that Christoph's symptoms were only relieved when he invoked the aid of a good object and was rewarded by a return of the unholy pact, which he received, torn in four pieces, from the hands of the Blessed Virgin in the chapel at Mariazell. He did not achieve freedom from relapses, however, until he had been received into a religious brotherhood and had thus replaced his pact with the Devil by solemn vows to the service of God. This was pre-sumably a triumph for the moral defence; but Freud's commentary fails to do justice to the significance of the cure no less than to the significance of the disease (which lay in the fact that the poor painter was 'possessed' by internalized bad objects). Freud is unquestionably correct when he writes in the introduction to his paper: 'Despite the somatic ideology of the era of "exact" science, the demonological theory of these dark ages has in the long run justified itself. Cases of demoniacal possession correspond to the neuroses of the present day.' Yet the chief point of the correspondence to which Freud refers is obscured when he adds: 'What in those days were thought to be evil spirits to us are base and evil wishes, the derivatives of impulses which have been rejected and repressed.' This comment reflects the inade-quacy of the classic conception that libido is primarily pleasure-seeking; for the whole point of a pact with the Devil lies in the fact that it involves a relationship with a bad object. Indeed, this is made perfectly plain in the terms of Christoph's bond; for, pathetically enough, what he sought from Satan in the depths of his depression was not the capacity to enjoy wine, women, and song, but per-mission, to quote the terms of the pact itself, 'sein leibeigner Sohn zu sein' ('for to be unto him euen as a sonne of his bodie'). What he sold his eternal soul to obtain, accordingly, was not gratification, but a father, albeit one who had been a bad object to him in his child-hood. While his actual father remained alive, the sinister influence of the bad father-figure whom he had internalized in his childhood was evidently corrected by some redeeming features in the real person; but after his father's death he was left at the mercy of the internalized bad father, whom he had either to embrace or else remain objectless and deserted.[1]

8. THE LIBIDINAL CATHEXIS OF BAD OBJECTS AS A SOURCE OF RESISTANCE

Reference has already been made to my attempt to recast the libido theory and to the considerations which led me to make this attempt. A recasting of the theory in conformity with the considerations in question is, in my opinion, an urgent necessity; for, although the heuristic, no less than the historical, importance of the libido theory would be difficult to exaggerate, a point has now been reached at which the theory has outworn its usefulness and, so far from providing impetus for further progress within the field of psychoanalytical thought, is actually operating as a brake upon the wheels. The theory in its original form may be shown to have many misleading implications; but the case of Christoph Haitzmann provides an admirable opportunity to illustrate one such misleading implication, which has an important bearing on the concept of repression. The classic form of the libido theory unquestionably implies that libido is irrevocably seeking to express itself in activities determined by zonal aims, and that, if it does not always succeed, it is only prevented from so doing by some form of inhibition, and in the last instance by repression. According to this view repressed libido can only manifest itself, if at all, in a disguised form, either in symptoms or sublimations or in a manner determined by character-formations (i.e. in a manner which is a cross between a sublimation and a symptom). Further, it follows from this view that the actual form assumed by any such manifestation will be determined by the nature of the original zonal aim. If, however, libido is primarily object-seeking, it will seek the object by whatever channels are most readily available in a manner which is not primarily determined by any presumptive aims dependent upon a zonal origin. On this view, the significance of the zones reduces itself to that of available channels by way of which libido may seek the object. The barriers to libidinal expression will likewise resolve themselves in great measure into

[1] It is very far from my intention to imply that guilt over aggressive wishes towards his father played no part in Christoph's depression; but it is implied that the part which it must undoubtedly have played is secondary from an *etiological* standpoint.

inhibitions against object-seeking. This being so, a peculiar situation arises when the object has been internalized and repressed; for, in these circumstances, we are confronted with a situation in which libido is seeking a repressed object. The bearing of this fact upon the concept of narcissism need not be stressed here. The phenomenon to which I desire to direct attention is that, in the circumstances mentioned, libido is, for practical purposes, operating in the same direction as repression. It is captivated by the repressed object; and, owing to the lure of the repressed object, it is driven into a state of repression by the very momentum of its own object-seeking. *When the object is a repressed object, accordingly, the object-cathexis operates as a resistance; and the resistance encountered in analytical therapy is thus maintained, not only by the agency of repression, but also by the dynamic qualities of libido itself.*

This last conclusion is in plain contradiction to Freud's statement: 'The unconscious, i.e. the "repressed" material, offers no resistance whatever to curative efforts; indeed, it has no other aim than to force its way through the pressure weighing on it, either to consciousness or to discharge by means of some real action.'[1] Nevertheless, it is a conclusion which follows as a necessary corollary from the view that libido is primarily object-seeking; and it possesses the special advantage of throwing additional light on the nature of the negative therapeutic reaction, which can now be seen to derive its significance largely from the fact that, in so far as the object is a repressed object, the libidinal aim is in direct conflict with the therapeutic aim. In a word, the negative therapeutic reaction involves a refusal on the part of libido to renounce its repressed objects; and, even in the absence of a negative therapeutic reaction, it is in the same direction that we must look in no small measure for an explanation of the extreme stubbornness of the resistance. The actual overcoming of repression as such would, accordingly, appear to constitute if anything a less formidable part of the analyst's difficult task than the overcoming of the patient's devotion to his repressed objects—a devotion which is all the more difficult to overcome because these objects are bad and he is afraid of their release from the unconscious. This being so, we may surmise that the analytical treatment of poor Christoph would have proved a somewhat formidable proposition in a twentieth-century consulting-room. It would have proved no easy task, we may be sure, to dissolve his pact with Satan; and it is not difficult to envisage the emergence of a stubborn negative therapeutic reaction in his case.

[1] *Beyond the Pleasure Principle* (1922), p. 19.

After all, even the intervention of the Blessed Virgin was insufficient to establish his cure upon a firm basis. It was only after his pact with the Devil was replaced by a pact with God that his freedom from symptoms was finally established. The moral would seem to be that the appeal of a good object is an indispensable factor in promoting a dissolution of the cathexis of internalized bad objects, and that the significance of the transference situation is partly derived from this fact.[1]

9. DISSOLUTION OF THE CATHEXIS OF BAD OBJECTS

It follows from what precedes that among the various aims of analytical technique should be (1) to enable the patient to release from his unconscious 'buried' bad objects which have been internalized because originally they seemed indispensable, and which have been repressed because originally they seemed intolerable, and (2) to promote a dissolution of the libidinal bonds whereby the patient is attached to these hitherto indispensable bad objects. So far as considerations of technique affect the fulfilment of these aims, principles to be borne in mind would appear to include the following: (1) that situations should be interpreted, not in terms of gratification, but in terms of object-relationships (including, of course, relationships with internalized objects); (2) that libidinal strivings should be represented to the patient as ultimately dictated by object-love and as, therefore, basically if not superficially 'good'; (3) that libidinal 'badness' should be related to the cathexis of bad objects ('sin' always being regarded, according to the Hebraic conception, as seeking after strange gods and, according to the Christian conception, as yielding to the Devil); (4) that 'guilt' situations should be related by interpretation to 'bad object' situations; (5) that caution should be exercised over interpretations in terms of aggression except perhaps in the case of depressives, who present a special problem for analytical technique.[2]

[1] It is of interest to record that, since this paper was originally written, the theme of a pact with the Devil has emerged quite explicitly and spontaneously in the case of several of my patients.

[2] Interpretations in terms of aggression are liable to have the undesirable effect of making the patient feel that the analyst thinks him 'bad'. In any case, they become less necessary in proportion as the repressed objects are released; for in such circumstances the patient's aggression makes itself obvious enough. It will then become the analyst's task to point out to the patient the libidinal factor that lies behind his aggression.

symptoms as a defence against the return of the repressed

10. THE PSYCHOPATHOLOGICAL RETURN OF BAD OBJECTS

Paradoxically enough, if it is an aim of analytical technique to promote a release of repressed bad objects from the unconscious, it is also fear of just such a release that characteristically drives the patient to seek analytical aid in the first instance. It is true that it is from his symptoms that he consciously desires to be relieved, and that a considerable proportion of psychopathological symptoms consist essentially in defences against a 'return of the repressed' (i.e. a return of repressed objects). Nevertheless, it is usually when his defences are wearing thin and are proving inadequate to safeguard him against anxiety over a threatened release of repressed objects that he is driven to seek analytical aid. From the patient's point of view, accordingly, the effect of analytical treatment is to promote the very situation from which he seeks to escape.[1] Hence the phenomenon of the transference neurosis, which involves in part a defence against, and in part a reaction to, a release of repressed bad objects. The release of such objects obtained in analytical treatment differs, however, from a spontaneous release of such objects in that it has a therapeutic aim— and ultimately a therapeutic effect in virtue of the fact that it is a release controlled by the analyst and safeguarded by the security imparted by the transference situation. Nevertheless, such fine distinctions are hard for the patient to appreciate at the time; and he is not slow to realize that he is being cured by means of a hair from the tail of the dog that bit him. It is only when the released bad objects are beginning to lose their terror for him that he really begins to appreciate the virtues of mental immunization therapy. Here it should be noted that the release of repressed objects of which I speak is by no means identical with that active externalization of internalized bad objects, which is the characteristic feature of the paranoid technique.[2] The phenomenon to which I specially refer is the escape

[1] This is well illustrated in a dream of one of my female patients. In this dream she saw a friend of her father digging in peaty ground. As her glance fell upon one of the cut surfaces, the loose and fibrous nature of the ground attracted her attention. Then, as she looked closer, she was horrified to see swarms of rats creeping out from the interstices between the roots and fibres. Whatever else this dream may have represented, it certainly represented the effects of analytical treatment. The man digging in the peaty ground was myself digging in her unconscious, and the rats were the repressed bad objects (actually penises, of course) which my digging had released.

[2] The paranoid technique consists, not in the projection of repressed impulses, as

of bad objects from the bonds imposed by repression. When such an escape of bad objects occurs, the patient finds himself confronted with terrifying situations which have hitherto been unconscious. External situations then acquire for him the significance of repressed situations involving relationships with bad objects. This phenomenon is accordingly not a phenomenon of projection, but one of 'transference'.

II. THE TRAUMATIC RELEASE OF BAD OBJECTS—WITH SPECIAL REFERENCE TO MILITARY CASES

The spontaneous and psychopathological (as against the induced and therapeutic) release of repressed objects may be observed to particular advantage in wartime in the case of military patients, amongst whom the phenomenon may be studied on a massive scale. Here I should add that, when I speak of a 'spontaneous' release of repressed objects, I do not mean to exclude the operation of precipitating factors in reality. On the contrary, the influence of such factors would appear to be extremely important. The position would appear to be that an unconscious situation involving internalized bad objects is liable to be activated by any situation in outer reality conforming to a pattern which renders it emotionally significant in the light of the unconscious situation. Such precipitating situations in outer reality must be regarded in the light of traumatic situations. The emotional intensity and specificity required to render an external situation traumatic varies, of course, in accordance with economic and dynamic factors in the endopsychic state. In military cases it is common to find that a traumatic situation is provided by the blast from an exploding shell or bomb, or else by a motor accident—and that quite irrespective of any question of cerebral concussion; but being caught in the cabin of a torpedoed troopship, seeing civilian refugees machine-gunned from the air or shelled in a crowded market-place, having to throttle an enemy sentry in order to escape captivity, being let down by a superior officer, being accused of homosexuality, and being refused compassionate leave to go home for a wife's confinement are all examples chosen at random from among the traumatic situations which have come under my notice. In many cases Army life in time of war itself constitutes a traumatic experience

is commonly supposed, but in the projection of repressed objects in the form of persecutors.

which approximates to the nature of a traumatic situation, and which may confer the quality of a traumatic situation upon some little incident of Army life. It is remarkable how common among psycho-neurotic and psychotic soldiers in wartime are the complaints, 'I can't bear being shouted at', and 'I can't eat Army food' (a remark which is commonly followed by, 'I can eat anything my wife cooks for me'). The effect of such traumatic situations and traumatic experiences in releasing bad objects from the unconscious is demonstrated nowhere better than in the wartime dreams of military patients. Amongst the commonest of such dreams, as would be expected, are nightmares about being chased or shot at by the enemy, and about being bombed by hostile aeroplanes (often described as 'great black planes'). The release of bad objects may, however, be represented in other ways, e.g. in nightmares about being crushed by great weights, about being strangled by someone, about being pursued by pre-historic animals, about being visited by ghosts and about being shouted at by the sergeant-major. The appearance of such dreams is sometimes accompanied by a revival of repressed memories of child-hood. One of the most remarkable cases of this kind in my experience was that of a psychopathic soldier, who passed into a schizoid state not long after being conscripted, and who then began to dream about prehistoric monsters and shapeless things and staring eyes that burned right through him. He became very childish in his behaviour; and simultaneously his consciousness became flooded with a host of forgotten memories of childhood, among which he became specially preoccupied by one of sitting in his pram on a station platform and seeing his mother enter a railway carriage with his older brother. In reality his mother was just seeing his brother off; but the impression created in the patient was that his mother was going off in the train too and thus leaving him deserted. The revival of this repressed memory of a deserting mother represented, of course, the release of a bad object from the unconscious. A few days after he told me of this memory a shop belonging to him was damaged by a bomb; and he was granted twenty-four hours' leave of absence to attend to business arising out of the incident. When he saw his damaged shop, he experienced a schizoid state of detachment; but that night, when he went to bed at home, he felt as if he were being choked and experienced a powerful impulse to smash up his house and murder his wife and children. His bad objects had returned with a vengeance.

12. A NOTE ON THE REPETITION COMPULSION

What has been said regarding the role of traumatic situations in precipitating psychopathological conditions in soldiers in wartime naturally recalls what Freud has to say regarding the traumatic neuroses in *Beyond the Pleasure Principle*. If, however, the views expressed in the present paper are well-founded, there is no need for us to go 'beyond the pleasure principle' and postulate a primal 'repetition compulsion' to explain the persistence of traumatic scenes in the mental life of those in whom it occurs. If it be true that libido is object-seeking and not pleasure-seeking, there is, of course, no pleasure principle to go beyond. Apart from that, however, it does not require any repetition compulsion to explain the revival of traumatic scenes. On the contrary, if the effect of a traumatic situation is to release bad objects from the unconscious, the difficulty will be to see how the patient can get away from these bad objects.[1] The fact is that he is haunted by them; and, since they are framed by the traumatic incident, he is haunted by this too. In the absence of a therapeutic dissolution of the cathexis of his bad objects, he can only achieve freedom from this haunting if his bad objects are once more banished to the unconscious through an access of repression. That this is the manner in which the ghosts are customarily laid is obvious from the attitude of those soldiers in whom traumatic memories have disappeared from waking life, if not from the life of dreams. Quite characteristic is the remark of one of them whom I questioned about his experiences: 'I don't want to talk about these things. I want to go home and forget about all that.'

13. A NOTE ON THE DEATH INSTINCTS

What applies to Freud's conception of the repetition compulsion applies also to his closely related conception of the death instincts. If libido is really object-seeking, this conception would appear superfluous. We have seen that libido is attached not only to good objects, but also to bad objects (witness Christoph's pact with the Devil). We have seen, furthermore, that libido may be attached to bad objects which have been internalized and repressed. Now a relation-

[1] It cannot be a coincidence that Freud should describe the expressions of a repetition compulsion as having, not only an instinctive, but also a 'daemonic' character (*Beyond the Pleasure Principle* (1922), p. 43).

ship with a bad object can hardly escape the alternative of being either of a sadistic or of a masochistic nature. What Freud describes under the category of 'death instincts' would thus appear to represent for the most part masochistic relationships with internalized bad objects. A sadistic relationship with a bad object which is internalized would also present the appearance of a death instinct. As a matter of fact, such relationships are usually of a sado-masochistic nature with a bias on the masochistic side of the scale; but in any case they are essentially libidinal manifestations. This may be well illustrated in the case of a patient of mine who came to me haunted by bad objects in the form of penises. In course of time, breasts began to rival penises in the role of haunting bad objects. Later the bad objects became grotesque figures which were obviously personifications of breasts and penises. Later still, the grotesque figures were replaced by devilish forms. These in turn were succeeded by numerous figures of a parental character; and eventually these figures were replaced in turn by recognizable images of her parents. 'They', as she always described them, seemed to forbid her under pain of death to express any feelings; and she was constantly saying, 'They will kill me if I let any feelings out.' It is, accordingly, interesting to note that, as the transference situation developed, she also began to beg me to kill her. 'You would kill me if you had any regard for me,' she cried, adding, 'If you won't kill me, it means that you don't care.' This phenomenon seems best interpreted as due, not to the operation of a death instinct, but to the transference of libido, albeit libido which still retained the masochistic complexion of her relationships with her original (bad) objects.

14. THE PSYCHONEUROSES AND PSYCHOSES OF WAR

The subject of the present paper can hardly be dismissed without a final note upon the psychoneuroses and psychoses of wartime. My experience of military cases leaves me in no doubt that the chief predisposing factor in determining the breakdown of a soldier (or for that matter a sailor or an airman) is infantile dependence upon his objects.[1] At the same time my experience leaves me in equally little

[1] As a matter of fact, this also applies to civilian cases, not only in time of war, but also in time of peace; and indeed it is one of the main theses of my paper entitled 'A Revised Psychopathology of the Psychoses and Psychoneuroses' that all psychopathological developments are ultimately based upon an infantile attitude of

doubt that the most distinctive feature of military breakdowns is separation-anxiety. Separation-anxiety must obviously present a special problem for democracies in time of war; for under a democratic regime the dependent individual can find no substitute for his accustomed objects under military conditions (the sergeant-major proving a very poor substitute, e.g., for an attentive wife). The problem of separation-anxiety in the soldier is anticipated under a totalitarian regime by a previous exploitation of infantile dependence, since it is part of the totalitarian technique to make the individual dependent upon the regime at the expense of dependence upon familial objects. Dependence upon familial objects is what really constitutes 'the degeneracy of the democracies' in totalitarian eyes. The totalitarian technique, however, has its weakness. It depends upon national success; for only under conditions of success can the regime remain a good object to the individual. Under conditions of failure the regime becomes a bad object to the individual; and the socially disintegrating effects of separation-anxiety then begin to assert themselves at the critical moment. On the other hand, it is in time of failure or defeat that a democracy has the advantage; for in a democracy the individual is less dependent upon the state, and, therefore, less subject to disillusionment regarding the 'goodness' of the state as an object. At the same time, the threat to familial objects inherent in defeat (so long as this is not too devastating) provides an incentive for effort, which is lacking under a totalitarian regime. Considered from the point of view of group psychology, accordingly, the great test of morale in a totalitarian state comes in time of failure, whereas in a democracy the great test of morale comes in time of success.[1]

If separation-anxiety is the most distinctive feature of breakdowns among soldiers, such breakdowns are at the same time characterized by another feature which is of no less importance from a national standpoint, and which can only be properly appreciated in the light

dependence. I had just reached this conclusion as the result of material provided by cases seen in private when I began to see military cases in large numbers; and I found my conclusion most opportunely confirmed on the grand scale. Military cases are specially illuminating for two reasons: (1) because in such cases phenomena detected in a narrow field under the high-power lens of the analytical microscope may be observed in a wide field under a less powerful lens, (2) because under military conditions in wartime large numbers of individuals may be observed in an 'experimental' state of artificial separation from their objects.

[1] The conclusions recorded in this paragraph now (1951) appear to have been justified by subsequent, no less than by previous, events.

of what has been said regarding the nature of the moral defence. No one who has read Freud's *Group Psychology and the Analysis of the Ego* can remain in doubt regarding the importance of the super-ego as a factor in determining the morale of a group. It is obvious, therefore, that the super-ego fulfils other functions besides that of providing the individual with a defence against bad objects. Above all, it is through the authority of the super-ego that the bonds which unite individuals into a group are forged and maintained. At the same time, it must be recognized that the super-ego does originate as a means of defence against bad objects. As such, the return of bad objects obviously implies a failure of the defence of repression; but it equally implies a failure of the moral defence and a collapse of the authority of the super-ego. The soldier who breaks down in time of war is thus characterized not only by separation-anxiety, but also by a condition in which the appeal of the super-ego, which bade him serve his country under arms, is replaced by the acute anxiety which a release of bad objects inspires. From a practical standpoint, accordingly, what happens is that for him the Army ceases to perform a super-ego function and reverts to the status of a bad object. It is for this reason that the psychoneurotic or psychotic soldier cannot bear to be shouted at by the sergeant-major and cannot bear to eat Army food. For in his eyes every word of command is equivalent to an assault by a malevolent father, and every spoonful of 'greasy' stew from the cookhouse is a drop of poison from the breast of a malevolent mother. No wonder that the 'war neuroses' are so recalcitrant! And no wonder, perhaps, that, after gaining some experience of psycho-neurotic and psychotic servicemen *en masse*, I was driven to remark, 'What these people need is not a psychotherapist, but an evangelist'; for, from a national point of view, the problem of the 'war neuroses' is not so much a problem of psychotherapy as a problem of group morale.

CHAPTER IV

Endopsychic Structure Considered in Terms of Object-Relationships[1] (1944)

OBJECT-RELATIONSHIP PSYCHOLOGY AS THE RATIONALE OF THE INTERNALIZATION OF OBJECTS

IN a previous paper (1941) I attempted to formulate a new version of the libido theory and to outline the general features which a systematic psychopathology based upon this re-formulation would appear to assume. The basic conception which I advanced on that occasion, and to which I still adhere, is to the effect that libido is primarily object-seeking (rather than pleasure-seeking, as in the classic theory), and that it is to disturbances in the object-relationships of the developing ego that we must look for the ultimate origin of all psychopathological conditions. This conception seems to me not only to be closer in accord with psychological facts and clinical data than that embodied in Freud's original libido theory, but also to represent a logical outcome of the present stage of psychoanalytical thought and a necessary step in the further development of psychoanalytical theory. In particular, it seems to me to constitute an inevitable implication of the illuminating conception of internalized objects, which has been so fruitfully developed by Melanie Klein, but which traces its scientific origin to Freud's theory of the superego (an endopsychic structure which was, of course, conceived by him as originating in the internalization of objects).

Quite apart from the considerations advanced in my previous paper or various other considerations which could be adduced, it may be claimed that the psychological introjection of objects and, in particular, the perpetuation of introjected objects in inner reality are processes which by their very nature imply that libido is essentially

[1] Originally published in *The International Journal of Psycho-Analysis*, Vol. XXV, Pts. 1 and 2.

object-seeking; for the mere presence of oral impulses is in itself quite insufficient to account for such a pronounced devotion to objects as these phenomena imply. A similar implication would appear to arise out of the mere possibility of an Œdipus situation being perpetuated in the unconscious; for unceasing devotion to an object constitutes the very essence of this situation. Nevertheless the conception of internalized objects has been developed without any significant modification of a libido theory with which there is no small reason to think that it is incompatible. Freud himself never saw fit to undertake any systematic re-formulation of his original libido theory, even after the introduction of his theory of the super-ego. At the same time there are innumerable passages in his works in which it appears to be taken for granted that libido is specifically object-seeking. Indeed it is possible to find passages in which this implicit view becomes explicit—as, for example, when he states quite simply (1929): 'Love seeks for objects.'[1] This statement occurs in a paragraph in which, referring to his original theory of instincts, he writes as follows: 'Thus first arose the contrast between ego instincts and object instincts. For the energy of the latter instincts and exclusively for them I introduced the term libido; an antithesis was then formed between the ego instincts and the libidinal instincts directed towards objects.' As Freud proceeds to point out, the distinction between these two groups of instincts was abandoned upon his 'introduction of the concept of narcissism, i.e. the idea that libido cathects the ego itself'; but in the light of the passage quoted it would appear no very revolutionary step to claim that libido is primarily object-seeking, especially if, as I have suggested in my previous paper, we conceive of narcissism as a state in which the ego is identified with objects.[2]

Nevertheless the ever-increasing concentration of psychoanalytical research upon object-relationships has left unmodified the original theory that libido is primarily pleasure-seeking, and with it the related conception that 'the course of mental processes is automatically regulated by "the pleasure principle"' (Freud, 1920).[3] The persistence of this view has raised various problems which might other-

[1] *Civilization and its Discontents* (London, 1930), p. 95.

[2] Quite apart from this suggestion, there is no necessary incompatibility between the view that libido is primarily object-seeking and the conception of libido cathecting the ego, since there is always the possibility of one part of the ego structure treating another part as an object—a possibility which cannot be ignored in the light of what follows regarding the splitting of the ego.

[3] *Beyond the Pleasure Principle* (London, 1922), p. 1.

wise have proved easier of solution. Prominent amongst these is the problem for which Freud set out to find a solution in *Beyond the Pleasure Principle* (1920) itself, viz. how it comes about that neurotics cling to painful experiences so assiduously. It was the difficulty of accounting for this phenomenon in terms of the pleasure principle that led Freud to fall back upon the conception of a 'repetition compulsion'. If, however, libido is regarded as primarily object-seeking, there is no need to resort to this expedient; and in a recent paper (1943) I attempted to show how the tendency to cling to painful experiences may be explained in terms of relationships with bad objects. In the same paper I also attempted to show how the difficulties involved in the conception of primary 'death instincts' (in contrast to the conception of a primary aggressive tendency) may be avoided if all the implications of libidinal relationships with bad objects are taken into account.

IMPULSE PSYCHOLOGY AND ITS LIMITATIONS

In actual fact, the 'object-relationship' standpoint which I have now come to adopt has resulted from an attempt, imposed upon me by circumstances, to gain a better understanding of the problems presented by patients displaying certain schizoid tendencies, i.e. a class of individuals for whom object-relationships present an especial difficulty; and here, in parenthesis, I venture to express the opinion that psychoanalytical research in its later phases has suffered from too great a preoccupation with the problems of melancholic depression. Previous to my reaching the above-mentioned standpoint, however, I had already become very much impressed by the limitations of 'impulse psychology' in general, and somewhat sceptical of the explanatory value of all theories of instinct in which the instincts are treated as existing *per se*. The limitations of impulse psychology make themselves felt in a very practical sense within the therapeutic field; for, whilst to reveal the nature of his 'impulses' to a patient by painstaking analysis is one proposition, to enable him to know what to do with these 'impulses' is quite another. What an individual shall do with his 'impulses' is clearly a problem of object-relationships. It is equally a problem of his own personality; but (constitutional factors apart) problems of the personality are themselves bound up with the relationships of the ego to its internalized objects—or, as I should prefer to say for reasons which will shortly appear, the relationships of various *parts* of the ego to internalized objects and to one another as objects. In a word 'impulses' cannot be considered apart from the endopsychic structures which they energize and the object-relationships which they enable these structures to establish; and, equally, 'instincts' cannot profitably be considered as anything more than forms of energy which constitute the dynamic of such endo-psychic structures.

From a practical psychotherapeutic standpoint the analysis of 'impulses' considered apart from structures proves itself a singularly sterile procedure, and particularly so in the case of patients with well-marked schizoid tendencies. By means of interpretations couched more or less exclusively in terms of 'impulses', it is sometimes quite easy in such cases to release a flood of associations (e.g. in the form of oral-sadistic phantasies), which appear singularly impressive as mani-festations of the unconscious, but which can be maintained indefin-itely without any real movement in the direction of integration and without any significant therapeutic development. The explanation of this phenomenon would appear to be that the ego (or, as I should prefer to say, *the central ego*) does not participate in the phantasies described except as a recording agent. When such a situation arises, the central ego, so to speak, sits back in the dress-circle and describes the dramas enacted upon the stage of inner reality without any effec-tive participation in them. At the same time it derives considerable narcissistic satisfaction from being the recorder of remarkable events and identifying itself with the analyst as observer while asserting a superiority over the analyst as mere observer by reason of the fact that it is not merely observing, but also furnishing the material for observation. This procedure is really a masterpiece of defensive tech-nique—one to which schizoid individuals are only too ready to resort at the best of times, but which constitutes an almost irresistible temp-tation to them when the analyst's interpretations are couched too exclusively in terms of 'impulses'. Such a technique provides the best of all means of enabling the patient to evade the central therapeutic problem, viz. how to release those dynamic charges known as 'impulses' in the context of reality. This problem is clearly one of object-relationships within the social order.

My point regarding the inadequacy of impulse psychology may be illustrated by a reference to one of the cases in the light of which my present views were developed. This patient was an unmarried woman with schizoid features which were none the less present because the clinical picture was dominated by well-marked phobic and hysterical symptoms, as well as by generalized anxiety. She was repressed in proportion to a high degree of unrelieved libidinal tension. When this libidinal tension rose during a session, it was no uncommon occurrence for her to complain of feeling sick. This sense of nausea was undoubtedly a transference phenomenon based upon an attitude towards her mother and her mother's breast mediated by her father and her father's penis, all as internalized objects; and it readily lent itself to interpretation in terms of oral impulses in so far as her associations had been characterized from the first by a considerable amount of oral material. Nevertheless the chief significance of her nausea seemed to reside, not so much in the oral nature of the reaction as in the influence shown by this reaction to be exercised upon her object-relationships (1) by a libidinal fixation upon her mother's breast, and (2) by an attitude of rejection towards the object of her libidinal need. It was true, of course, that the oral nature of her reaction was related to a severe repression of genital sexuality; and she was probably right when, on more than one occasion, she hazarded the opinion that she would be frigid in intercourse, although the correctness of this surmise had never been put to the test. At the same time, her difficulty in achieving a genital attitude seemed best understood, not in terms of any fixation at an oral stage, but rather in terms of a rejection of her father's penis based partly on an identification of this object with the bad breast, partly on a preferential fixation on the breast, and partly on the emotional 'badness' of her father as a whole object. The scales were further weighted against a genital attitude by the fact that an oral attitude involves a lesser degree of commitment to the object whilst conferring a greater measure of power over it. It was not uncommon for the same patient to say during a session: 'I want to go to the lavatory.' In the first instance this statement had quite a literal significance; but later in the analysis it came increasingly to mean that she was experiencing a desire to express libidinal feelings mobilized by the transference situation. Here again, it was not in the nature of the 'impulse' considered in terms of phases (this time urinary and anal) that the chief significance of the phenomenon lay. It lay rather in the quality of the object-relationship involved. 'Going to the lavatory', like 'being sick', undoubtedly signified a rejection of the libidinal object considered as contents. Nevertheless, as compared with 'being sick', it signified a lesser measure of rejection; for, although in both cases a cathartic discharge of libidinal tension was also involved, the discharge of contents represented by 'going to the lavatory', being a discharge of assimilated contents, indicated a greater willingness to express libidinal feelings *before* an external object, albeit falling short of that direct discharge of feelings *towards* an object, which characterizes the genital attitude.

The scientific validity of a psychological theory cannot, of course, be assessed solely in terms of psychotherapeutic success or failure; for the scientific significance of therapeutic results can only be judged when it is known exactly how these results are obtained. Impulse psychology cannot be regarded as providing any exception to this general rule; but it is significant that, where psychoanalysis is concerned, it is now generally recognized that therapeutic results are closely related to the phenomenon of transference, i.e. to the establishment of an object-relationship of a special kind with the analyst on the part of the patient. On the other hand, it is an accepted article of the psychoanalytical technique that the analyst should be unusually self-effacing. As we know, there are very good reasons for the adoption of such an attitude on his part; but it inevitably has the effect of rendering the object-relationship between patient and analyst somewhat one-sided from the patient's point of view and thus contributing to the resistance. A certain one-sidedness in the relationship between patient and analyst is, of course, inherent in the analytical situation; but it would appear that, when the self-effacing attitude of the analyst is combined with a mode of interpretation based upon a psychology of impulse, a considerable strain is imposed upon the patient's capacity for establishing satisfactory object-relationships (a capacity which must be regarded as already compromised in virtue of the fact that the patient is a patient at all). At the same time, the patient is placed under a considerable temptation to adopt, among other defences, that to which reference has already been made, viz. the technique of describing scenes enacted on the stage of inner reality without any significant participation on the part of the central ego either in these scenes or in an effective object-relationship with the analyst. One of my patients, who was a past master in this technique, said to me one day, after providing a comprehensive intellectual description of the state of impulse-tension in which he felt himself to be placed: 'Well, what are you going to do about it?' By way of reply I explained that the real question was what he himself was going to do about it. This reply proved highly disconcerting to him, as indeed it was intended to be. It was disconcerting to him because it faced him abruptly with the real problem of the analysis and of his life. How an individual is going to dispose of impulse-tension is, as already stated, clearly a problem of object-relationships, but equally a problem of the personality, since an object-relationship necessarily involves a subject as well as an object. The theory of object-relationships thus inevitably leads us to the position that, if 'impulses' cannot be considered apart from objects, whether external or internal, it is equally impossible to consider them apart from ego structures. Indeed it is even more impossible to consider 'impulses' apart from ego structures, since it is only ego structures that can seek relationships with objects. We are thus brought back to the conclusion, already recorded, that 'impulses' are but the dynamic aspect of endopsychic structures and cannot be said to exist in the absence of such structures, however immature these may turn out to be. Ultimately 'impulses' must be simply regarded as constituting the forms of activity in which the life of ego structures consists.

STRUCTURE PSYCHOLOGY AND THE REPRESSION OF STRUCTURES[1]

Once the position now indicated has been reached, it obviously becomes incumbent upon us to review afresh our theory of the mental apparatus. In particular, it becomes a question how far Freud's description of mental structure in terms of id, ego, and super-ego can be retained without modification. The moment this question is raised, it is, of course, plainly in relation to the status of the id that doubts will first arise; for, if it be true that no 'impulses' can be regarded as existing in the absence of an ego structure, it will no longer be possible to preserve any psychological distinction between the id and the ego. Freud's conception of the *origin* of the ego as a structure which develops on the surface of the psyche for the purpose of regulating id-impulses in relation to reality will thus give place to a conception of the ego as the source of impulse-tension from the beginning. This inclusion of the id in the ego will, of course, leave essentially unaffected Freud's conception of the *function* served by the 'ego' in regulating the discharge of impulse-tension in deference to

[1] It is now obvious in retrospect that some of the conclusions recorded in this, as also in the previous, section of the present paper were already adumbrated in my paper entitled 'Features in the Analysis of a Patient with a Physical Genital Abnormality', which was written as long ago as in 1931, and which is included in this volume.

the conditions of outer reality. It will, however, involve the view that 'impulses' are oriented towards reality, and thus to some extent determined by the 'reality principle', from the very beginning. Thus, for example, the child's earliest oral behaviour will be regarded as oriented *ab initio* towards the breast. In accordance with this point of view, the pleasure principle will cease to be regarded as the primary principle of behaviour and will come to be regarded as a subsidiary principle of behaviour involving an impoverishment of object-relationships and coming into operation in proportion as the reality principle fails to operate, whether this be on account of the immaturity of the ego structure or on account of a failure of development on its part. Questions regarding the extent to which the reality principle has superseded the pleasure principle will then give place to questions regarding the extent to which an originally immature reality principle has progressed towards maturity; and questions regarding the capacity of the ego to regulate id-impulses in deference to reality will give place to questions regarding the measure in which the ego structure within which impulse-tension arises has been organized in accordance with the reality principle, or, in default of this, has resorted to the pleasure principle as a means of organization.

If, then, 'impulse' is to be regarded as inseparably associated with an ego structure from the beginning, what becomes of Freud's conception of repression as a function exercised by the ego in its dealings with impulses originating in the id? I have already elsewhere (1943) considered the implications of my theory of object-relationships for the concept of repression. There I advanced the view that repression is primarily exercised, not against impulses which have come to appear painful or 'bad' (as in Freud's final view) or even against painful memories (as in Freud's earlier view), but against *internalized objects* which have come to be treated as bad. I still feel justified in regarding this view as correct; but in certain other respects my views regarding repression have undergone a change. In particular, I have come to regard repression as exercised, not only against internalized objects (which, incidentally, must be regarded as endopsychic structures, albeit not ego structures), but also against parts of the 'ego' which seek relationships with these internal objects. Here it may occur to the reader to pass the criticism that, since repression is a function of the 'ego', this view involves the anomaly of the ego repressing itself. How, it may be asked, can the ego be conceived as repressing the ego? The answer to this question is that, whilst it is inconceivable that the ego as a whole should repress itself, it is not inconceivable that one part of the 'ego' with a dynamic charge should repress another part of the 'ego' with a dynamic charge. This is, of course, quite a different proposition from one set of impulses repressing another set—a conception rightly rejected by Freud when engaged in the task of formulating his theory of the mental apparatus. In order to account for repression Freud found himself compelled to postulate the existence of a *structure* capable of instigating repression —viz. the super-ego. It is, therefore, only another step in the same direction to postulate the existence of structures which are repressed. Apart from any theoretical reasons such as those already advanced, there are very good clinical reasons for making such an assumption. Prominent among these is the difficulty experienced in effecting the 'sublimation' of libidinal 'impulses'. This difficulty cannot be adequately explained as due to an inveterate and inherent obstinacy on the part of 'impulses' themselves, especially once we have come to regard 'impulses' as just forms of energy at the disposal of the ego structure. On the contrary, it can only be satisfactorily explained on the assumption that the repressed 'impulses' are inseparable from an ego structure with a definite pattern. The correctness of this assumption is confirmed by the phenomena of multiple personality, in which the linkage of repressed 'impulses' with a submerged ego structure is beyond question; but such a linkage may also be detected in the less extensive forms of dissociation, which are so characteristic of the hysterical individual. In order to account for repression, we thus appear to be driven to the necessity of assuming a certain multiplicity of egos. This should not really prove a particularly difficult conception for any one familiar with the problems presented by schizoid patients. But here, as so often, we are reminded of the limitations imposed upon psychoanalytical theory in some of its later developments by a preoccupation with the phenomena of melancholic depression.

THE SCHIZOID POSITION

That Freud's theory of mental structure is itself based in no small measure upon a consideration of the phenomena of melancholia can hardly escape the notice of any reader of *The Ego and the Id* (1923), the work which contains the classic exposition of the theory; and, in conformity with this fact, it is in his paper entitled 'Mourning and

Melancholia' (1917)¹ that we find the final link in the chain of thought which culminated in the exposition in question. Correspondingly the 'depressive position' is accorded a place of central importance in the views of Melanie Klein and her collaborators. Here I must confess that the accordance of such a central place to the depressive position is difficult to reconcile with my own experience. It would be idle, of course, to deny the importance of the depressive position in individuals suffering from true depression or, for that matter, in individuals of a depressive type. So far as my experience goes, however, such individuals do not constitute any appreciable proportion of the analyst's clientèle, although, of course, they are common enough in ordinary psychiatric practice. So far as concerns the usual run of patients suffering from anxiety states, psychoneurotic symptoms and character difficulties, the central position seems to me to be schizoid rather than depressive in the vast majority of those who embark upon and persist in analytical treatment.

At this point I feel it necessary to refer to the distinction which I have already drawn (1941) between the characteristically melancholic affect of 'depression' and the 'sense of futility' which I have come to regard as the characteristically schizoid affect. From the point of view of the observer there is, admittedly, sufficient superficial similarity between the two affects to render the distinction difficult to draw in many cases, especially since the schizoid individual so commonly describes himself as 'depressed'; and consequently the familiar term 'depressed' is frequently applied in clinical practice to patients who should properly be described as suffering from a sense of futility. In this way a confusion of classification is liable to occur, with the result that a number of patients with psychoneurotic symptoms come to be regarded as belonging to the depressive type when the type to which they belong is really schizoid. Apart from this source of confusion, however, it is a common thing for a basic schizoid position to escape notice in the case of 'psychoneurotic' patients owing to the strength of psychoneurotic defences and the resulting prominence of psychoneurotic (e.g. hysterical) symptoms in the clinical picture. Yet, when we consider the cases cited by Janet in illustration of the material upon the basis of which he formulated the conception of hysteria as a clinical entity, it is difficult to avoid concluding that quite a number of the individuals concerned displayed remarkably schizoid characteristics; and indeed it may be surmised that an

¹ *Collected Papers* (London, 1925), Vol. IV, pp. 152 f.

appreciable proportion would actually be diagnosed as frank schizophrenics if they appeared in a modern psychiatric clinic. Here it may be added that my own investigations of patients with hysterical symptoms leave me in no doubt whatever that the dissociation phenomena of 'hysteria' involve a split of the ego fundamentally identical with that which confers upon the term 'schizoid' its etymological significance.

'BACK TO HYSTERIA'

At this point it seems apposite to recall that Freud's earliest researches within the realm of psychopathology were concerned almost exclusively with hysterical (and *not* with melancholic) phenomena, and that it is upon a basis of these phenomena, accordingly, that psychoanalytical theory and practice were originally founded. It would doubtless be idle to speculate to what extent the development of psychoanalytical theory would have pursued a different course if hysterical phenomena had retained the central place which they originally occupied in Freud's researches; but it may at least be surmised that the importance subsequently assumed by the depressive position would have been assumed in large measure by the schizoid position. It was, of course, when Freud turned from the study of the repressed to a study of the agency of repression that the problems of melancholia began to oust problems of hysteria from the central position which the latter had hitherto occupied. That this should have been the case is not difficult to understand in view of (*a*) the close association which appears to exist between guilt and repression, on the one hand, and (*b*) the outstanding prominence which guilt assumes in the melancholic state, on the other. Be that as it may, Freud's theory of the super-ego certainly represents an attempt to trace the genesis of guilt and the instigation of repression to a common source in the Œdipus situation. This fact gives rise to a serious incompatibility between Freud's views regarding the origin of repression and Abraham's 'phase' theory of libidinal development; for, whilst Freud conceived the Œdipus situation, to which he looked for the rationale of repression, as essentially a genital situation, his account of the origin of the super-ego, which he regarded as the instigator of repression, is conceived in terms of an oral situation, i.e. a situation corresponding to a stage which, according to the 'phase' theory, must necessarily be pregenital. Melanie Klein has, of course, come to regard the Œdipus situation as originating at a very much earlier stage than was formerly supposed. Her resolution of the difficulty must accordingly be interpreted as having been achieved at the expense of the 'phase' theory. This theory has already been the subject of detailed criticism on my part (1941). At the same time I have now come to look for the source of repression not only beyond the genital attitude, but also beyond the Œdipus situation, and even beyond the level at which the super-ego is established. Thus I not only attempted elsewhere (1943) to show that *repression* originates primarily as a defence against 'bad' internalized objects (and not against 'impulses', whether incestuous in the genital sense or otherwise), but also that *guilt* originates as an *additional* defence against situations involving bad internalized objects. According to this view, guilt originates on the principle that the child finds it more tolerable to regard himself as conditionally (i.e. morally) bad than to regard his parents as unconditionally (i.e. libidinally) bad. To describe the process whereby the change from the latter to the former attitude is effected, I introduced the term 'moral defence'; and, according to my view, it is only at the instance of the 'moral defence' that the super-ego is established.[1] The establishment of the super-ego accordingly represents the attainment of a new level of structural organization, beneath which the old level persists. Thus, in my opinion, beneath the level at which the central ego finds itself confronted with the super-ego as an internal object of moral significance lies a level at which parts of the ego find themselves confronted with internal objects which are not simply devoid of moral significance, but unconditionally bad from the libidinal standpoint of the central ego whether in the role of an exciting or that of a rejecting object (internal persecutors of one kind or the other). Whilst, therefore, the main phenomenon of melancholic depression may be regarded as receiving a relatively satisfactory explanation at the super-ego level, some of the accompanying

[1] I should add that, in my opinion, it is always 'bad' objects that are internalized in the first instance, since it is difficult to find any adequate motive for the internalization of objects which are satisfying and 'good'. Thus it would be a pointless procedure on the part of the infant to internalize the breast of a mother with whom he already had a perfect relationship in the absence of such internalization, and whose milk proved sufficient to satisfy his incorporative needs. According to this line of thought it is only in so far as his mother's breast fails to satisfy his physical and emotional needs and thus becomes a bad object that it becomes necessary for the infant to internalize it. It is only later that good objects are internalized to defend the child's ego against bad objects which have been internalized already; and the super-ego is a 'good object' of this nature.

phenomena are not so easily explained. Thus the paranoid and hypo-chrondriacal trends which so frequently manifest themselves in melancholics represent an orientation towards internal objects which are in no sense 'good', but are unconditionally (i.e. libidinally) bad. The same may be said of the obsessional features which are so characteristic of individuals in the initial stages of depression; for the obsessional defence is not primarily moral. On the contrary, this defence is essentially a defence against the 'unlucky', i.e. against situations involving relationships with unconditionally bad (internal) objects. It is equally difficult to find a satisfactory explanation of the symptoms of 'hysteria' at the super-ego level—if for no other reason than that in 'hysteria' the libidinal inhibitions which occur are out of all proportion to the measure of guilt which is found to be present. Since, therefore, it was in an effort on Freud's part to explain hysterical phenomena that psychoanalysis originated, it may not be without profit to return to a consideration of this material, encouraging ourselves, if encouragement be needed, with the slogan 'Back to hysteria'.

A MULTIPLICITY OF EGOS

Attention has already been drawn to the fact that, whereas the repressed was eventually described by Freud as consisting essentially of impulses, he found it necessary to fall back upon structural conceptions (the ego and the super-ego) when he came to seek an explanation of the agency of repression. Reduced to its simplest terms, Freud's conception of repression is to the following effect: (*a*) that the agency of repression is the ego, (*b*) that repression is instigated and maintained by the pressure of the super-ego (an internalized parental figure) upon the ego, (*c*) that the repressed consists essentially in libidinal impulses, and (*d*) that repression arises as a means of defence against impulses involved in the Œdipus situation and treated by the ego as 'guilty' in terms of the pressure of the super-ego. That the agent and the instigator of repression should both be regarded as structures whilst the repressed is regarded as consisting of impulses involves a certain anomaly which appears so far to have escaped attention. The extent of this anomaly may perhaps best be appreciated in the light of the fact that the super-ego, which is described as the instigator of repression, is itself largely unconscious; for this raises the difficult question whether the super-ego itself is not also repressed. Freud himself was by no means oblivious to this problem; and he

94

expressly envisages the possibility of the super-ego being in some measure subject to repression. Repression of the super-ego would, of course, represent the repression of a structure. It would thus appear that the general possibility of the repression of a structure is recognized by Freud; and, in the light of the considerations already advanced, it becomes reasonable to ask whether the repressed is not invariably and inherently structural. In this event the anomaly to which I have referred would be avoided.

That the repressed is essentially structural in nature is implicit in the view which I have already advanced (1943) to the effect that repression is primarily directed against internalized objects which are treated as bad; for, unless it is assumed that internalized objects are structures, the conception of the existence of such objects becomes utterly meaningless. In the light of further experience, my view that repression is primarily directed against bad internalized objects has proved to require considerable elaboration in a direction which has eventually led me to a revised conception of psychical structure. What actually provided the occasion of my chief step in this direction was the analysis of a dream recorded by one of my patients. This patient was a married woman who originally came to me for analysis on account of frigidity. Her frigidity was unquestionably a phenomenon of hysterical dissociation (hysterical anæsthesia combined with hysterical paresis of the vagina); but, like all such phenomena, it represented but one part of a general personality problem. The dream itself was simple enough; but it struck me in the light of one of those simple manifestations which have so often in the history of science been found to embody fundamental truths.

The (manifest) dream to which I refer consisted in a brief scene in which the dreamer saw the figure of herself being viciously attacked by a well-known actress in a venerable building which had belonged to her family for generations. Her husband was looking on; but he seemed quite helpless and quite incapable of protecting her. After delivering the attack the actress turned away and resumed playing a stage part, which, as seemed to be implied, she had momentarily set aside in order to deliver the attack by way of interlude. The dreamer then found herself gazing at the figure of herself lying bleeding on the floor; but, as she gazed, she noticed that this figure turned for an instant into that of a man. Thereafter the figure alternated between herself and this man until eventually she awoke in a state of acute anxiety.

It came as no great surprise to me to learn from the dreamer's associations that the man into whom the figure of herself turned was wearing a suit closely resembling one which her husband had recently acquired, and that, whilst he had acquired this suit at her instigation, he had taken 'one of his blondes' to the fitting. This fact, taken in conjunction with the fact that in the dream he was a helpless spectator of the attack, at once confirmed a natural suspicion that the attack was directed no less against him than against herself. This suspicion was amply confirmed by further associations which need not be detailed. The course followed by the associations also confirmed an additional suspicion that the actress who delivered the attack belonged as much to the personality of the dreamer as did the figure of herself against which the attack was delivered. In actual fact, the figure of an actress was well suited to represent a certain aspect of herself; for she was essentially a shut-in and withdrawn personality who displayed very little genuine feeling towards others, but who had perfected the technique of presenting façades to a point at which these assumed a remarkably genuine appearance and achieved for her a remarkable popularity. Such libidinal affect as she experienced had, since childhood, manifested itself predominantly in a secret phantasy life of masochistic complexion; but in the life of outer reality she had largely devoted herself to the playing of roles—e.g. the roles of good wife, good mother, good hostess, and good business woman. From this fact the helplessness attributed to her husband in the dream derived additional significance; for, although she played the role of good wife with conspicuous success, her real personality was quite inaccessible to him and the good wife whom he knew was for the most part only the good actress. This held true not only within the sphere of emotional relationships, but also within the sphere of marital relations; for, whilst she remained frigid during intercourse, she had acquired the capacity of conveying the impression of sexual excitement and sexual satisfaction. Further, as the analysis revealed beyond all question, her frigidity represented not only an attack upon the libidinal component in herself, but also a hostile attitude towards her husband as a libidinal object. It is clear, therefore, that a measure of hidden aggression against her husband was involved in her assumption of the role of actress as this was portrayed in the dream. It is equally clear from the dream that, in a libidinal capacity, she was identified with her husband as the object of her own aggression. At this point it should be mentioned that, when the dream occurred, her husband was a member of one of the combatant Services and was about to return home on leave. On the eve of his return, and just before the occurrence of the dream, she had developed a sore throat. This was a conjunction of events which had occurred so frequently in the past as to preclude coincidence on this occasion, and which accordingly served to confirm her identification with her husband as the object of her aggression. The situation represented in the dream is thus one in which the dreamer in one capacity, so far unspecified, vents her aggression directly against herself in another capacity, viz., a libidinal capacity, whilst, at the same time, venting her aggression indirectly against her husband as a libidinal object. At a superficial level, of course, this situation readily lent itself to being interpreted in the sense that the dreamer, being ambivalent towards her husband, had diverted the aggressive component in her ambivalent attitude from her husband to herself at the instance of guilt over her aggression in conformity with the melancholic pattern. Nevertheless, during the actual session in which the dream was recorded this interpretation did not commend itself to me as exhaustive, even at a superficial level.

It is obvious, of course, that the situation represented in the dream lent itself to a deeper interpretation than that to which reference has just been made. The situation was described a moment ago as one in which the dreamer in a capacity so far unspecified vented her aggression directly against herself in a libidinal capacity, whilst, at the same time, venting her aggression indirectly against her husband as a libidinal object. This description is, of course, incomplete in that it leaves unspecified the capacity in which she expressed her aggression; and it is when we come to consider the nature of this unspecified capacity that the deeper significance of the dream becomes a matter of moment. According to the manifest content of the dream, it was as an actress that she delivered the attack; and we have already seen how well suited the figure of an actress was to represent an aspect of herself hostile to libidinal relationships. However, abundant material had already emerged during the analysis to make it plain that the figure of an actress was at least equally well suited to represent the dreamer's mother—an artificial woman who had neither displayed any natural and spontaneous affection towards her children nor welcomed any such display on their part towards herself, and for whom the fashionable world provided a stage upon which she had spent her life in playing parts. It was thus easy to see that, in the capacity of

97

actress, the dreamer was closely identified with her mother as a repressive figure. The introduction of her mother into the drama as an apparently 'super-ego' figure at once raises the question whether the deeper interpretation of the dream should not be couched in terms of the Œdipus situation; and it becomes natural to ask whether her father is not also represented. In reality her father had been killed on active service during the war of 1914–18, at a time when she was only six years of age; and analysis had revealed the presence of considerable resentment towards him as a libidinal object who had proved at once exciting and rejecting (this resentment being focused particularly upon the memory of an early dressing-room scene). If then we are to look for a representation of her father in the dream, our choice is obviously limited to a single figure—the man who alternated with the figure of the dreamer as the object of attack. We have seen, of course, that this figure represented her husband; but analysis had already revealed how closely her husband was identified by transference with her father. For this, as well as for other reasons which need not be detailed, it was safe to infer that the man who was involved in the attack represented her father at the deeper level of interpretation. At this level, accordingly, the dream was capable of being interpreted as a phantasy in which both she and her father were portrayed as being killed by her mother on account of a guilty incestuous relationship. At the same time the dream was equally capable of being interpreted in terms of psychical structure, and thus as representing the repression of her libido on account of its incestuous attachment to her father at the instigation of a super-ego modelled upon her mother. Nevertheless, neither of these interpretations seemed to me to do justice to the material, although the structural interpretation seemed to offer the more fruitful line of approach.

At this point I feel it necessary to make some reference to the development of my own views regarding phantasy in general and dreams in particular. Many years ago I had the opportunity to analyse a most unusual woman, who was a most prolific dreamer.[1]

---

[1] This case is described at some length in my paper entitled, 'Features in the Analysis of a Patient with a Physical Genital Abnormality' (included in the present volume). It is also the third case described in 'The Effect of a King's Death upon Patients Undergoing Analysis' (also included in this volume). Although the patient in question displayed symptoms which were mainly of a manic-depressive nature, I consider in retrospect that she was basically a schizoid personality.

Among the dreams recorded by this woman were a number which defied all efforts to bring them into conformity with the 'wish-fulfilment' theory, and which she herself came to describe quite spontaneously as 'state of affairs' dreams, intending by this description to imply that they represented actually existing endopsychic situations. Doubtless this made an impression on me. At any rate, much later, after Freud's theory of psychical structure had become familiar, after Melanie Klein had elaborated the conceptions of psychical reality and internal objects and after I myself had become impressed by the prevalence and importance of schizoid phenomena, I tentatively formulated the view that all the figures appearing in dreams represented either parts of the dreamer's own personality (conceived in terms of ego, super-ego, and id) or else identifications on the part of the ego. A further development of this view was to the effect that dreams are essentially, not wish-fulfilments, but dramatizations or 'shorts' (in the cinematographic sense) of situations existing in inner reality. To the view that dreams are essentially 'shorts' of situations existing in inner reality I still adhere in conformity with the general line of thought pursued in this article; but, so far as the figures appearing in dreams are concerned, I have now modified my view to the effect that such figures represent either parts of the 'ego' or internalized objects. According to my present view, therefore, the situations depicted in dreams represent relationships existing between endopsychic structures; and the same applies to situations depicted in waking phantasies. This conclusion is the natural outcome of my theory of object-relationships taken in conjunction with a realization of the inescapable fact that internalized objects must be regarded as endopsychic structures if any theoretic significance whatever is to be attached to them.

After this explanatory digression I must return to the specific dream under discussion with a view to giving some account of the conclusions which I subsequently reached, in no small measure as the result of an attempt to solve the theoretic problems which it raised in my mind. As I have already stated, none of the obvious interpretations seemed to me entirely satisfactory, although the structural type of interpretation seemed to offer the most fruitful line of approach. The reader will, of course, bear in mind what I have already said regarding psychical structures; and he will also recall my having already formulated the view that all psychopathological developments originate at a stage antecedent to that at which the super-ego develops and proceed from a level beneath that at which the super-ego operates. Thus no reference will be made in what follows either to the super-ego or to the id as explanatory concepts. On the contrary, whilst adopting a structural approach, I shall attempt to elucidate the significance of the dream quite simply in terms of the data which it itself provides.

In the manifest dream the actual drama involves four figures: (1) the figure of the dreamer subjected to attack, (2) the man into whom this figure turns, and who then alternates with it, (3) the attacking actress, and (4) the dreamer's husband as a helpless onlooker. In our pre-occupation with the actual drama, however, we must not forget our only witness of its occurrence—the dreamer herself, the observing ego. Including her, there are five figures to be reckoned with. At this juncture I venture to suggest that, if the dream had ended a few seconds earlier, there would only have been four figures, even on the assumption that the 'I' of the dream is taken into account; for it was only in the fifth act, so to speak, that a man began to alternate with the figure of the dreamer as the object of attack. This is an interesting reflection; for we must conclude that, up to the point of the emergence of this man, the object of attack was a composite figure. The special interest of this phenomenon resides in the fact that, as we have seen, there is good reason to regard a second figure as composite; for the attacking actress undoubtedly represented both another figure of the dreamer and the dreamer's mother. I venture, therefore, to hazard a further suggestion—that, if the dream had lasted a few seconds longer, there might well have been six figures, instead of five. It is safe, at any rate, to infer that there were six figures in the latent content; and this, after all, is what matters for purposes of interpretation. Assuming then that six figures are represented in the dream, let us proceed to consider the nature of these figures. When we do so, our first observation is that the figures fall into two classes—ego structures and object structures. Interestingly enough there are three members of each class. The ego structures are (1) the observing ego or 'I', (2) the attacked ego, and (3) the attacking ego. The object structures are (1) the dreamer's husband as an observing object, (2) the attacked object, and (3) the attacking object. This leads us to make a second observation—that the ego structures naturally lend themselves to be paired off with the object structures. There are three such pairs: (1) the observing ego and the dreamer's husband, who also figured as an observer; (2) the attacking ego and the attacking object representing her mother, and (3) the attacked ego and the attacked object representing her father (for at this point it is to the deeper level of interpretation that we must adhere).

Bearing these two main observations in mind, let us now consider the conclusions to which I was led in an attempt to interpret the dream to my satisfaction. They are as follows. The three ego figures which appear as separate in the dream actually represent separate ego structures in the dreamer's mind. The dreamer's 'ego' is therefore split in conformity with the schizoid position; and it is split into three separate egos—a central ego and two other subsidiary egos which are both, relatively speaking, cut off from the central ego. Of these two subsidiary egos, one is the object of aggression on the part of the other. Since the ego which is attacked is closely related to the dreamer's father (and by transference to her husband), it is safe to infer that this ego is highly endowed with libido; and it may thus be appropriately described as a 'libidinal ego'. Since the attacking ego is closely related to the dreamer's mother as a repressive figure, its behaviour is quite in accord with that traditionally ascribed to the super-ego in the setting of the Œdipus situation. Since, however, the attack bears all the marks of being vindictive, rather than moral, and gives rise to an affect, not of guilt, but of plain anxiety, there is no justification (apart from preconceptions) for equating the attacking ego with the super-ego. In any case, as I have already indicated, there is reason to attach overriding psychopathological importance to a level beneath that at which the super-ego functions. At the same time, it was shown by the circumstances in which the dream occurred that the dreamer's libidinal relationship with her husband was severely compromised; and, so far as the dream is concerned, it is clearly to the operation of the attacking ego that we must look for the compromising factor. Consequently, the attacking ego may perhaps be most appropriately described as an 'internal saboteur'. In an attempt to discover what this dream was stating and to determine the structural significance of what was stated, I was accordingly led to set aside the traditional classification of mental structure in terms of ego, id, and super-ego in favour of a classification couched in terms of an ego-structure split into three separate egos—(1) a central ego (the 'I'), (2) a libidinal ego, and (3) an aggressive, persecutory ego which I designate as the internal saboteur. Subsequent experience has led me to regard this classification as having a universal application.

An Object-Relations Theory of the Personality

THE OBJECT-RELATIONSHIPS OF THE CENTRAL EGO AND THE SUBSIDIARY EGOS

Such being my conclusions regarding the ego structures represented in the dream, let us now pass on to consider my conclusions regarding the object-relationships of these ego structures. As already indicated, each of the three egos in question naturally lends itself to being paired off with a special object. The special object of the central ego was the dreamer's husband; and it is convenient to begin by considering the nature of the attitude adopted by the dreamer's central ego towards him. Since the central ego was the observing 'I' of the dream, who was felt to be continuous with the waking 'I' by whom the dream was subsequently described, it is safe to infer that this ego is in no small measure preconscious—which is, in any case, what one would naturally expect of an ego deserving the title of 'central'. This inference gains further support from the fact that the dreamer's husband was a supremely important object in outer reality and was very much in the dreamer's conscious thoughts on the eve of the dream. Although the figure representing him in the dream must be regarded as an internalized object, this object must obviously occupy a much more superficial position in the psyche than the other objects represented (parental objects internalized in childhood); and it must correspond comparatively closely to the relative object in outer reality. Accordingly, the dreamer's attitude to her husband as an external object assumes considerable significance for our present purpose. This attitude was essentially ambivalent, especially where marital relations were concerned. Active manifestations of aggression towards him were, however, conspicuously absent. Equally, her libidinal attachment to him bore the marks of severe repression; and, in associating to the dream, she reproached herself over her lack of deep feeling towards him and her failure to give to him of herself, albeit her conscious capacity to remedy these deficiencies was restricted to an assumption of the role of 'good wife'. The question therefore arises whether, since her hidden aggression towards him and her hidden libidinal need of him do not declare themselves directly in the dream, they may not manifest themselves in some indirect fashion. No sooner is this question raised than we are at once reminded of the metamorphosis undergone by the figure of the libidinal ego after this was attacked by the figure of the internal saboteur. The libidinal ego changed into, and then began alternating with, a man who, whilst representing the dreamer's father at a deep level, was nevertheless closely associated with her husband. It is thus evident that, instead of being directed against her husband as an external object, a considerable proportion of her aggression was absorbed in an attack directed, not simply against the libidinal ego, but also against an internal object closely connected with the libidinal ego. It is likewise evident that this volume of aggression had come to be at the disposal, not of the central ego, but of the internal saboteur. What then of the libidinal component in her ambivalence? As we have seen, her libidinal attitude to her husband showed signs of considerable impoverishment in spite of good intentions at a conscious level. It is obvious, accordingly, that what held true of her aggression also held true of her libido. A considerable proportion had ceased to be at the disposal of the central ego. The object towards whom this volume of libido is directed can hardly remain in doubt. In terms of the dream, it must surely be the man who alternated with the libidinal self as the object of aggression. Unlike the aggression, however, this libido is not at the disposal of the internal saboteur. On the contrary we must regard it as being at the disposal of the libidinal ego; and indeed it is precisely for this reason that the term 'libidinal ego' has come to commend itself to me for adoption. At this point it becomes desirable to formulate a suspicion which must be already present in the mind of the reader—that, although it is represented otherwise in the dream, the attack delivered by the internal saboteur is only secondarily directed against the libidinal ego and is primarily directed against the libidinal object which alternates with this ego. Assuming this suspicion to be correct, we must regard the ordeal to which the libidinal ego is subjected as evidence of a very complete identification with, and therefore a very strong libidinal attachment to, the attacked object on the part of the libidinal ego. It is evidence of the measure of 'suffering' which the libidinal ego is prepared to endure out of devotion to its object. The anxiety experienced by the dreamer on waking may be interpreted in a similar sense; and indeed I venture to suggest that this anxiety represented an irruption into consciousness of such 'suffering' on the part of the libidinal ego. Here we are at once reminded of Freud's original conception of neurotic anxiety as libido converted into suffering. This is a view which at one time presented the greatest theoretic difficulty to me, but which I have now come to appreciate in the light of my present standpoint, and substantially to accept in preference to the modified view which Freud later (and, as I think, rather reluctantly) came to adopt.

The position regarding the object-relationships of the three egos represented in the dream has now been to some extent clarified; but the process of clarification is not yet complete. Up to date, the position which has emerged would appear to be as follows. The dreamer's preconscious attitude towards her husband is ambivalent; and this is the attitude adopted by her central ego towards its external object, as well as towards the internalized representative of this object. However, both the libidinal and the aggressive components in the object-relationship of the central ego are predominantly passive. On the other hand, a considerable proportion of the dreamer's active libido is at the disposal of the libidinal ego and is directed towards an internalized object which, for purposes of nomenclature, may perhaps best be described as 'the (internal) exciting object'. At the same time, a considerable proportion of her aggression is at the disposal of the internal saboteur and is directed (a) towards the libidinal ego, and (b) towards the exciting object (i.e. towards the object of the libidinal ego). It cannot fail to be noticed, however, that this summary of the position leaves out of account certain endopsychic relationships which may be presumed to exist—notably (1) the relationship of the central ego to the other egos, and (2) the relationship of the internal saboteur to the internalized object with which it is so closely associated, and which is represented by the maternal component in the actress figure. Taking the latter relationship first, we have no difficulty in seeing that, since the actress in the dream was a composite figure representing both the dreamer's mother and herself, the internal saboteur is closely identified with its object and must therefore be regarded as bound to this object by a strong libidinal attachment. For purposes of description we must give the object a name; and I propose to describe it as 'the (internal) rejecting object'. I have chosen this term primarily for a reason which will emerge later; but meanwhile my justification will be that the dreamer's mother, who provided the original model of this internalized object, was essentially a rejecting figure, and that it is, so to speak, in the name of this object that the aggression of the internal saboteur is directed against the libidinal ego. As regards the relationship of the central ego to the other egos, our most important clue to its nature lies in the fact that, whereas the central ego must be regarded as comprising pre-conscious and conscious, as well as unconscious, elements, the other egos must equally be regarded as essentially unconscious. From this we may infer that the libidinal ego and the internal saboteur are both rejected by the central ego; and this inference is confirmed by the fact that, as we have seen, the considerable volume of libido and of aggression which has ceased to be at the disposal of the central ego is now at the disposal of the subsidiary egos. Assuming then that the subsidiary egos are rejected by the central ego, it becomes a question of the dynamic of this rejection. Obviously the dynamic of rejection cannot be libido. So there is no alternative but to regard it as aggression. Aggression must, accordingly, be regarded as the characteristic determinant of the attitude of the central ego towards the subsidiary egos.

I have now completed the account of my attempt to reconstruct, in terms of dynamic structure, the endopsychic situation represented in a patient's dream. The account has been cast in the form of a reasoned statement; and, as such, it should serve to give some indication of what is involved in my view that dreams are essentially 'shorts' of inner reality (rather than wish-fulfilments). However, it is not primarily with the aim of substantiating my views on dreams in general that I have claimed so much of the reader's attention for a single dream. On the contrary, it is because the dream in question seems to me to represent an endopsychic situation of a classic order, and indeed of a basic character which entitles it to be regarded as the paradigm of all endopsychic situations. For convenience, the general features of this situation are illustrated in the accompanying diagram.

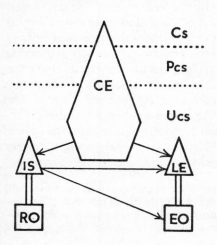

CE, Central Ego; IS, Internal Saboteur; LE, Libidinal Ego; RO, Rejecting Object; EO, Exciting Object. Cs, Conscious; Pcs, Preconscious; Ucs, Unconscious. ——→, Aggression; =, Libido.

THE BASIC ENDOPSYCHIC SITUATION AND A REVISED THEORY OF MENTAL STRUCTURE FOUNDED THEREON

I myself feel convinced that the basic endopsychic situation above described is the situation underlying Freud's description of the mental apparatus in terms of ego, id, and super-ego. It is certainly the endopsychic situation upon which I deliberately base the revised theory of mental structure which I now submit, and which is couched in terms of central ego, libidinal ego, and internal saboteur. As it would, of course, be natural to expect, there is a general correspondence between Freud's concepts and those which I have now come to adopt. In the case of 'the central ego' the correspondence to Freud's 'ego' is fairly close from a functional standpoint; but there are important differences between the two concepts. Unlike Freud's 'ego', the 'central ego' is not conceived as originating out of something else (the 'id'), or as constituting a passive structure dependent for its activity upon impulses proceeding from the matrix out of which it originated, and on the surface of which it rests.[1] On the contrary, the 'central ego' is conceived as a primary and dynamic structure, from which, as we shall shortly see, the other mental structures are subsequently derived. The 'libidinal ego' corresponds, of course, to Freud's 'id'; but, whereas according to Freud's view the 'ego' is a derivative of the 'id', according to my view the 'libidinal ego' (which corresponds to the 'id') is a derivative of the 'central ego' (which corresponds to the 'ego'). The 'libidinal ego' also differs from the 'id' in that it is conceived, not as a mere reservoir of instinctive impulses, but as a dynamic structure comparable to the 'central ego', although differing from the latter in various respects, e.g. in its more infantile character, in a lesser degree of organization, in a smaller measure of adaptation to reality and in a greater devotion to internalized objects. The 'internal saboteur' differs from the 'super-ego' in a number of respects. For one thing it is in no sense conceived as an internal object. It is wholly an ego structure, although, as we have seen, it is very closely associated with an internal object. Actually, the 'super-ego'

---

[1] Freud's conception of the ego was, of course, borrowed from Groddeck; but, if there is any truth in the conclusions which will shortly be recorded, it is a conception based upon an endopsychic situation resulting from repression, and therefore is anomalous in terms of Freud's own views, since it implies that repression is responsible for the origin of the ego.

corresponds not so much to the 'internal saboteur' as to a compound of this structure and its associated object (like the figure of the actress in the dream). At the same time, the 'internal saboteur' is unlike the 'super-ego' in that it is conceived as, in itself, devoid of all moral significance. Thus I do not attribute the affect of guilt to its activity, although this activity is unquestionably a prolific source of anxiety. Such anxiety may, of course, merge with guilt; but the two affects are theoretically distinct. Here it should be noted that, whilst introducing the conception of the internal saboteur, I am not prepared to abandon the conception of the super-ego as I have now come to abandon that of the id. On the contrary, it seems to me impossible to offer any satisfactory psychological explanation of guilt in the absence of the super-ego; but the super-ego must be regarded as originating at a higher level of mental organization than that at which the internal saboteur operates. Exactly how the activities of the two structures are related must in the meantime remain an open question; but, for the most recent expression of my views regarding the origin and the function of the super-ego I must refer the reader to a previous paper (1943).

SPLITTING OF THE EGO AND REPRESSION CONSIDERED AS ASPECTS OF AN IDENTICAL PROCESS OPERATIVE IN BOTH SCHIZOID AND HYSTERICAL CONDITIONS

Before proceeding to consider the origin of what I have called 'the basic endopsychic situation', I feel it necessary to record some general conclusions which seem to follow from the inherent nature of the situation itself. The first and most obvious of these conclusions is that the ego is split. In this respect, therefore, the basic endopsychic situation which has now emerged conforms to the pattern of the schizoid position—a position which, as already indicated, I have come to regard as central (in preference to the depressive position). Freud's theory of the mental apparatus was, of course, developed upon a basis of the depressive position; and it is on a similar basis that Melanie Klein has developed her views. By contrast, it is the schizoid position that constitutes the basis of the theory of mental structure which I now advance. It is to be noted, further, that, whilst conforming to the pattern of the schizoid position, the endopsychic situation revealed in my patient's dream also provided a satisfactory explanation of the dreamer's hysterical frigidity in terms of dynamic structure. Here we are reminded of the common association of hysterical symptoms with an underlying schizoid attitude—an association to which reference has already been made. There would, accordingly, appear to be good grounds for our second conclusion—that hysterical developments are inherently based upon an underlying and fundamental schizoid position. Our third conclusion follows from what has already been said regarding the aggressive attitude of the central ego towards the subsidiary egos. It is to the effect that the splitting of the ego observed in the schizoid position is due to the operation of a certain volume of aggression which remains at the disposal of the central ego. It is this aggression that provides the dynamic of the severance of the subsidiary egos from the central ego. The subsidiary egos are, of course, ordinarily unconscious; and their unconscious status at once raises the suspicion that they are subject to repression. This is obviously so in the case of the libidinal ego (which corresponds to Freud's id); but, if one of the subsidiary ego structures can be repressed, there is no reason for regarding the other as immune from similar treatment at the hands of the central ego. Consequently our fourth conclusion is that the internal saboteur (which largely corresponds to Freud's super-ego in function) is repressed no less than the libidinal ego. This conclusion may at first sight appear to be in conflict with the theory which I previously advanced (1943), to the effect that repression is primarily directed against internalized bad objects. There is no real inconsistency, however; for I regard the repression of the subsidiary egos, which I now envisage, as secondary to the repression of internalized bad objects. Here we find a helpful analogy in the attack of the internal saboteur on the libidinal ego; for, as we have seen, the aggression involved in this attack is primarily directed against the exciting object to which the libidinal ego is related, and only secondarily against the libidinal ego itself. Similarly, I regard repression of the libidinal ego on the part of the central ego as secondary to repression of the exciting object. Our fifth conclusion needs no elaboration in the light of what precedes. It is to the effect that the dynamic of repression is aggression. Our sixth, and last, conclusion, which follows equally from preceding conclusions, is that splitting of the ego, on the one hand, and repression of the subsidiary egos by the central ego, on the other, constitute essentially the same phenomenon considered from different points of view. Here it is apposite to recall that, whilst the concept of splitting of the ego was formulated by Bleuler in an attempt to explain the phenomena of what was known as 'dementia præcox' until he introduced the term 'schizophrenia' to take its place, the concept of repression was formulated by Freud in an attempt to explain the phenomena of hysteria. Our final conclusion thus serves to substantiate the view that the position underlying the development of hysterical symptoms is essentially a schizoid position.

THE ORIGIN OF THE BASIC ENDOPSYCHIC SITUATION AND OF THE MULTIPLICITY OF EGOS

It is now time for us to turn our attention to questions regarding the origin of the basic endopsychic situation which found a classic expression in my patient's dream. In the light of considerations which have already emerged, it will be obvious that whatever explanation we may reach regarding the origin of this situation will also serve as an explanation of the origin of the schizoid position, the origin of repression and the differentiation of the various fundamental endopsychic structures. As we have seen, the patient whose dream has occupied so much of our attention was essentially ambivalent towards her husband as an external object; and it is from the establishment of a state of ambivalence towards objects in early life that the basic endopsychic situation springs. The first libidinal object of the infant is, of course, his mother's breast, although there can be no doubt that the form of his mother as a person soon begins to take shape round the original nucleus of this maternal organ. Under theoretically perfect conditions the libidinal relationship of the infant to his mother would be so satisfactory that a state of libidinal frustration could hardly arise; and, as I see it, there would consequently be no ambivalence on the part of the infant towards his object. At this point I must explain that, whilst I regard aggression as a primary dynamic factor in that it does not appear capable of being resolved into libido (as Jung, for example, sought to resolve it), at the same time I regard it as ultimately subordinate to libido, not only metaphysically, but also psychologically. Thus I do not consider that the infant directs aggression spontaneously towards his libidinal object in the absence of some kind of frustration; and my observation of the behaviour of animals confirms me in this view. It should be added that in a state of nature the infant would never normally experience that separation from his mother which appears to be imposed upon him increasingly by conditions of civilization. Indeed, it may be inferred that in a state of nature it would be rare for the infant to be deprived of the shelter of his mother's arms and of ready access to her breast until, in the ordinary course of development, he himself became increasingly disposed to dispense with them.[1] Such perfect conditions are, however, only theoretically possible for the human infant born into a civilized cultural group; and in actual fact the libidinal relationship of the infant to his mother is disturbed from the first by a considerable measure of frustration, although, of course, the degree of such frustration varies in different cases. It is the experience of libidinal frustration that calls forth the infant's aggression in relation to his libidinal object and thus gives rise to a state of ambivalence. To content ourselves with saying simply that the infant becomes ambivalent would, however, be to give an incomplete and partial picture of the situation which now arises; for it would be a picture conceived exclusively from the point of view of the observer. From the subjective point of view of the infant himself it is a case of his mother becoming an ambivalent object, i.e. an object which is both good and bad. Since it proves intolerable to him to have a good object which is also bad, he seeks to alleviate the situation by splitting the figure of his mother into two objects. Then, in so far as she satisfies him libidinally, she is a 'good' object, and, in so far as she fails to satisfy him libidinally, she is a 'bad' object. The situation in which he now finds himself placed proves, however, in its turn to be one which imposes a severe strain upon his capacity for endurance and his power of adjustment. Being a situation in outer reality, it is one which he finds himself impotent to control, and which, accordingly, he seeks to mitigate by such means as are at his disposal. The means at his disposal are limited; and the technique which he adopts is more or less dictated by this limitation. He accordingly follows the only path open to him and, since outer reality seems unyielding, he does his best to transfer the traumatic factor in the situation to the field of inner reality, within which he feels situations to be more under his own control. This means that he internalizes his mother as a 'bad' object. Here I would remind the reader that, in my opinion, it is

---

[1] It must be recognized, of course, that, under any conditions, a profound sense of separation and loss of security must be experienced by the infant at the time of birth; and it may be presumed that some measure of aggression, in addition to anxiety, is called forth by this experience. There is no reason, however, to think that this experience in itself would give rise to a state of ambivalence in the absence of further experience of libidinal frustration during infancy.

always the 'bad' object (i.e., at this stage, the unsatisfying object) that is internalized in the first instance; for (as already indicated in a footnote) I find it difficult to attach any meaning to the primary internalization of a 'good' object which is both satisfying and amenable from the infant's point of view. There are those, of course, who would argue that it would be natural for the infant, when in a state of deprivation, to internalize the good object on the wish-fulfilment principle; but, as it seems to me, internalization of objects is essentially a measure of coercion and it is not the satisfying object, but the unsatisfying object that the infant seeks to coerce. I speak here of 'the satisfying object' and 'the unsatisfying object', rather than of 'the good object' and 'the bad object', because I consider that, in this connection, the terms 'good object' and 'bad object' tend to be misleading. They tend to be misleading because they are liable to be understood in the sense of 'desired object' and 'undesired object' respectively. There can be no doubt, however, that a bad (viz. unsatisfying) object may be desired. Indeed it is just because the infant's bad object is desired as well as felt to be bad that it is internalized. The trouble is that it remains bad after it has been internalized, i.e. it remains unsatisfying. At this point an important consideration arises. Unlike the satisfying object, the unsatisfying object has, so to speak, two facets. On the one hand, it frustrates; and, on the other hand, it tempts and allures. Indeed its essential 'badness' consists precisely in the fact that it combines allurement with frustration. Further, it retains both these qualities after internalization. After internalizing the unsatisfying object, accordingly, the infant finds himself in the quandary of 'out of the frying-pan into the fire'. In his attempts to control the unsatisfying object, he has introduced into the inner economy of his mind an object which not only continues to frustrate his need, but also continues to whet it. He thus finds himself confronted with another intolerable situation—this time an internal one. How does he seek to deal with it? As we have seen, in his attempt to deal with the intolerable external situation with which he was originally faced his technique was to split the maternal object into two objects, (*a*) the 'good' and (*b*) the 'bad', and then proceed to internalize the bad object; and in his attempt to deal with the intolerable internal situation which subsequently arises he adopts a technique which is not altogether dissimilar. He splits the internal bad object into two objects—(*a*) the needed or exciting object and (*b*) the frustrating or rejecting object; and then he represses both these objects (employing aggression, of course, as the dynamic of repression). Here a complication arises, however; for his libidinal attachment to the undivided object is shared, albeit not in equal proportions, by the objects resulting from division. The consequence is that, in the process of repressing the resultant objects, the ego, so to speak, develops pseudopodia by means of which it still maintains libidinal attachments to the objects undergoing repression. The development of these pseudopodia represents the initial stage of a division of the ego. As repression of the objects proceeds, the incipient division of the ego becomes an accomplished fact. The two pseudopodia are rejected by the part of the ego which remains central on account of their connection with the rejected objects; and with their associated objects they share the fate of repression. It is in this way that the two subsidiary egos, the libidinal ego and the internal saboteur, come to be split off from the central ego, and that a multiplicity of egos arises.

THE 'DIVIDE ET IMPERA' TECHNIQUE FOR THE DISPOSAL OF LIBIDO AND AGGRESSION

It will be noted that the situation resulting from the sequence of processes which has just been described has now assumed the *structural* pattern of what I have called 'the basic endopsychic situation'. It has also assumed the *dynamic* pattern of this situation except in one important respect—that the aggressive attitude adopted by the internal saboteur towards the libidinal ego and its associated object (the exciting object) is still left out of the picture. In order to explain the origin of this feature of the situation, we must return to the original ambivalence of the child towards his mother and consider from a fresh angle what this involves. This time we shall consider the child's reactions, less in their conative, and more in their affective aspect. It is natural for the child, not only to be impulsive, but also to express his feelings in no uncertain terms. Moreover, it is through the expression of his feelings that he makes his chief impression upon his objects. Once ambivalence has been established, however, the expression of feeling towards his mother involves him in a position which must seem to him singularly precarious. Here it must be pointed out that what presents itself to him from a strictly conative standpoint as *frustration* at the hands of his mother presents itself to him in a very different light from a strictly affective standpoint. From the latter standpoint, what he experiences is a sense of lack of love, and indeed emotional *rejection* on his mother's part. This being so, the expression of hate towards her as a rejecting object becomes in his eyes a very dangerous procedure. On the one hand, it is calculated to make her reject him all the more, and thus to increase her 'badness' and make her seem *more real* in her capacity of bad object. On the other hand, it is calculated to make her love him less, and thus to decrease her 'goodness' and make her seem *less real* (i.e. destroy her) in her capacity of good object. At the same time, it also becomes a dangerous procedure for the child to express his libidinal need, i.e. his nascent love, of his mother in face of rejection at her hands; for it is equivalent to discharging his libido into an emotional vacuum. Such a discharge is accompanied by an affective experience which is singularly devastating. In the older child this experience is one of intense humiliation over the depreciation of his love, which seems to be involved. At a somewhat deeper level (or at an earlier stage) the experience is one of shame over the display of needs which are disregarded or belittled. In virtue of these experiences of humiliation and shame he feels reduced to a state of worthlessness, destitution or beggardom. His sense of his own value is threatened; and he feels bad in the sense of 'inferior'. The intensity of these experiences is, of course, proportionate to the intensity of his need; and intensity of need itself increases his sense of badness by contributing to it the quality of 'demanding too much'. At the same time his sense of badness is further complicated by the sense of utter impotence which he also experiences. At a still deeper level (or at a still earlier stage) the child's experience is one of, so to speak, exploding ineffectively and being completely emptied of libido. It is thus an experience of disintegration and of imminent psychical death.

We can understand accordingly how precarious a matter it becomes for the child, when confronted with the experience of rejection by his mother, to express either aggressive or libidinal affect towards her. Reduced to its simplest terms, the position in which he finds himself placed would appear to be one in which, if, on the one hand, he expresses aggression, he is threatened with loss of his good object, and, if, on the other hand, he expresses libidinal need, he is threatened with loss of his libido (which for him constitutes his own goodness) and ultimately with loss of the ego structure which constitutes himself. Of these two threats by which the child feels menaced, the former (i.e. loss of the good object) would appear to be that which gives rise to the affect of depression, and which provides a basis for the subsequent development of a melancholic state in individuals for whom the disposal of aggression presents greater difficulties than the disposal of libido. On the other hand, the latter threat (i.e. loss of libido and of ego structure) would appear to be that which gives rise to the affect of futility, and which provides a basis for the subsequent development of a schizoid state in individuals for whom the disposal of libido presents greater difficulties than the disposal of aggression.

So far as the ætiology of depressive and schizoid states is concerned, views similar to those just indicated have already been developed by me at some length previously (1941). In the present instance, however, our immediate concern is with the measures adopted by the child to circumvent the various dangers which appear to him to attend the expression of affect, whether libidinal or aggressive, towards his mother when he is faced with the experience of rejection at her hands. As we have already seen, he attempts to deal with the ambivalent situation successively (1) by splitting the figure of his mother into two objects, a good and a bad, (2) by internalizing the bad object in an endeavour to control it, (3) by splitting the internalized bad object in turn into two objects, viz. (a) the exciting or needed object, and (b) the rejecting object, (4) by repressing both these objects and employing a certain volume of his aggression in the process, and (5) by employing a further volume of his aggression in splitting off from his central ego and repressing two subsidiary egos which remain attached to these respective internalized objects by libidinal ties. These various measures, based upon the techniques of internalization and splitting, serve to mitigate the asperities of the situation resulting from the child's experience of frustration in his relationship with his mother and his sense of rejection at her hands; but, except in the most extreme cases, they do not succeed in eliminating the child's need of his mother as an object in outer reality, or in robbing her of all significance—which, after all, is just as well. In conformity with this fact, his libido and his aggression are very far from being wholly absorbed in the processes so far described; and, consequently, the risks involved in the expression of libidinal and aggressive affect towards his mother as a rejecting object still remain to be met. The measures so far described thus require to be supplemented. Actually they are supplemented by a very obvious technique which is closely akin to the well-known principle of 'Divide et impera'. The child seeks to circumvent the dangers of expressing both libidinal and aggressive affect towards his object by *using a maximum of his aggression to subdue a maximum of his libidinal need.* In this way he reduces the volume of affect, both libidinal and aggressive, demanding outward expression. As has already been pointed out, of course, neither libido nor aggression can be considered as existing in a state of divorce from structure. Accordingly, what remains for us to decide is to which of the ego structures already described the child's excess of libido and excess of aggression are to be respectively allotted. This is a question to which the answer can be in no doubt. The excess of libido is taken over by the libidinal ego; and the excess of aggression is taken over by the internal saboteur. The child's technique of using aggression to subdue libidinal need thus resolves itself into an attack by the internal saboteur upon the libidinal ego. The libidinal ego in its turn directs the excess of libido with which it becomes charged towards its associated object, the exciting object. On the other hand, the attack of the internal saboteur upon this object represents a persistence of the child's original resentment towards his mother as a temptress inciting the very need which she fails to satisfy and thus reducing him to bondage—just as, indeed, the attack of the internal saboteur upon the libidinal ego represents a persistence of the hatred which the child comes to feel towards himself for the dependence dictated by his need. It should be added that the processes just described take place simultaneously with those which they are designed to supplement, although, in the interests of clarity of exposition, they have been described separately.

DIRECT REPRESSION, LIBIDINAL RESISTANCE AND INDIRECT REPRESSION

Now that the origin of the aggressive attitude adopted by the internal saboteur towards the libidinal ego and the exciting object has been described, our account of the processes which determine the dynamic pattern of the basic endopsychic situation is complete. At this point, however, something requires to be added to what has already been said regarding the nature and origin of repression. In terms of the line of thought so far developed, repression is a process originating in a rejection of both the exciting object and the rejecting object on the part of the undivided ego. This primary process of repression is accompanied by a secondary process of repression whereby the ego splits off and rejects two parts of itself, which remain attached respectively to one and the other of the repressed internal objects. The resulting situation is one in which the central ego (the residue of the undivided ego) adopts an attitude of rejection, not only towards the exciting object and the rejecting object, but also towards the split off and subsidiary egos attached to these respective objects, i.e. the libidinal ego and the internal saboteur. This attitude of rejection adopted by the central ego constitutes repression; and the dynamic of the rejection is aggression. So far so good. But this explanation of the nature and origin of repression is incomplete in so far as it has not yet taken into account what is involved in the technique of reducing the volume of libido and aggression available for expression towards external objects by employing a maximum of aggression to subdue a maximum of libido. As we have seen, this technique resolves itself into a process whereby (*a*) the excess of aggression is taken over by the internal saboteur and devoted to an attack upon the libidinal ego, and (*b*) the excess of libido is taken over by the libidinal ego and directed towards the exciting object. When the full significance of this process is considered, it becomes at once plain that the relentless attack of the internal saboteur upon the libidinal ego must operate as a very powerful factor in furthering the aims of repression. Indeed, so far as dynamic is concerned, it seems more than likely that this is the most important factor in the maintenance of repression. Obviously it is upon the phenomenon just mentioned that Freud's conception of the super-ego and its repressive functions is based; for the uncompromising hostility which, according to Freud, characterizes the attitude of the super-ego towards id impulses coincides exactly with the uncompromisingly aggressive attitude adopted by the internal saboteur towards the libidinal ego. Similarly, Freud's observation that the self-reproaches of the melancholic are ultimately reproaches directed against the loved object falls readily into line with the aggressive attitude adopted towards the exciting object by the internal saboteur.

There is no need at this point to repeat the criticisms already passed upon Freud's conceptions of the super-ego and the id, and upon all that is involved in these conceptions. It does, however, seem desirable to draw attention to the fact that, in his description of repression, Freud left completely out of account all that is involved in the phenomenon which I have described as the attachment of the libidinal ego to the exciting object. As we have seen, this attachment comes to absorb a considerable volume of libido. Further, the volume of libido in question is directed towards an object which is both internal and repressed; and, in conformity with this fact, it is inevitably oriented away from outer reality. Such being the case, the object-seeking of the libidinal ego operates as a resistance which powerfully reinforces the resistance directly resulting from repression, and which is thus no less in conflict with therapeutic aims than is the latter resistance. This is a theme which I have already developed, *mutatis mutandis*, in an earlier paper (1943). I add the proviso '*mutatis mutandis*' here, because, at the time when I wrote the paper referred to, I had not yet formulated my present views regarding endopsychic structures; but the effect of these latter views is to give greater point, rather than otherwise, to the original theme. This theme is, of course, in direct conflict with Freud's statement (1920)[1]: 'The unconscious, i.e. the "repressed" material, offers no resistance whatever to curative efforts.' It is, however, a theme which develops naturally out of the view that libido is primarily object-seeking, once we come to consider what happens when the object sought is a repressed internal object; and, in terms of my present standpoint, there can be no room for doubt that the obstinate attachment of the libidinal ego to the exciting object and its reluctance to renounce this object constitute a particularly formidable source of resistance—and one which plays no small part in determining what is known as the negative therapeutic reaction. The attachment in question, being libidinal in character, cannot, of course, be regarded as in itself a repressive phenomenon; but, whilst itself a resultant of repression exercised by the central ego, it also functions as a powerful aid to this process of repression. The attack of the internal saboteur upon the object of the libidinal ego (the exciting object) serves, of course, to perpetuate the attachment of the libidinal ego to its object by virtue of the fact that this object is being constantly threatened. Here we catch a glimpse of the original wolf under its sheep's clothing, i.e. we catch a glimpse of the original ambivalent situation persisting underneath all its disguises; for what the obstinate attachment of the libidinal ego to the exciting object and the equally obstinate aggression of the internal saboteur towards the same object really represent is the obstinacy of the original ambivalent attitude. The truth is that, however well the fact may be disguised, the individual is extremely reluctant to abandon his original hate, no less than his original need, of his original objects in childhood. This holds particularly true of psychoneurotic and

[1] *Beyond the Pleasure Principle* (London, 1922), p. 19.

psychotic individuals, not to mention those who fall into the category of psychopathic personality.

If the attachment of the libidinal ego to the exciting object serves as a powerful aid to repression, the same may equally be said of the aggressive attitude adopted towards this internal object by the internal saboteur. So far as the actual process of repression is concerned, however, the latter differs from the former in one important respect; for not only does it forward the aim of repression, but it also actually operates in the same manner as repression. In its attack upon the exciting object it performs a function which constitutes it a co-belligerent, albeit not an ally, of the central ego, whose repression of the exciting object represents, as we have seen, a manifestation of aggression. The internal saboteur functions further as a co-belligerent of the central ego in respect of its attack upon the libidinal ego—an attack which serves to supplement that involved in the repression of this ego by the central ego. There is a sense, therefore, in which it would be true to say that the attacks of the internal saboteur upon the libidinal ego and upon its associated object represent an *indirect form of repression*, whereby the direct repression of these structures by the central ego is both supplemented and facilitated.

As we have already seen, the subsidiary egos owe their origin to a split of the undivided ego; but, as we have also seen, what presents itself from a topographic standpoint as simply a split of the ego presents itself from a dynamic standpoint as an active rejection and repression of both the subsidiary egos on the part of the central ego. It thus becomes a matter for some comment that, whilst both the libidinal ego and the internal saboteur share a common fate so far as direct repression is concerned, only one of the subsidiary egos, viz. the libidinal ego, should be subjected to the process of indirect repression. When the difference between direct and indirect repression is considered in the light of what has already been said, it is, of course, plain that the process of repression described by Freud corresponds very much more closely to what I have described as indirect repression than to what I have described as direct repression. Nevertheless, when Freud's conception of repression is compared with my conception of the total phenomenon of repression, both direct and indirect, this common feature may be detected—that the libidinal components in the psyche are subjected to a much greater measure of repression than the aggressive components. There can be no doubt, of course, that the repression of aggressive components does occur;

but it is difficult to see how this fact can be consistently explained in terms of Freud's theory of the mental apparatus. This theory, conceived as it is in terms of a fundamental divorce between impulse and structure, would appear to permit only of the repression of libido; for, in terms of Freud's theory, the repression of aggression would involve the anomaly of aggression being used to repress aggression. By contrast, if, in conformity with the point of view which I advocate, we conceive of impulse as inseparable from structure and as representing simply the dynamic aspect of structure, the repression of aggressive components in the psyche is no more difficult to account for than the repression of libidinal components. It then becomes a question, not of aggression repressing aggression, but of one ego structure using aggression to repress another ego structure charged with aggression. This being so, my view to the effect that the internal saboteur, no less than the libidinal ego, is repressed by the central ego provides a satisfactory explanation of the repression of aggressive components. At the same time, the fact that libidinal components are subject to a greater measure of repression than aggressive components is satisfactorily explained by means of the conception of indirect repression. The truth would appear to be that, if *the principle of repression* governs the disposal of *excess libido* in greater measure than it governs the disposal of excess aggression, *the principle of topographical redistribution* governs the disposal of *excess aggression* in greater measure than it governs the disposal of excess libido.

THE SIGNIFICANCE OF THE ŒDIPUS SITUATION

I have already said enough to indicate that the technique whereby aggression is employed to subdue libido is a process which finds a common place in Freud's conception of 'repression' and my own conception of 'indirect repression'. At the same time, my views regarding the origin of this technique differ from those of Freud. According to Freud, the technique originates as a means of averting or reducing the expression of libidinal (incestuous) impulses towards the parent of opposite sex and aggressive (parenticidal) impulses towards the parent of similar sex in the setting of the Œdipus situation. According to my view, on the other hand, the technique originates in infancy as a means of reducing the expression of both libido and aggression on the part of the infant towards his mother, who at this stage constitutes his only significant object, and upon whom he is wholly dependent. This discrepancy of view will be interpreted, quite correctly, in the sense that I have departed from Freud in my evaluation of the Œdipus situation as an explanatory concept. For Freud, the Œdipus situation is, so to speak, an ultimate cause; but this is a view with which I no longer find it possible to agree. So far from agreeing, I now consider that the role of ultimate cause, which Freud allotted to the Œdipus situation, should properly be allotted to the phenomenon of infantile dependence. In conformity with this standpoint, the Œdipus situation presents itself, not so much in the light of a causal phenomenon as in the light of an end-product. It is not a basic situation, but the derivative of a situation which has priority over it not only in the logical, but also in the temporal sense. This prior situation is one which issues directly out of the physical and emotional dependence of the infant upon his mother, and which declares itself in the relationship of the infant to his mother long before his father becomes a significant object. The present is no occasion for an elaboration of the views which I have now reached regarding the Œdipus situation—views which have been in some measure adumbrated already (1941). Nevertheless, in view of the comparison which I have just drawn between my own conception of repression and Freud's conception, formulated as it is in terms of the Œdipus situation, it seems desirable that I should indicate briefly how I propose to introduce this classic situation into the general scheme which I have outlined. It will hardly be necessary to remind the reader that I have dispensed with the Œdipus situation as an explanatory concept not only in my account of the origin of repression, but also in my account of the genesis of the basic endopsychic situation and in my account of the differentiation of endopsychic structure. These accounts have been formulated exclusively in terms of the measures adopted by the child in an attempt to cope with the difficulties inherent in the ambivalent situation which develops during his infancy in his relationship with his mother as his original object. The various measures which the child adopts in his attempt to deal with this ambivalent situation have all been adopted before the Œdipus situation develops. It is in the setting of the child's relationship to his mother that the basic endopsychic situation is established, that the differentiation of endopsychic structure is accomplished and that repression is originated; and it is only after these developments have occurred that the child is called upon to meet the particular difficulties which attend the Œdipus situation. So far from furnishing an explanatory concept, therefore, the Œdipus situation is rather a phenomenon to be explained in terms of an endopsychic situation which has already developed.

The chief novelty introduced into the child's world by the Œdipus situation, as this materializes in outer reality, is that he is now confronted with two distinct parental objects instead of with only one as formerly. His relationship with his new object, viz: his father, is, of course, inevitably fraught with vicissitudes similar to those which he previously experienced in his relationship with his mother—and in particular, the vicissitudes of need, frustration and rejection. In view of these vicissitudes, his father becomes an ambivalent object to him, whilst at the same time he himself becomes ambivalent towards his father. In his relationship with his father he is thus faced with the same problem of adjustment as that with which he was originally faced in his relationship with his mother. The original situation is reinstated, albeit this time in relation to a fresh object; and, very naturally, he seeks to meet the difficulties of the reinstated situation by means of the same series of techniques which he learned to adopt in meeting the difficulties of the original situation. He splits the figure of his father into a good and a bad object, internalizes the bad object and splits the internalized bad object into (a) an exciting object associated with the libidinal ego and (b) a rejecting object associated with the internal saboteur. It should be added that the new paternal exciting object would appear to be partly superimposed upon, and partly fused with the old maternal exciting object, and that similarly the paternal rejecting object is partly superimposed upon, and partly fused with the maternal rejecting object.

The adjustment which the child is called upon to make in relation to his father differs, of course, in one important respect from that which he was previously called upon to make in relation to his mother. It differs in the extent to which it has to be achieved upon an emotional plane. The new adjustment must be almost exclusively emotional; for in his relationship with his father the child is necessarily precluded from the experience of feeding at the breast. We are thus introduced to a further important respect in which his adjustment to his father must differ from his previous adjustment to his mother. His father is a man, whereas his mother is a woman. It is more than doubtful, however, whether the child at first appreciates the genital difference between the two parents. It would appear rather that the difference which he does appreciate is that his father has no breasts. His father thus first presents himself to the child as a parent without breasts; and this is one of the chief reasons that his relationship with his father has to be established so much more on an emotional plane than his relationship with his mother. On the other hand, it is because the child does have the experience of a physical relationship with his mother's breast, while also experiencing a varying degree of frustration in this relationship, that his need for his mother persists so obstinately beneath his need for his father and all subsequent genital needs. When the child comes to appreciate, in some measure at least, the genital difference between his parents, and as, in the course of his own development, his physical need tends to flow increasingly (albeit in varying degrees) through genital channels, his need for his mother comes to include a need for her vagina. At the same time, his need for his father comes to include a need for his father's penis. The strength of these physical needs for his parents' genitals varies, however, in inverse proportion to the satisfaction of his emotional needs. Thus, the more satisfactory his emotional relations with his parents, the less urgent are his physical needs for their genitals. These latter needs are, of course, never satisfied, although substitutive satisfactions may be sought, e.g. those of sexual curiosity. Consequently, some measure of ambivalence necessarily develops in relation to his mother's vagina and his father's penis. This ambivalence is reflected incidentally, in sadistic conceptions of the primal scene. By the time the primal scene is envisaged, however, the relationships of his parents to one another have become a matter of moment for the child; and jealousy of each of his parents in relation to the other begins to assert itself. The chief incidence of his jealousy is, of course, partly determined by the biological sex of the child; but it is also in no small measure determined by the state of his emotional relationships with his respective parents. Be this as it may, the child is now called upon to meet the difficulties of two ambivalent situations at the same time; and he seeks to meet these difficulties by the familiar series of techniques. The result is that he internalizes both a bad maternal genital figure and a bad paternal genital figure and splits each of these into two figures, which are embodied respectively in the structures of the exciting object and the rejecting object. It will thus be seen that, before the child is very old, these internal objects have already assumed the form of complex composite structures. They are built up partly on a basis of the superimposition of one object upon another, and partly on a basis of the fusion of objects. The extent to which the internal objects are built up respectively on a basis of *layering* and on a basis of *fusion* differs, of course, from individual to individual; and the extent to which either layering or fusion predominates would appear to be a matter of no small importance. Thus, in conjunction with the proportioning of the various component objects, it would appear to play an important part in determining the psychosexual attitude of the individual in so far as this is not determined by biological sexual factors. Likewise, in conjunction with the proportioning of the component objects, it would appear to be the chief determining factor in the ætiology of the sexual perversions. We may thus envisage an ætiology of the perversions conceived in terms of object-relationship psychology.

It will be noticed that in the preceding account the personal pronoun employed to indicate the child has been consistently masculine. This must not be taken to imply that the account applies only to the boy. It applies equally to the girl; and the masculine pronoun has been used only because the advantages of a personal pronoun of some kind appear to outweigh those of the impersonal pronoun, however noncommittal this may be. It will also be noticed that the classic Œdipus situation has not yet emerged. The stage which was last described was one at which, whilst the relations of his parents with one another had become significant to the child, his position was essentially one of ambivalence towards both parents. We have seen, however, that the child seeks to deal with both ambivalent situations by a series of processes in consequence of which genital figures of each of his parents come to be embodied both in the structure of the exciting object and in that of the rejecting object. It must be recognized, of course, that the biological sex of the child must play some part in determining his attitude to his respective parents; but that this is very far from being the sole determining factor is obvious from the frequency of inverted and mixed Œdipus situations. Considered in terms of the views which I have outlined, these inverted and mixed Œdipus situations must necessarily be determined by the constitution of the exciting object and the rejecting object. It is, therefore, only taking a further step in the same direction to conclude that the same consideration applies to the positive Œdipus situation. The fact then would appear to be that *the Œdipus situation is not really an external situation at all, but an internal situation*—one which may be transferred in varying degrees to the actual external situation. Once the Œdipus situation comes to be regarded as essentially an internal situation, it is not difficult to see that the maternal components of both the internal objects have, so to speak, a great initial advantage over the paternal components; and this, of course, applies to children of both sexes. The strong position of the maternal components is, of course, due to the fact that the nuclei of both the internal objects are derivatives of the original ambivalent mother and her ambivalent breasts. In conformity with this fact, *a sufficiently deep analysis of the Œdipus situation invariably reveals that this situation is built up around the figures of an internal exciting mother and an internal rejecting mother.* It was, of course, on a basis of hysterical phenomena that Freud originally formulated the concept of the Œdipus situation; and according to Abraham's 'phase' theory the origin of hysteria is to be traced to a fixation in the genital (phallic) phase. I have already (1941) passed various criticisms on Abraham's 'phase' theory; and so I shall be merely passing a further criticism, if only by implication, when I say that I have yet to analyse the hysteric, male or female, who does not turn out to be an inveterate breast-seeker at heart. I venture to suggest that the deep analysis of a positive Œdipus situation may be regarded as taking place at three main levels. At the first level the picture is dominated by the Œdipus situation itself. At the next level it is dominated by ambivalence towards the heterosexual parent; and at the deepest level it is dominated by ambivalence towards the mother. Traces of all these stages may be detected in the classic drama of *Hamlet*; but there can be no doubt that, both in the role of exciting and tempting object and in that of rejecting object, the Queen is the real villain of the piece. The position then would appear to be this. The child finds it intolerable enough to be called upon to deal with a single ambivalent object; but, when he is called upon to deal with two, he finds it still more intolerable. He, therefore, seeks to simplify a complex situation, in which he finds himself confronted with two exciting objects and two rejecting objects, by converting it into one in which he will only be confronted with a single exciting object and a single rejecting object; and he achieves this aim, with, of course, a varying measure of success, by concentrating upon the exciting aspect of one parent and the rejecting aspect of the other. He thus, for all practical purposes, comes to equate one parental object with the exciting object, and the other with the rejecting object; and by so doing *the child constitutes the Œdipus situation for himself.* Ambivalence to both parents persists, however, in the background; and at rock bottom both the exciting object and the rejecting object remain what they originally were, viz. figures of his mother.

NEUROTIC ANXIETY AND HYSTERICAL SUFFERING

I have spoken of the *divide et impera* technique as a means of reducing the volume of affect (both libidinal and aggressive) which demands outward expression; and at this point it would be both relevant and profitable to consider in some detail what happens when the attack of the internal saboteur upon the libidinal ego fails to subdue libidinal need sufficiently to meet the requirements of the central ego, i.e. sufficiently to reduce the volume of available libidinal affect to manageable proportions. It is impossible, however, to embark upon so large a theme on the present occasion. Suffice it to say that, when the technique in question does not succeed in reducing the volume of libidinal affect sufficiently and so fails to fulfil its primary function, it appears to assume a secondary function, in virtue of which it imposes a change of quality upon such libidinal affect as insists upon emerging and thereby disguises the quality of the original affect. Thus, when the dynamic tension within the libidinal ego rises above a certain threshold value and an excess of libidinal need threatens to assert itself, the emergent libidinal affect is converted into (neurotic) *anxiety* by the impact of the aggression which is directed against the libidinal ego by the internal saboteur. When the dynamic tension within the libidinal ego continues to rise until it reaches a further threshold value, it becomes no longer possible for a libidinal discharge to be averted; and the attack of the internal saboteur upon the libidinal ego then has the effect of imparting a *painful* quality to the libidinal affect accompanying the inevitable discharge. Such, at any rate, would appear to be the process involved in the hysterical mode of expressing affect—a process which demands that the expression of libidinal need shall be experienced as suffering.

THE PSYCHOLOGY OF DYNAMIC STRUCTURE AND ITS GENERAL SCIENTIFIC BACKGROUND

In the light of what has just been said regarding the genesis of (neurotic) anxiety, it will be noted that my conception of the nature of anxiety is closely in accord with Freud's original conception, viz. that anxiety is a converted form of undischarged libido. Here we find but one example of the somewhat remarkable fact that, if the general standpoint which I have now come to adopt represents a departure from some of Freud's later views, it has had the effect of revivifying some of Freud's earlier views (views which, in some cases, have latterly been in abeyance). The explanation of this general phenomenon would appear to be that, whilst at every point there is a recognizable analogy between my present views and those of Freud, the development of my views follows a path which diverges gradually from that followed by the historical development of Freud's views. This divergence of paths itself admits of only one explanation —a difference in certain basic theoretic principles. The central points of difference are not difficult to localize. They are two in number. In the first place, although Freud's whole system of thought was concerned with object-relationships, he adhered theoretically to the principle that libido is primarily pleasure-seeking, i.e. that it is directionless. By contrast, I adhere to the principle that libido is primarily object-seeking, i.e. that it has direction. For that matter, I regard aggression as having direction also, whereas, by implication at any rate, Freud regards aggression as, like libido, theoretically directionless. In the second place, Freud regards impulse (i.e. psychical energy) as theoretically distinct from structure, whereas I do not accept this distinction as valid and adhere to the principle of dynamic structure. Of these two central points of difference between Freud's views and those which I have now come to adopt, the latter is the more fundamental; and indeed the former would appear to depend upon the latter. Thus Freud's view that libido is primarily pleasure-seeking follows directly from his divorce of energy from structure; for, once energy is divorced from structure, the only psychical change which can be envisaged as other than disturbing, i.e. as pleasant, is one which makes for the establishment of an equilibrium of forces, i.e. a directionless change. By contrast, if we conceive of energy as inseparable from structure, then the only changes which are intelligible are changes in structural relationships and in relationships between structures; and such changes are essentially directional.

No man, even the greatest and most original, can remain wholly independent of the scientific background of his day; and it cannot be claimed that Freud provides any exception to this rule. Here we must remind ourselves of the scientific atmosphere of the nineteenth century in which Freud was nurtured. This atmosphere was dominated by the Helmholtzian conception that the physical universe consisted in a conglomeration of inert, immutable and indivisible particles to which motion was imparted by a fixed quantity of energy separate from the particles themselves. The energy in question was conceived as having been, for some unknown reason, unevenly distributed at the beginning and as subsequently undergoing a gradual process of redistribution calculated to lead eventually to an equilibrium of forces and an immobilization of the solid particles. Such being the prevailing conception of the contemporary physicist, it is not difficult to understand how it came about that, when Freud, in advance of his time, set himself the arduous task of introducing order into the hitherto confused realm of psychopathology, he should have remained sufficiently under the influence of the scientific atmosphere of his day to conceive impulse (psychical energy) as separate from structure and to cast his libido theory in an equilibrium-seeking mould. In my opinion, however, this feature constitutes a limitation imposed by outside influences upon his thought, which otherwise represented an historic advance upon prevailing conceptions in the psychological field, and which was much more in the spirit of the new scientific outlook at present emerging; for during the twentieth century the scientific conception of the physical universe has alrea˙ʝ undergone a profound change. The inert and indivisible particles or atoms, of which the physical universe was formerly thought to be composed, are now known to be structures of the greatest complexity embodying almost incredible quantities of energy—energy in the absence of which the structures themselves would be unintelligible, but which is equally difficult to explain in the absence of the structures. This intra-atomic energy has effects which not only determine intra-atomic relationships, but also influence bodies at enormous distances. The most remarkable of these effects is radiation; and it has been found necessary to call in radiation to explain certain of the phenomena of light, which defied explanation on the basis of the wave theory of the previous scientific epoch. Interestingly enough, radiation has proved to possess at least one of the properties formerly regarded as a prerogative of solid matter, viz. mass; and the occurrence of radiation affects the structure of both the emitting and the receiving atoms. Further, the universe itself is conceived as undergoing a process of change other than that involved in the establishment of an equilibrium within a closed system. Thus it would appear that the universe is expanding at a terrific speed. The major forces at work are attraction and repulsion (cf. libido and aggression); but, although attraction has the effect of producing local condensations of matter, the dominant force, at any rate during the present phase, is repulsion. So far from being in process of establishing a non-directional equilibrium, therefore, the universe is in process of expanding towards a limit at which no further expansion will be possible and everything will be so attentuated that no further mutual influences will occur and nothing more will be able to happen. The change which the universe is undergoing is thus a directional change. Such being the general scientific background of the present day, it seems to me a demand of the times, if nothing else, that our psychological ideas should be reformulated in terms of a relationship psychology conceived on a basis of dynamic structure.

THE PSYCHOLOGY OF DYNAMIC STRUCTURE AS AN EXPLANATORY SYSTEM

As an explanatory system, the psychology of dynamic structure which I envisage seems to me to have many advantages, among which by no means the least is that it provides a more satisfactory basis than does any other type of psychology for the explanation of group phenomena. However, this is a theme which, like certain others touched upon in this paper, must be left for another occasion. It remains for me, in my concluding remarks, to say something regarding the advantages which appear to accrue from the particular theory of mental structure which I have advanced in place of Freud's classic theory. It is obvious, of course, that, from a topographic standpoint, Freud's theory only admits of the operation of three factors (id, ego and super-ego) in the production of the variety of clinical states with which we are familiar. By contrast, my theory admits of the operation of five factors (central ego, libidinal ego, internal saboteur, exciting object and rejecting object)—even when the super-ego as I conceive it is left out of account. My theory, accordingly, offers a greater range of ætiological possibilities. In actual practice, the difference between the two theories as regards ætiological possibilities is even greater than at first appears; for, of the three factors envisaged in Freud's theory, only two (the ego and the super-ego) are structures properly speaking—the third (viz. the id) being only a source of energy. The energy proceeding from the id is, of course, conceived by Freud as assuming two forms—libido and aggression. Consequently, Freud's theory admits of the operation of two structural and two dynamic factors in all. Freud's two dynamic factors find a place, of course, in my own theory; but, according to my theory, the number of the structural factors is not two, but five. Thus, with five structural factors and two dynamic factors to conjure with, my theory permits of a much greater range of permutations and combinations than does Freud's theory. Actually, however, the possibilities left open by Freud's theory in the abstract are still further limited by his conception of the function of the super-ego, which he regards not only as characteristically aggressive, but also as characteristically anti-libidinal. According to Freud, therefore, the endopsychic drama largely resolves itself into a conflict between the ego in a libidinal capacity and the super-ego in an anti-libidinal capacity. The original dualism inherent in Freud's earliest views regarding repression thus remains substantially unaffected by his subsequent theory of mental structure. Such a conception of the endopsychic drama is unduly limiting, not only so far as its implications for social psychology are concerned (e.g. the implication that social institutions are primarily repressive), but also so far as concerns its explanatory value within the psychopathological and characterological fields. Within these fields explanation reduces itself to an account of the attitudes adopted by the ego in a libidinal capacity *vis-à-vis* the super-ego. By contrast, my theory possesses all the features of an explanatory system enabling psychopathological and characterological phenomena of all kinds to be described in terms of the patterns assumed by a complex of relationships between a variety of structures. It also possesses the advantage of enabling psychopathological symptoms to be explained directly in terms of structural conformations, and thus of doing justice to the unquestionable fact that, so far from being independent phenomena, symptoms are but expressions of the personality as a whole.

At this juncture it becomes necessary to point out (if indeed it has not already become sufficiently obvious) that the basic endopsychic situation which I have described, and to which I have attached such importance, is by no means conceived as immutable from the economic standpoint. From the topographic standpoint, it must be regarded as relatively immutable, although I conceive it as one of the chief aims of psychoanalytical therapy to introduce some change into its topography by way of territorial adjustment. Thus I conceive it as among the most important functions of psychoanalytical therapy (a) to reduce the split of the original ego by restoring to the central ego a maximum of the territories ceded to the libidinal ego and the internal saboteur, and (b) to bring the exciting object and the rejecting object so far as possible together within the sphere of influence of the central ego. The extent to which such changes can be effected appears, however, to be strictly limited. In its economic aspect, by contrast, the basic endopsychic situation is capable of very extensive modification. In conformity with this fact, I conceive it as another of the chief aims of psychoanalytical therapy to reduce to a minimum (a) the attachment of the subsidiary egos to their respective associated objects, (b) the aggression of the central ego towards the subsidiary egos and their objects, and (c) the aggression of the internal saboteur towards the libidinal ego and its object. On the other hand, the basic endopsychic situation is undoubtedly capable of considerable modification in a psychopathological direction. As I have already indicated, the economic pattern of the basic endopsychic situation is the pattern which prevails in hysterical states. Of this I have no doubt whatsoever in my own mind. I have, however, come across cases of hysterical individuals who displayed remarkably paranoid traits (even to the point of having been previously diagnosed as paranoid) and who were found, on analysis, to oscillate between paranoid and hysterical attitudes. Such oscillations appeared to be accompanied by changes in the economic pattern of the endopsychic situation— the paranoid phases being characterized by a departure from the economic pattern of what I have called the *basic* endopsychic situation. What economic pattern the endopsychic situation assumes in the paranoid state I do not feel in a position to say; but I do venture to suggest that corresponding to every distinguishable clinical state there is a characteristic pattern of the endopsychic situation. It must be recognized, of course, that various patterns may exist side by side or be superimposed one upon the other. It must also be recognized that patterning of the endopsychic situation may either be rigid or flexible—extreme rigidity and extreme flexibility being alike unfavourable features. At the same time, it must be stressed that the *basic* (and original) endopsychic situation is that which is found in hysterical states. In conformity with this consideration, I take the view that the earliest psychopathological symptoms to manifest themselves are hysterical in character; and I interpret the screaming fits of the infant in this sense. If I am right in this, Freud showed no mean insight in choosing hysterical phenomena as the material out of which to build the foundations of psychoanalytical theory.

In the light of considerations already advanced it will be understood, of course, that, although the basic endopsychic situation is the situation underlying hysterical states, it is itself the product of a split of the original ego, and is, therefore, a schizoid phenomenon. Thus, although the earliest psychopathological *symptoms* are hysterical, the earliest psychopathological *process* is schizoid. Repression itself is a schizoid process; and splitting of the ego is a universal phenomenon, although, of course, the degree of such splitting varies in different individuals. It is not to be inferred, however, that overt schizoid states are the earliest psychopathological states to develop. On the contrary, the earliest of such states are hysterical in nature. An actual schizoid state is a much later development—one which only materializes when the schizoid process is pushed to a point at which a massive repression of affect occurs and even an hysterical expression of affect is thereby precluded. Thus it is only when a massive repression of affect occurs that the individual becomes unduly detached and experiences a pronounced sense of futility. What is involved in the development of schizoid states cannot, however, be discussed further on the present occasion.

THE DYNAMIC QUALITY OF INTERNALIZED OBJECTS

The feature of Freud's theory of the mental apparatus presenting the greatest anomaly is one to which reference has not yet been made. It is this—that the only part of the psyche which he describes in terms at all approximating to those of dynamic structure is the super-ego. The id is, of course, described as a source of energy without structure; and the ego is described as a passive structure without energy except such as invades it from the id. By contrast, the super-ego is described as a structure endowed with a fund of energy. It is true that the energy in question is conceived as being ultimately derived from the id; but this in no way alters the fact that Freud attributes to the super-ego a considerable measure of independent functional activity. So much is this the case that he speaks of the super-ego and the id as diametrically opposed to one another in the aims of their activities, and of the ego as buffetted between these two endopsychic entities. The odd thing about all this is that the super-ego is really only a naturalized alien, as it were, within the realm of the individual mind, an immigrant from outer reality. Its whole significance resides in the fact that it is essentially an internalized object. That the only part of the psyche which Freud treats as a dynamic structure should be an internalized object is, to my mind an anomaly sufficient in itself to justify my attempt to formulate an alternative theory of psychical structure. It will be observed that, in formulating such an alternative theory, I have so far followed a line opposite to that followed by Freud in that, whereas an internalized object is the only part of the psyche which Freud treats as a dynamic structure, the internalized objects which I envisage are the only parts of the psyche which I have *not* treated as dynamic structures. I have treated the internalized objects simply as *objects* of the dynamic ego structures, i.e. as endopsychic structures which are not themselves dynamic. I have done this deliberately, not only to avoid complications of exposition, but also to bring into focus the activity of the ego structures which I find it necessary to postulate, and to avoid all risk of under-rating the primary importance of this activity; for, after all, it is only through this activity that objects ever come to be internalized. However, in the interests of consistency, I must now draw the logical conclusion of my theory of dynamic structure and acknowledge that, since internal objects are structures, they must necessarily be, in some measure at least, dynamic. In drawing this conclusion and making this acknowledgement, I shall not only be here following the precedent of Freud, but also, it would seem, conforming to the demands of such psychological facts as are revealed, e.g. in dreams and in the phenomena of paranoia. This further step will enhance the explanatory value of my theory of mental structure by introducing additional possibilities into the endopsychic situation by way of permutation and combination. It must be recognized, however, that, in practice, it is very difficult to differentiate between the activity of internalized objects and the activity of the ego structures with which they are associated; and, with a view to avoiding any appearance of demonology, it seems wise to err, if anything, on the side of overweighting the activity of the ego structures rather than otherwise. It remains true, nevertheless, that under certain conditions internalized objects may acquire a dynamic independence which cannot be ignored. It is doubtless in this direction that we must look for an explanation of the fundamental animism of human beings, which is none the less persistent under the surface even when it is hidden under the veneers of civilization and science, but which significantly betrays itself even in the most sophisticated forms of art.

ADDENDUM
(1951)

As has been stated in the preface, the series of papers which constitute Part 1 of this book, and among which the above paper finds a place, is a series representing, not the systematic elaboration of an already established point of view, but the progressive development of a line of thought. In these circumstances it is inevitable that certain of the views expressed later in the series will be found to conflict with, and even contradict, views expressed earlier in the series. Actually, very few of the contradictions which have arisen are of serious moment, since in most cases the reasons for the replacement of one view by another are clearly stated in the argument for the later view. Unfortunately, however, this does not hold true in every case; and, in retrospect, I cannot help recognizing the presence of two serious contradictions between views expressed in the above paper and views expressed in 'A Revised Psychopathology of the Psychoses and Psychoneuroses'. Thus in the earlier paper my classification of the four 'transitional' defensive techniques is based upon a distinction between two internalized objects which I describe as 'the accepted object' and 'the rejected object' respectively; and the distinctive features of each technique is related to a characteristic method of dealing with these two objects according as they are treated, separately or together, as internal or external. In the later paper I do not speak of 'the accepted object' and 'the rejected object'; but I do speak of 'the exciting object' and 'the rejecting object' in describing the establishment of 'the basic endopsychic situation'. It will be noticed that, in previously describing internal objects as 'accepted and rejected', I was considering their status from the point of view of the attitude adopted by the ego towards them, whereas, in describing internal objects as 'exciting' and 'rejecting', I was considering their status from the point of view of the light in which they presented themselves to the ego. These two points of view are different; but I do not think that they are irreconcilable, since the attitude adopted by an ego-structure towards an object must necessarily be related to the light in which the object presents itself. However, the contrast between 'accepted' and 'rejected' is not strictly parallel to the contrast between 'exciting' and 'rejecting'; for, whilst 'rejecting' is the obverse of 'rejected', 'exciting' cannot be regarded as the obverse of '*accept*ed', especially since 'the exciting object' is described as 'bad' in the sense of 'unsatisfying'. Here then some readjustment of views would appear to be required in the interests of consistency of systematization; for, whilst I do not feel prepared to sacrifice the concept of exciting and rejecting objects, I should be reluctant to abandon the general basis of my classification of the transitional techniques.

At this point it becomes appropriate to direct attention to the second, and more serious, of the contradictions to which I have referred. It will be recalled that I described the exciting and rejecting objects as resulting from a split in the internalized 'bad' or unsatisfying object, which I regarded as the first object to be internalized, and, therefore, as the original internal object. However, in speaking of the 'accepted' and 'rejected' objects in the earlier paper, I was proceeding on the assumption that a 'good', as well as a 'bad', object had already been internalized. This apparent inconsistency could, of course, be explained on the grounds that in the two contexts I was speaking of different stages of development; for, even from the standpoint adopted in the later paper, I recognized that a 'good' or satisfying object could be internalized subsequently to the original internalization of the 'bad' or unsatisfying object to compensate for the inner effects produced by the latter. And, of course, the stage of development which I was discussing when I spoke of 'accepted' and 'rejected' objects was the 'transitional' stage—a stage subsequent to that which I was discussing when I described the differentiation of the 'exciting' and 'rejecting' objects. At the same time, it is not easy to relate the two conceptions involved. It might appear at first sight as though the 'unsatisfying' and the 'rejected' objects might be equated; but the stage which I had in mind when I spoke of 'the rejected object' corresponds to one at which, according to my later view, 'the unsatisfying object' has already been split into the 'exciting' and 'rejecting' objects —so that no solution of the difficulty seems possible along these lines.

It now occurs to me, however, that a solution of the difficulty may be found in a revision of views to the effect that the object which is originally internalized is, not an object embodying the exclusively 'bad' and unsatisfying aspect of the external object, but the pre-ambivalent object; and indeed this is the assumption on which I proceeded in my paper entitled 'Schizoid Factors in the Personality' (included in this volume). The internalization of the pre-ambivalent object would then be explained on the grounds that it presented itself as unsatisfying in some measure as well as in some measure satisfying. On this assumption ambivalence will be a state first arising in the original unsplit ego in relation, not to the external object, but to an internalized pre-ambivalent object. The resulting situation will then be one in which the unsplit ego is confronted with an internal ambivalent object. At this point it is necessary to recall that, in the basic endopsychic situation which I have envisaged, *both* the exciting and the rejecting objects are 'rejected objects' from the point of view of the central ego, although the former is 'accepted' by the libidinal ego and the latter 'accepted' by the internal saboteur. Bearing this consideration in mind, we may conceive that the next step in the development of the internal situation, viz. the splitting of the internal object, occurs in the following manner. Since both the *over-exciting* and the *over-frustrating* elements in the internal (ambivalent) object are unacceptable to the original ego, these elements are both split off from the main body of the object and repressed in such a way as to give rise to 'the exciting object' and 'the rejecting object'. The libidinal cathexes of these two objects, persisting in spite of their rejection, will then give rise to a splitting of the ego along the lines described in the later paper. A part of the original ego cathecting the exciting object will be rejected and repressed by the central part of the ego, and thus give rise to 'the libidinal ego'; and a part of the original ego cathecting the rejecting object will be rejected and repressed by the central part of the ego, and thus give rise to 'the internal saboteur'. It will be noticed, however, that, after the over-exciting and over-frustrating elements have been split off from the internal ambivalent object, there remains a nucleus of the object shorn of its over-exciting and over-frustrating elements. This nucleus will then assume the status of an 'accepted object' in the eyes of the central ego, which will maintain the cathexis of this object and retain it for itself. This conception of the development of the basic endopsychic situation seems to me to represent an advance upon that put forward in the above paper, and is one which I now desire to substitute for the latter.

It will be noticed that, in accordance with my revised conception, the central ego's 'accepted object', being shorn of its over-exciting and over-rejecting elements, assumes the form of a desexualized and idealized object which the central ego can safely love after divesting itself of the elements which give rise to the libidinal ego and the internal saboteur. It is significant, accordingly, that this is just the sort of object into which the hysterical patient seeks to convert the analyst—and the sort of object into which the child seeks to convert his parents, usually with a considerable measure of success. It now seems to me, therefore, that this is the object which forms the nucleus of the super-ego as I have come to conceive it (in contrast to 'the internal saboteur'). It would, however, seem more appropriate to the nature of this object to describe it as 'the ego-ideal' rather than 'the super-ego' (and thus to revive the earlier term).

There still remains the problem of relating the 'accepted' and 'rejected' objects of my earlier paper to my revised conception, and thus finding a place in this conception for my description of the transitional defensive techniques. When all considerations are taken into account, it would appear best to regard 'the accepted object' as equivalent to the nucleus of the internal ambivalent object, which remains cathected by the central ego after the repression of the exciting and rejecting objects, and which I now envisage as the nucleus round which the super-ego is eventually built up; and the term 'accepted object' may conveniently be used to describe this nucleus. Once this equivalence is established, it will then be necessary to regard the 'exciting' and 'rejecting' objects of the later paper as both included in the concept of 'the rejected object' of the earlier paper; for, as we have seen, both these objects are rejected by the central ego. The term 'rejected objects' (in the plural) will then require to be substituted in the earlier paper for the term 'rejected object' (in the singular). The use of the plural term would appear to be quite justifiable, since reflection now suggests that, in the case of each of the 'transitional' techniques, the 'exciting' and 'rejecting' objects are both treated in the same way. Thus in the paranoid and phobic techniques they are both treated as external; and in the obsessional and hysterical techniques they are both treated as internal. It should be added that these various techniques must all be regarded as techniques employed by the central ego.

CHAPTER V

Object-Relationships and Dynamic Structure[1]
(1946)

THE aim of the present contribution is to give some general
account of the special point of view which I have now come
to adopt, and which was developed in a series of papers published during the course of the 1939–45 war.[2] These papers do not represent the elaboration of a definitely established point of view so
much as the progressive development of a line of thought. Nevertheless, the ultimate principle from which the whole of my special views
are derived may be formulated in the general proposition that libido
is not primarily pleasure-seeking, but object-seeking. The clinical
material on which this proposition is based may be summarized in
the protesting cry of a patient to this effect—'You're always talking
about my wanting this and that desire satisfied; but what I really
want is a father.' It was reflection upon the implications of such
phenomena as this that formed the real starting point of my present
line of thought. I suppose there are very few analysts nowadays who
would not feel indignant if criticized on the grounds of minimizing
the importance of object-relationships in practice. Yet it is not so
easy to find an analyst whose acknowledgement of the importance
of object-relationships has influenced his adherence to the *theoretic*
principle upon which the classic libido theory is based, viz., that
libido is primarily pleasure-seeking. It will, of course, at once occur
to the reader that what is meant by 'pleasure-seeking' in the classic
theory is really 'relief of libidinal tension'; but my point is that such
tension is inherently the tension of object-seeking needs. The claim

---

[1] Read before the British Psycho-Analytical Society on 5th June 1946, and subsequently published in *The International Journal of Psycho-Analysis*, Vol. XXVII,
Pts. 1 and 2.

Viz. the three papers immediately preceding in this volume.

that pleasure-seeking is inherent in the state of tension itself seems to me an argument based on the principle that *post hoc* necessarily means *propter hoc*. At the same time, this claim may be seen to reduce itself to the mere statement that tension is tension, since tension naturally seeks discharge, and discharge naturally brings relief; and this statement leaves quite unanswered the question of the nature of the forces under tension, and the direction or aim of these forces. It also leaves out of account the question how far relief of tension in itself involves fulfilment of the libidinal aim. Freud spoke, of course, of libidinal aims and defined these aims in terms of erotogenic zones—as oral aims, anal aims and so on. What he so described, however, are not really aims, but modes of dealing with objects; and the zones in question should properly be regarded, not as the dictators of aims, but as the servants of aims—bodily organs which serve as channels whereby personal aims may be achieved. The real libidinal aim is the establishment of satisfactory relationships with objects; and it is, accordingly, the object that constitutes the true libidinal goal. At the same time, the form assumed by the libidinal approach is determined by the nature of the object. Thus it is owing to the nature of the breast that the infant's inherent incorporative tendency assumes the form of sucking with the mouth. Strictly speaking, of course, the mother's breast and the instinctive oral endowment of the infant have been evolved in mutual adaptation to one another; but this fact in itself implies that libidinal aims are inherently bound up with object-relationships. Actually some of the activities to which so-called libidinal aims have been attributed are activities which I should hesitate to describe as primarily libidinal at all, e.g. anal and urinary activities; for the inherent aim of these activities, in common with that of vomiting, is not the establishment of a relationship with objects, but the rejection of objects which, from the point of view of the organism, constitute foreign bodies. This fact does not, of course, prevent such activities constituting a source of pleasure, since pleasure has no special connection with libido, but is a natural accompaniment of relief of tension irrespective of the nature of the forces whose tension is relieved. The conception of erotogenic zones raises other critical considerations, to some of which I must now refer.

The conception of erotogenic zones is based upon an atomic or molecular conception of the organism—the conception that the organism is initially a conglomeration of separate entities, which can only become related and integrated as the result of a process of

development. Within the functional sphere, a corresponding atomism has given rise to a tendency to describe dynamic processes in
terms of isolated impulses and isolated instincts. It has led to the common practice of hypostatizing 'libido' by endowing it with the
definite article, and describing it as '*the* libido.' Similar atomism
seems to me to underlie Marjorie Brierley's 'process theory'[1], as
also the epistemology adopted by Adrian Stephen in his 'Note on
Ambivalence'[2], in which he selected my views as the text for a
critical consideration of the conception of 'good and bad objects'.
Such atomism seems to me a legacy of the past quite alien to modern
biological conceptions, in accordance with which the organism is
regarded as functioning as a whole from the start. When the organism
is functioning normally, it is only from the artificial point of view
of scientific analysis that it can be regarded as consisting of separately
functioning parts; and, in cases in which parts actually do turn out to
be functioning separately, this only happens as the result of a pathological process. Similarly, it is impossible to gain any adequate conception of the nature of an individual organism if it is considered
apart from its relationships to its natural objects; for it is only in its
relationships to these objects that its true nature is displayed. It was
neglect of this fact that vitiated Behaviourist experiments on infants
isolated in glass rooms; for a child isolated from his mother in a glass
room has already ceased to be a normally functioning human child,
since he is deprived of his natural objects. Many Pavlovian experiments would appear to have been similarly vitiated.

In the second place, the conception of erotogenic zones does less
than justice to the capacity of the individual to dispense with pleasurable satisfaction. According to the classic theories, such a capacity
is to be attributed either (*a*) to repression, or (*b*) to the substitution
of the reality principle for the pleasure principle. So far as repression
is concerned, there can be no doubt, of course, about the influence
of this technique in enabling the individual to dispense with pleasure,
and indeed in promoting a renunciation of pleasure on his part.
On the other hand, from the point of view of object-relationship
psychology, explicit pleasure-seeking represents a deterioration of
behaviour. I speak here of a 'deterioration', rather than of a 'regres-

[1] Marjorie Brierley, 'Notes on Metapsychology as Process Theory', *The International Journal of Psycho-Analysis*, Vol. XXV, Pts. 3 and 4 (1944).
[2] Adrian Stephen, 'A Note on Ambivalence', *The International Journal of Psycho-
Analysis*, Vol. XXVI, Pts. 1 and 2 (1945).

sion', of behaviour because, if object-seeking is primary, pleasure-seeking can hardly be described as 'regressive', but is more appropriately described as partaking of the nature of deterioration. Explicit pleasure-seeking has as its essential aim the relieving of the tension of libidinal need for the mere sake of relieving this tension. Such a process does, of course, occur commonly enough; but, since libidinal need is object-need, simple tension-relieving implies some failure of object-relationships. The fact is that simple tension-relieving is really a safety-valve process. It is thus, not a means of achieving libidinal aims, but a means of mitigating the failure of these aims.

As already mentioned, the capacity to dispense with pleasurable satisfaction may, according to classic theory, be due not only to repression, but also to a substitution of the reality principle for the pleasure principle. If, however, libido is primarily object-seeking, it follows that behaviour must be oriented towards outer reality, and thus determined by a reality principle from the first. If this is not obvious in the case of the human infant, it is largely because, in man as contrasted with the animals, the patterns of instinctive behaviour are not rigid, but are only laid down in broad outline. Thus the instinctive drives of man only assume the form of general trends; and these only acquire a more rigid and differentiated pattern as the result of experience. What the child lacks above all is experience of reality; and it is this, rather than any lack of orientation towards reality, that gives the adult observer the impression that the child's behaviour is primarily determined by a pleasure principle. It must be recognized, of course, that with the child's inexperience goes a tendency to be more emotional and impulsive, i.e. less controlled, than the adult; and this, combined with the amount of frustration which he encounters, leads him to be more prone than the adult to resort to tension-relieving behaviour. In my opinion, however, it is erroneous to conclude that his behaviour is primarily determined by a pleasure principle which has later to be replaced by a reality principle. No such distinction between principles of behaviour can be drawn in the case of animals, whose instinctive behaviour follows rigid patterns relatively independent of experience, and for whom object-seeking thus represents little difficulty. The human child seeks his objects with no less insistence than the animal; but, in his case, the path to the object is only roughly charted; and he is thus liable to lose his way. At this point, the example of the moth seeking the flame may be cited as a critical instance. This may be regarded at first sight as an unfortunate instance for me to quote, since it may be said that, in seeking the flame, the moth displays a remarkable lack of reality sense. It can hardly be said, on the other hand, that the moth is guided to the flame by pleasure. On the contrary, its behaviour is essentially object-seeking. What it is seeking, however, is not the flame but the light. Thus it is not actuated by a pleasure principle, but by a reality sense which is severely limited, since it cannot differentiate between one source of light and another. The fact is that reality sense is essentially a matter of degree. Characteristically the child's sense of reality is of low degree compared with that of the adult; but he is none the less actuated by a reality sense from the beginning, even if he is all too liable, in face of frustration, to stray into tension-relieving sidetracks.

A further reflection suggests itself with regard to the conception of erotogenic zones and the related conception that libido is primarily pleasure-seeking. This is that these conceptions do scant justice to that specificity of instinctive object-seeking, which is best observed in animals, but which is in no sense compromised, although it may be obscured, by human adaptability. The nesting-habits of birds may be cited in this connection. The objects which birds collect as material for their nests are remarkably specific. Thus one species may collect sticks, another straws and another clay. Similarly, the completed nests have a characteristic structure in the case of every species. And here it must be remembered that a nest is no less an object to a bird, just as a house is no less an object to a man, because it is an object which has to be constructed. It is an object which is sought, even if, to be found, it has first to be made. Of course, the houses of men display a much greater latitude of design and a much greater diversity of material than do the nests of any given species of birds. Nevertheless, a house is always a house; and the variety of human houses must be interpreted as a sign of that adaptability which is the counterpart of the absence of rigid patterns in the instinctive endowment of man. Adaptability implies, of course, a capacity to learn by experience, i.e. to improve an inherent reality sense, in the interests of object-seeking. It also puts at the disposal of object-seeking a considerable latitude of techniques. These advantages have their inevitable dangers since they involve a greater risk of deviations from normality; but this must not be allowed to obscure the object-seeking principle. At this point I am reminded of a man for whose medical care I was at one time responsible, and whose limbs were completely paralysed as the result of a fracture of the cervical spine. This man was an assiduous reader whose access to the world of literature depended upon a technique of turning the pages of his book with his tongue. Such behaviour on his part does not, of course, lend itself to be explained in terms of an intense oral fixation or of an overwhelming predominance of oral components in his character. He used his mouth to turn the pages because this organ was the only organic channel open to him for the purpose. On a somewhat similar principle the child uses his mouth for the purpose of breast-seeking because it is the only available organ whereby this purpose can be achieved. He is, of course, all the more disposed to do this because, as the result of a long evolutionary process, his mouth has been specially fashioned to serve this very purpose at the instance of object-seeking aims. *Pari passu*, by means of the same evolutionary process, the use of the mouth for purposes of breast-seeking has been established as a pattern in his instinctive endowment. But, if on this account he is to be described as oral, it must be acknowledged that he is only oral because he is breast-seeking, and not *vice versa*. The general position would thus appear to be that, for the achievement of his libidinal aims, i.e. for the establishment of the desired relationships with his objects, the individual employs bodily organs, the choice of which is determined by the following principles in order of priority: (*a*) That the organ is one which is appropriate to the aim, and preferably one which has been specially adapted for the achievement of the aim in the course of the evolutionary process; (*b*) that the organ is available (and, when I say 'available', I mean, of course, 'psychologically as well as biologically available'); (*c*) that the organ is one which has received the sanction of experience, and not least if such experience has been traumatic. The general mode of operation of these principles may be illustrated as follows. Where an adult is concerned, the organ of choice for a sexual relationship with the object is a genital organ; and normally the genital organ will provide the main libidinal channel in the relationship. If, however, for psychological reasons the genital organ is not available, libido will tend to be diverted into some other available channel or channels. It may be diverted, for example, to the mouth, which was in infancy the organ of choice, and which then received the sanction of experience. Alternatively, it may be diverted to the anus, which, although never a channel of choice, may nevertheless have received the sanction of experience in infancy—perhaps in traumatic fashion as the result of the administration of enemas. Here it may perhaps be remarked that, just as libido may be diverted from the genitals to the mouth in an adult, so in infancy it may be prematurely diverted from the mouth to the genitals, if the availability of the mouth is compromised by situations of frustration. This particular diversion is associated with infantile masturbation; and it would appear to be an important feature of hysterical psychopathology.

I have now attempted to give some account of my reasons for dissatisfaction with certain features of the classic libido theory. I have also attempted to give some indication of the direction in which, in my opinion, the theory requires to be modified. The major change which I advocate is the adoption of the principle that libido is primarily object-seeking; and all the other changes follow directly from that. It will be readily understood that these various changes involve a point of view which is incompatible with Abraham's theory of libidinal development, based as it is upon the conception of erotogenic zones. I do not propose on the present occasion to enter into any detailed criticism of Abraham's scheme, such as appeared in my paper, 'A Revised Psychopathology of the Psychoses and Psychoneuroses'; but it is obvious that, if there is something wrong with the conception of erotogenic zones, there will also be something wrong with a scheme of development based upon this conception. This is not to say that Abraham was indifferent to the importance of object-relationships; for his recognition of their importance is obvious in his writings. In my opinion, however, he made the general mistake of conferring the status of libidinal phases upon what are really *techniques* employed by the individual in his object-relationships; and this was mainly due to his uncritical acceptance of the conception of erotogenic zones. Here it must be remembered that, although he was far from indifferent to the importance of object-relationships, he suffered from a great disadvantage; for he had already formulated his theory before attention had been drawn to the supreme importance of *internalized* objects through the work of Melanie Klein. In the light of Melanie Klein's work and of developments consequent upon it, it is impossible to do justice to the object-relationships of the individual without taking into account, and attaching due importance to, his relationships with internal objects. It is only when this is done that it is possible to recognize the true significance of the phenomena which Abraham interpreted in terms of phases, but which, in my view, should largely be interpreted in terms of techniques.

From the point of view of object-relationship psychology, it is axiomatic that no scheme of libidinal development can be satisfactory unless it is based upon a consideration of the natural and biological objects of the developing individual at various stages. There can be no dispute, of course, about the fact that at the earliest stage the child's natural object is his mother—and more specifically her breast, although, as development proceeds, the libidinal focus alters in such a manner that interest which was predominantly directed to her breast at the outset becomes increasingly directed to his mother as a whole. There can be equally little dispute that, at the other end of the scale of development, the genital organs of a heterosexual object other than a parent should occupy a place in libidinal interest corresponding to that occupied by the mother's breast at the outset, albeit there is something very far wrong if interest is as predominantly concerned with a bodily organ at the later stage as at the earlier. Here then we have two recognizable stages (one at the lower, and one at the upper end of the scale) which can be readily distinguished in terms of *the appropriate biological object*. The problem then arises by what steps the individual passes from one stage to the other. Now it is impossible to find any appropriate biological objects which play an intermediate role in the developmental process between the objects of the initial and final stages. It thus becomes a question of a transitional process between the one stage and the other. This transitional process is, however, so prolonged and complicated that we must regard it as representing a special intermediate stage between the other two stages. We thus arrive at a theory of libidinal development in which a place is found for three stages—(1) a stage at which the appropriate biological object is the breast, (2) a transitional stage, and (3) a stage at which the heterosexual genital organs constitute the appropriate biological object. Throughout this sequence there is a gradual expansion and development of personal relationships with objects, beginning with an almost exclusive and very dependent relationship with the mother, and maturing into a very complex system of social relationships of all degrees of intimacy. These personal relationships are profoundly influenced by, but are not exclusively dependent upon, the relationships established with the appropriate biological objects, although, the younger the child, the greater the influence of the latter upon the former. From the social point of view, of course, personal relationships are of overriding importance; and, therefore, they must be taken into account in assessing the significance of the various stages. Further, their importance is such as to claim some recognition in nomenclature. At the earliest stage, the attitude of the child to the breast may, admittedly, be described as oral; but it is only oral because it is *incorporative* and the organ of incorporation is the mouth. The outstanding feature of the child's personal relationship to his mother is, however, one of extreme *dependence*; and this dependence is reflected in a psychological process of *primary identification*[1], in the light of which separation from his object becomes the child's greatest source of anxiety (as in my experience of war psychiatry it proved to be the greatest source of anxiety to the neurotic soldier). In the light of these various considerations, it seems most appropriate to describe the first stage as one of *Infantile Dependence*, without prejudice to the fact that this dependence is chiefly manifested in an attitude of oral incorporation towards, and an attitude of primary emotional identification with the object. By contrast, the final stage appears best described as a stage of *Mature Dependence*— 'mature dependence' rather than 'independence', since a capacity for relationships necessarily implies dependence of some sort. What distinguishes mature dependence from infantile dependence is that it is characterized neither by a one-sided attitude of incorporation nor by an attitude of primary emotional identification. On the contrary, it is characterized by a capacity on the part of a differentiated individual for co-operative relationships with differentiated objects. So far as the *appropriate biological object* is concerned, the relationship, is, of course, genital; but it is a relationship involving evenly matched giving and taking between two differentiated individuals who are mutually dependent, and between whom there is no disparity of dependence. Further, the relationship is characterized by an absence of primary identification and an absence of incorporation. At least, this is the ideal picture; but it is, of course, never completely realized in practice, since there is no one whose libidinal development proceeds wholly without a hitch. The intermediate stage has already been described as *Transitional*; and it appears best so named, since it is a stage of vicissitudes arising out of the difficulties and conflicts of transition. As might be expected, therefore, it is not only characteristi-

[1] I employ the term 'primary identification' here to signify the cathexis of an object which has not yet been differentiated (or has been only partly differentiated) from himself by the cathecting subject. This process differs, of course, from the process ordinarily described as 'identification', viz. an emotionally determined tendency to treat a differentiated (or partly differentiated) object as if it were not differentiated, when it is cathected. The latter process should properly be described as 'secondary identification'.

cally the stage of conflict, but also characteristically the stage of *defensive techniques*. Among these techniques, four classic techniques stand out conspicuously from the rest—the paranoid, the obsessional, the hysterical and the phobic. As I see it, however, these four techniques do not correspond to any recognizable libidinal phases, but are four alternative methods for attempting to deal with the difficulties of the transitional stage. At this point it is necessary for us to remind ourselves of the importance of the part played by an incorporative attitude at the stage from which transition is being attempted. This incorporative attitude manifests itself, not only in the ingestion of milk, but also in the psychological internalization of objects, i.e. the psychological incorporation of representations of objects into the psychical structure. The result is that the great task of the transitional period comes to be one, not only of establishing relationships with differentiated external objects, but also of coming to terms with objects which have already been internalized. The situation is complicated by the fact that the task of the transitional stage also includes the renunciation of relationships established during the first stage. It is further complicated by the previous establishment of ambivalence and the splitting of the object into a good and a bad object. Consequently, attempts to get rid of objects become a marked feature of the transitional stage; and this applies not only to external, but also to internal objects. And it is for this reason, and not on account of the emergence of any inherently anal stage, that techniques based upon the expulsive, excretory processes come to be employed so freely, especially during the earlier phase of the transitional stage, when the attempt to get rid of early objects naturally plays a more prominent role than in the later phase. What must be emphasized, however, is that the various techniques which form the basis of psychopathological developments during the transitional stage represent varying and alternative methods of dealing with internalized objects—really methods of trying to get rid of early objects, which have been internalized, without losing them.

It is impossible on the present occasion to discuss the characteristic features of the various transitional techniques; and I must therefore content myself with the bald statement that it is in their varying modes of dealing with internal objects that their essential differences lie. Nor is it possible to discuss at any length the processes which form the basis of psychopathological developments during the stage of infantile dependence. It must suffice if I draw attention to the supreme importance I attach to the earliest developments which take place during this first stage, and which, in my opinion, include the following series of processes:

(1) The splitting of the internalized bad object into (*a*) an exciting and (*b*) a rejecting object;

(2) The repression of both these objects by the ego;

(3) The splitting off and repression of parts of the ego which remain attached to the repressed objects and, so to speak, follow them into repression, and which I describe as respectively the *libidinal ego* and the *internal saboteur*;

(4) A resulting situation, which I call the *Basic Endopsychic Situation*, and in which we find a *Central Ego* employing aggression in the exercise of *Direct Repression* (*a*) over the *Libidinal Ego* attached to an *Exciting Object*, and (*b*) over the *Internal Saboteur* attached to a *Rejecting Object*;

(5) The operation of a process which I describe as *Indirect Repression*, and which consists in the exercise of aggression on the part of the internal saboteur, aligned with the rejecting object, against the libidinal ego, aligned with the exciting object.

The outstanding feature of the basic endopsychic situation, to which I have so briefly referred, is that it is produced by means of a *splitting of the ego* and therefore involves the establishment of a *Schizoid Position*. This position becomes established in the earlier part of the first stage and antecedes the depressive position which has been so fully described by Melanie Klein, and which can only emerge after the original unitary ego has been split and the schizoid position has been established. At this point it becomes necessary to explain what no opportunity has been found to explain earlier— that I regard the first stage as falling into two phases, the latter of which is differentiated from the former by the emergence of the tendency to bite side by side with the original tendency to suck. This differentiation of phases corresponds, of course, to Abraham's differentiation of the earlier and later oral phases. It is only during the latter of these two phases that the depressive position can arise, i.e. when the child becomes able to envisage situations arising out of destructive biting as well as situations arising out of incorporative sucking. What I feel disposed to maintain, however, is that the schizoid position, as represented in the basic endopsychic situation, forms the ultimate basis of all psychopathological developments which may subsequently take place. For it is only after such a position has been established that there can be any differentiation of endopsychic structures such as Freud attempted to formulate in terms of the ego, the super-ego and the id.

The conception of endopsychic structure at which I have arrived will be seen to differ considerably from that formulated by Freud. It differs conspicuously, of course, in that it is ultimately based upon the repression of internalized objects. If, however, the repression of such objects is left out of account, it is clear that there is a general correspondence. Thus the central ego corresponds to Freud's 'ego', the libidinal ego to Freud's 'id', and the internal saboteur to Freud's 'super-ego'. Nevertheless, underlying this correspondence there is a profound difference of conception. For the ego-structures which I envisage (i.e. the central ego and the two subsidiary egos) are all conceived as inherently *dynamic* structures resulting from the splitting of an original and single dynamic ego-structure present at the beginning. By contrast, the three parts of the mental apparatus, as described by Freud, are not all inherently dynamic structures. For the 'ego' is conceived as a structure without any energy in its own rights; and the 'id' is conceived as a source of energy without structure. As regards the 'super-ego', its behaviour is certainly described in terms which imply that it is a dynamic structure; but, since all energy in the psyche is regarded as proceeding ultimately from the 'id', it becomes obvious that the 'super-ego', like the 'ego', is really an energiless structure deriving energy from a source outside itself. A further feature of Freud's theory of the mental apparatus is that the 'ego' is not an original structure, but a structure developing on the surface of the undifferentiated matrix of the 'id', from which it continues to derive its energy in the form of so-called 'impulses'. According to my theory, by contrast, all the ego-structures are conceived as inherently dynamic; and the central ego represents the central portion of an original unitary, dynamic ego-structure, from which the subsidiary egos come to be subsequently split off. Thus, whilst Freud regards the structural 'ego' as a derivative of the structureless 'id', I regard the libidinal ego (which corresponds to the 'id') as a split off portion of the original, dynamic ego. The 'super-ego' was, of course, always regarded by Freud as in a sense a derivative of the 'ego', so that in this respect it does not differ from its *vis-à-vis* the internal saboteur, except, of course, in so far as its energy is derivative. However, Freud also describes the super-ego as an internalized object; and in this capacity it plays a part somewhat similar to that played by what I describe as the rejecting object (to which the internal saboteur is attached). At the same time, I do not regard the concept of the 'super-ego' as covered by the concepts of the internal saboteur and the rejecting object; and indeed I would introduce the term 'super-ego' into my scheme to designate an internalized object which remains cathected and accepted as 'good' by the central ego when it rejects and represses the exciting and rejecting objects.

I have drawn attention to various points of difference, some more general and some more particular, between my own theory of endopsychic structure and Freud's theory of the mental apparatus; but the fundamental difference is one derived from the fact that, whilst I, of course, employ Freud's psychoanalytical method of approach to the phenomena in question, I have come to adopt underlying scientific principles which differ from his. It is the accompaniment of this similarity of method by a difference of underlying principles that accounts for the fact that my views simultaneously correspond with and diverge from his. The real position would thus appear to be that my views consist largely in a reinterpretation of Freud's views on the basis of a differing set of underlying scientific principles. The central points of difference are two in number:

(1) Although Freud's whole system of thought was concerned with object-relationships, he adhered theoretically to the principle that libido is primarily concerned with pleasure-seeking, i.e. with the relief of its own tension. This means that for him libido is theoretically directionless, although some of his statements undoubtedly imply the contrary. By contrast, I adhere to the principle that libido is primarily object-seeking, and that the tension which demands relief is the tension of object-seeking tendencies. This means that for me libido has direction.

(2) Freud approached psychological problems from the *a priori* standpoint that psychical energy is essentially distinct from psychical structure. On the other hand, I have come to adopt the principle of dynamic structure, in terms of which both structure divorced from energy and energy divorced from structure are meaningless concepts.

Of those two central points of difference, the latter is the more fundamental, since the former would appear to depend upon the latter. Thus Freud's view that libido is primarily pleasure-seeking follows directly from his divorce of energy from structure; for, once energy is divorced from structure, the only psychical change which can be regarded as other than disturbing is one which makes for the establishment of an equilibrium of forces, i.e. a directionless change. If, however, we conceive energy as inseparable from structure, the only changes which are intelligible are changes in structural relationships and in relationships between structures; and such changes are inherently directional. On consideration it becomes obvious, of course, that Freud's divorce of energy from structure represents a limitation imposed upon his thought by the general scientific atmosphere of his day. It is a curious feature of modern times that the scientific atmosphere of a period appears to be always dominated by the current conceptions of physics. Be that as it may, the scientific atmosphere of Freud's day was largely dominated by the Helmholtzian conception that the universe consisted in a conglomeration of inert, immutable and indivisible particles to which motion was imparted by a fixed quantity of energy separate from these particles. However, modern atomic physics has changed all that; and, if psychology has not yet succeeded in setting the pace for physics, it is perhaps not too much to expect that psychology should at least try to keep in step. So far as psychoanalysis is concerned, one of the unfortunate results of the divorce of energy from structure is that, in its dynamic aspects, psychoanalytical theory has been unduly permeated by conceptions of hypothetical 'impulses' and 'instincts' which bombard passive structures, much as if an air-raid were in progress. Thus, to choose a random example, we find Marjorie Brierley (*op. cit.*) speaking of 'instinct as the stimulus to psychic activity.' From the standpoint of dynamic structure, however, 'instinct' is *not the stimulus to* psychic activity, but itself consists in characteristic activity on the part of a psychical structure. Similarly, 'impulse' is not, so to speak, a kick in the pants administered out of the blue to a surprised, and perhaps somewhat pained, ego, but a psychical structure in action—a psychical structure doing something to something or somebody. Actually, from the point of view of dynamic structure, the terms, 'instinct' and 'impulse', like so many terms used in psychology, are misleading hypostatizations which only serve to confuse the issue. Still more misleading are the plural forms 'instincts' and 'impulses'. The fact is that such terms only serve a useful purpose when employed in their adjectival forms, as when we speak of 'an instinctive tendency' or of 'impulsive behaviour'; for it is only then that they imply a reference to a psychical structure on the one hand, and to an object-relationship on the other.

Object-Relationships and Dynamic Structure

I have now attempted to give some account of the most fundamental of the various theoretical conclusions at which I arrived during the war years of 1939–45, in the circumstances of which I found myself provided with a special opportunity to reconsider classic problems from a new approach. The approach which I was led, quite deliberately, to adopt was that of an explicit object-relationship psychology—albeit, in retrospect, I can see that this standpoint was already heralded in some of my earlier papers. As it has turned out, however, the results obtained by this approach raised issues which necessitated a further change of outlook leading to the explicit adoption of a psychology of dynamic structure. I can only hope that the preceding account will afford some indication, not only of my main conclusions, but also of the process whereby a psychology of dynamic structure has developed out of a psychology of object-relationships.

CHAPTER VI

Steps in the Development of an Object-Relations Theory of the Personality[1] (1949)

O N my first introduction to the academic study of psychology in 1909 I was immediately intrigued by the prospect of acquiring some insight into the mainsprings of human behaviour; but it did not take me long to observe some remarkable omissions in the account of mental life presented to me. In particular, I noted an almost complete absence of reference to two important groups of phenomena which, even at that time, I found it difficult to believe that any account of mental life could ignore. I refer to the respective phenomena of sex and conscience. Years subsequently I discovered in Freud a psychologist who could scarcely be accused of any such remarkable omissions; and thereafter it was in the direction opened up by his researches that my psychological interest was preponderantly drawn—and all the more so because the field of psychopathology, in which his researches were conducted, was one which had meanwhile come to occupy my own special attention. There was, however, one cardinal feature of Freud's theories which I always found great difficulty in accepting, viz. his psychological hedonism. This was, partly at least, because, in the course of a philosophical training, I had already become acquainted with the dilemma confronting the theory of hedonism as originally propounded by John Stuart Mill, and had observed the inconsistent, but inevitable, process of transition in this writer's thought from the psychological principle of pleasure-seeking to the ethical principle of 'the greatest happiness of the greatest number'. It was, of course, in deference to the inexorable facts of social life that this transition was effected; and

[1] A lecture delivered at the Twelfth International Congress of Psychology in Edinburgh on 26th July 1948, and subsequently published in *The British Journal of Medical Psychology*, Vol. XXII, Pts. 1 and 2.

its necessity reveals the difficulty of giving any satisfactory account of object-relationships in terms of the pleasure-seeking principle. In the development of Freud's thought a similar transition may be observed —a transition from the libido theory, in which libido is conceived as primarily pleasure-seeking, to the super-ego theory, which is designed to explain how pleasure-seeking becomes subordinated to a moral principle under the pressure of object-relationships. Here again it was the inexorability of the facts of social life that revealed the inadequacy of the theory of pleasure-seeking; and it was only after his formulation of the super-ego theory that Freud was able to embark upon a systematic attempt to explain the phenomena of group life in *Group Psychology and the Analysis of the Ego*. In this work he explained the cohesion of the social group in terms of common loyalty to a leader conceived as functioning as an outer representative of the individual super-ego. The group leader was, of course, also conceived as a father-figure; and this is a reflection of the fact that Freud already regarded the super-ego as an endopsychic representative of parental figures internalized during childhood at the instance of an inner necessity for the control of the Œdipus situation. It will be observed that the Œdipus situation itself implies the existence of object-relationships and the existence of the family as a social group. At the same time the super-ego is obviously a product of the child's object-relationships as well as a means of controlling them; and, of course, it is itself an internal object. It is further to be noted that Freud's theory of the ego is bound up with his theory of the super-ego as the instigator of repression; for it was upon a study of the agency of repression that his theory of the ego was based. The progress of Freud's thought is thus seen to lead from his original theory that behaviour is determined by pleasure-seeking to a theory of the personality conceived in terms of relationships between the ego and objects, both external and internal. According to this latter theory, the nature of the personality is determined by the internalization of an external object, and the nature of group relationships is in turn determined by the externalization or projection of an internal object. In such a development then we detect the germ of an 'object-relations' theory of the personality—a theory based upon the conception that object-relationships exist within the personality as well as between the personality and external objects.

This development was carried a stage further by Melanie Klein, whose analytical researches led her to ascribe ever-increasing importance to the influence of internal objects in the development of the personality. In Freud's theory the only internal object to be recognized was the super-ego; and the role attributed to this structure was that of an internal parent exercising the function of a conscience. Melanie Klein, of course, accepts the concept of the super-ego; but she also envisages the presence of a multiplicity of other introjected objects—good objects and bad objects, benign objects and persecuting objects, whole objects and part objects. The introjection of these various objects is regarded by her as the result of phantasies of oral incorporation occurring primarily and characteristically during the oral phase of infancy. This conception has given rise to controversies into which I shall not enter; but, as it seems to me, Melanie Klein has never satisfactorily explained how phantasies of incorporating objects orally can give rise to the establishment of internal objects as endopsychic structures—and, unless they are such structures, they cannot be properly spoken of as internal objects at all, since otherwise they will remain mere figments of phantasy. Be that as it may, Melanie Klein goes on to attribute the goodness and badness of internal objects to components in the child's own oral activities— their goodness being related to a libidinal factor, and their badness to an aggressive factor in conformity with Freud's dualistic theory of instinct. At the same time, whilst developing and expanding the conception of internal objects, Melanie Klein also develops and expands the conception of introjection and projection in such a way as to represent the mental life of the child in terms of a constant interplay between the introjection of external objects and the projection of internalized objects. The form assumed by the child's developing personality thus comes to be largely explained in terms of object-relationships.

In general, Melanie Klein's views seemed to me from the first to represent an important advance in the development of psychoanalytical theory. In due course, however, it occurred to me with increasing conviction that, in certain important respects, she had failed to push her views to their logical conclusions. First and foremost, she continued to adhere uncritically to Freud's hedonistic libido theory. This seemed to me an inconsistency; for, if the introjection of objects and the perpetuation of such objects in the inner world are as important as her views imply, it is difficult to be satisfied with attributing this simply to the presence of oral impulses in the child or to the compulsions of libidinal pleasure-seeking. On the contrary, it seems to point inevitably to the conclusion that libido is not primarily pleasure-seeking, but object-seeking. This is a conclusion which I registered in a paper published in 1941[1], and to which I have subsequently adhered. It is a conclusion which involves a modification of Freud's conception of erotogenic zones—a modification to the effect that these zones cannot properly be regarded as themselves the sources of pleasure-seeking aims in the interests of which objects are more or less adventitiously exploited, but rather that they constitute channels adapted for the fulfilment of libidinal aims which have their source in the ego and are directed towards the establishment of satisfactory relationships with objects.

A second conception which Melanie Klein has, to my mind inconsistently, retained is Abraham's theory of libidinal development. This theory, based as it is upon Freud's theory of erotogenic zones, postulates a developmental series of libidinal phases, each characterized by the dominance of a specific zone. It would be unfair to Abraham to say that he is indifferent to object-relationships; for each of his phases is intended to represent not only a stage in libidinal organization, but also a stage in the development of object-love. Nevertheless, his phases are described, not in terms of appropriate objects, but in terms of erotogenic zones. Thus, instead of speaking of a 'breast' phase, he speaks of an 'oral' phase. Another feature of Abraham's theory is, of course, that he attributes each of the classic psychoses and psychoneuroses to a fixation at a specific phase. Both of these features were subjected to criticism on my part in the paper to which I have referred. At the same time I ventured to put forward alternative views. In place of Abraham's theory of libidinal development I formulated a theory based upon the nature of dependence upon objects; and I outlined a process of development in terms of which an original state of infantile dependence gave place to a final state of adult dependence during the course of an intermediate stage of transition. I also formulated the view that, with the two exceptions of schizophrenia and depression, the various classic psychopathological conditions represented, not fixations at specific libidinal phases, but specific *techniques* for regulating relationships with *internal* objects; and I described these techniques as originating during the developmental stage of transition from infantile dependence to adult dependence for the purpose of defending the growing personality against the effects of the conflicts involved in early object-relationships. On the other

[1] Included in the present volume.

hand, I interpreted schizophrenia and depression as representing the emergence of psychological states which these techniques were designed to avert, and whose etiological origin I ascribed to the primary stage of infantile dependence.

The impulse-psychology which Freud originally adopted and never abandoned constitutes another feature of pre-existing psychoanalytical thought which Melanie Klein has allowed to remain unquestioned, but which I have now come to regard as an anachronism in the light of her researches. In retrospect it is easy to see that the first step in my renunciation of impulse-psychology was taken when I reformulated the libido theory in terms of object-seeking; but I took a more obvious step in this direction when, in a paper published in 1943,[1] I went on to consider the implications of this revision of the libido theory for the classic theory of repression. In doing so, I took as my text Freud's statement, 'The super-ego is, however, not merely a deposit left by the earliest object-choices of the id; it also represents an energetic reaction formation against these choices.' Now, whilst in describing the super-ego as a deposit of object-choices Freud is describing it as an internal object, in describing it as a reaction formation *against* object-choices he is, of course, describing it as the instigator of repression. It therefore seemed to me obvious that, if repression involved a reaction against object-choices, it must be directed against objects—objects which, like the super-ego, were internal, but which, unlike the super-ego, were rejected by the ego. Accordingly, I proceeded to give explicit formulation to this view, which seemed to me a more logical conclusion from Freud's premises than his own view that repression was directed against guilty impulses. From this standpoint, guilt, or the sense of personal moral badness, became secondary to a sense of badness in the object; and it appeared to represent a product of tension arising from a conflict between the relationship of the ego with the super-ego as an internal object accepted as good and its relationships with other internal objects regarded, *pari passu*, as bad. Guilt thus resolved itself into a defence against relationships with bad objects. In the light of these conclusions it become important to determine why the child should incorporate objects which presented themselves to him as bad; and the answer to this question seemed to me to be that the child internalized bad objects partly with a view to controlling them (an aggressive motive), but chiefly because he experienced a libidinal need of them. Accordingly I

[1] Included in the present volume.

directed attention to the part played by positive libidinal attachments to internal bad objects in the phenomenon of resistance encountered in psychotherapy; and in doing so, of course, I departed from Freud's principle that resistance is exclusively a manifestation of repression.

The subject of repression is one to which I returned in a paper published in 1944[1]. In this paper I directed more specific attention to the weakness of impulse-psychology, adopting the general standpoint that it is impossible to isolate so-called 'impulses' from the endo-psychic structures which they energize and the relationships which they enable these structures to establish with objects. I suggested further that similar considerations applied to so-called 'instincts'. In conformity with this line of thought, I envisaged a replacement of the outmoded impulse-psychology, which, once adopted, Freud had never seen fit to abandon, by a new psychology of dynamic structure. This step involved a critical examination of Freud's description of mental structure in terms of id, ego and super-ego. Such an examination reveals at the outset an inherent incompatibility between any psychology of dynamic structure and Freud's conceptions of the id as a reservoir of instinctive impulses, and of the ego as a structure which develops on the surface of the id for the regulation of id-impulses in relation to outer reality. Obviously the principle of dynamic structure can only be maintained if the distinction between id and ego is abolished and the ego is regarded as an original structure which is itself the source of impulse-tension. At the same time impulse-tension in the ego must be regarded as inherently oriented towards outer reality, and thus initially determined by the reality principle. From this point of view, inadequacies in the child's capacity for adaptation will be explained as largely due to lack of experience combined with the fact that the instinctive endowment of mankind only assumes the form of general trends which require experience to enable them to acquire a more differentiated and rigid pattern. With the child's inexperience goes a tendency on his part to be more emotional and impulsive, and to be less tolerant of the many frustrations which he encounters. These various factors must all be taken into account; and it is only in so far as conditions of adaptation become too difficult for the child that the reality principle gives place to the pleasure principle as a secondary, and deteriorative (as against regressive) principle of behaviour calculated to relieve tension and provide compensatory satisfactions. And here I may perhaps add

[1] Included in the present volume.

that, in somewhat similar fashion, I have come to regard aggression as secondary to libido, thus departing from Freud, who regarded it as an independent primary factor (viz. as a separate 'instinct').

The revised conception of the ego which arises at this point involves a reconsideration of the theory of repression. According to Freud, of course, repression was directed against *impulses*; but, in order to explain the agency of repression, he felt compelled to postulate the existence of a *structure* (the super-ego) capable of instigating repression. I was only taking another step in the same direction, therefore, when I postulated the existence of *structures* which are repressed—as I did in recording the conclusion that what are primarily repressed are internal bad objects. At the time when I took this step I considered that impulses also became subjected to repression in a secondary sense. After my adoption of a psychology of dynamic structure, however, this view could no longer be maintained; and I substituted the view that what became subjected to secondary repression was that part of the ego which was most closely involved in a relationship with repressed objects. This conception presents us with the phenomenon of a split in the ego characterized by the repression of one dynamic part of the ego by another dynamic, but more central, part of the ego.

Here it becomes relevant to observe that, whilst Freud's earlier researches into the nature of the *repressed* were based upon a study of hysteria, his later researches into the nature of the *agency of repression* were based upon a study of melancholia. Whilst it would be presumptuous to suggest that this change of ground has proved a historical mistake, it seems a matter for regret that Freud was not able to pursue his study of the agency of repression on the same ground as his study of the repressed, and so to make the phenomena of hysteria the basis of his theory of mental structure. This is a regret which I registered in the slogan 'Back to hysteria' in my 1944 paper. In my opinion, what led Freud to change his ground was an impasse created by the psychological hedonism and the related impulse-psychology to which he adhered, and which prevented him from envisaging the presence of such a process as splitting of the ego in hysteria. Splitting of the ego is, of course, a phenomenon associated characteristically with schizophrenia. It may thus be said that, whilst Freud's conception of repression was based upon what Melanie Klein subsequently described as 'the depressive position', my conception is based upon what may be described as 'the schizoid position.'

My conception may, therefore, be regarded as having a more fundamental basis than Freud's in proportion as schizophrenia is a more primal condition than melancholia; and, at the same time, a theory of the personality based upon the conception of splitting of the ego would appear to be more fundamental than one based upon Freud's conception of the repression of impulses by an unsplit ego. The theory which I now envisage is, of course, obviously adapted to explain such extreme manifestations as are found in cases of multiple personality; but, as Janet has pointed out, these extreme manifestations are only exaggerated examples of the dissociation phenomena characteristic of hysteria. Thus, if we implement the slogan 'Back to hysteria', we find ourselves confronted with the very phenomenon of splitting upon which my theory of repression is based.

At this point it also becomes material to note that, according to Freud, the super-ego as the instigator of repression is no less unconscious than the repressed itself. Why the super-ego should be unconscious is a problem to which Freud never gave any really satisfactory answer; and the question now arises whether the super-ego itself is not repressed. That a structure corresponding to Freud's 'super-ego' is actually repressed was another of the conclusions which I drew in my 1944 paper. The situation which I envisaged was one based upon a split in the internalized bad object. I have already explained how I reached the conclusion that repression of an internalized bad object led to repression of that part of the ego which was most intimately bound by libidinal ties to the object in question; but, if the object is split, it follows that two parts of the ego will also be split off from the central ego, one attached to each of the partial objects. According to my conception, the internalized bad object has two aspects—an exciting aspect and a rejecting aspect; and this duality of aspects forms the basis of a split of the object into an *exciting* object and a *rejecting* object. Repression of the exciting object is accompanied by the splitting off and repression of a part of the original ego, which I have described as the 'libidinal ego'; and repression of the rejecting object is accompanied by the splitting off and repression of another part of the original ego, which I have described as the 'internal saboteur'. The conception of the internal saboteur is by no means identical with that of the super-ego;[1] but, being allied to the rejecting object,

---

[1] I retain the term 'super-ego' to describe an internal object which is cathected and accepted as 'good' by the central ego, and which appears to function as an ego-ideal at a level of organization established subsequently to the basic level now under

this part of the ego has aims contrary to those of the libidinal ego, which thus becomes subject to its hostility. This hostility of the internal saboteur to the libidinal ego operates in the same direction as the repression exercised over the libidinal ego by the central ego; and accordingly I have described it as a process of 'indirect repression'. This indirect repression would appear to be the aspect of repression upon which Freud chiefly concentrated, and upon which he based his theory of repression as a whole.

The internal situation resulting from the processes which I have just outlined is one which I have described as 'the basic endopsychic situation'. The three ego structures involved (viz. the central and the two subsidiary egos) correspond roughly to Freud's ego, id and super-ego; but they are all conceived as inherently dynamic ego-structures assuming a dynamic pattern in relation to one another, whereas the id is conceived as a source of energy without structure, and the ego and the super-ego as structures without any energy except such as they derive at second-hand from the id. The super-ego is, of course, conceived by Freud as an internalized object which achieves quasi-ego status; but, since the primal id is not conceived as fundamentally object-seeking, it is difficult to see how the internalization of the super-ego can be consistently explained by Freud on theoretic grounds. According to the conception which I have formulated, however, the internalization of objects is the direct expression of the libidinal needs of an original object-seeking ego in the face of the vicissitudes of its early object-relationships. The internal differentiation of structure within the personality through splitting of the ego is also explained in terms of relationships with objects which have been internalized; and these relationships are seen to give rise to relationships between the various parts into which the original ego becomes split. It will be appreciated, accordingly, how appropriate it is for the theory whose genesis and development I have been outlining to be described as 'an object-relations theory of the personality.'

A final word regarding the basic endopsychic situation to which I have just referred. Although, once it has been established, this situation would appear to be relatively immutable from a topographic standpoint, from an economic standpoint it would appear to

consideration. I regard the cathexis of this object by the central ego as constituting a defence against the cathexis of internal bad objects by the subsidiary egos, and as providing the basis for the establishment of moral values in the inner world.

admit of a considerable variety of dynamic patterns; and it may be assumed that the more characteristic of such patterns will correspond to the various psychopathological conditions described in textbooks of psychiatry. The details of these patterns and their relation to symptomatology could, however, only be established after considerable research. Meanwhile, it is in the case of hysteria that the dynamic configuration is clearest. Be that as it may, the general account which I have given must suffice to indicate what is meant by 'an object-relations theory of the personality'; and the historical form in which this account has been cast will, I trust, justify its aim—which is to indicate the *raison d'être* of a theory of this kind by describing the various considerations which have determined the steps in its progressive development.

CHAPTER VII

A Synopsis of the Development of the Author's Views Regarding the Structure of the Personality (1951)

IN 1941 (*A Revised Psychopathology of the Psychoses and Psycho-neuroses*) I recorded the observation that evidence of splitting of the ego was to be found not only in overtly schizoid states, but also in the psychoneuroses, and indeed in psychopathological conditions generally. The data upon which this observation was founded also led me to question the validity of Freud's libido theory in respect of (1) his thesis that libido is essentially pleasure-seeking, and (2) the significance which he attributed to erotogenic zones in determining ego-development. It followed inevitably that I should also question the validity of Abraham's 'phase' theory of ego-development and the etiological theory based upon it. I accordingly attempted to reformulate these basic psychoanalytical concepts (the libido theory, the theory of ego-development and the etiological theory) in such a way as to bring them more into conformity with observed clinical data and so to enhance their explanatory value. The main features of my reformulation were to the following effect:

(1) Libido is essentially object-seeking;

(2) Erotogenic zones are not themselves primary determinants of libidinal aims, but channels mediating the primary object-seeking aims of the ego;

(3) Any theory of ego-development that is to be satisfactory must be conceived in terms of relationships with objects, and in particular relationships with objects which have been internalized during early life under the pressure of deprivation and frustration;

(4) What are described by Abraham as 'phases' are, with the exception of his 'oral phases', really *techniques* employed by the ego for

162

regulating relationships with objects, and in particular with internalized objects;

(5) The psychopathological conditions ascribed by Abraham to fixations at specific phases are, with the exception of schizophrenia and depression, really conditions associated with the employment of *specific techniques*.

In the light of these considerations I proceeded to outline a theory of ego–development conceived in terms of object–relationships, and embodying the following features:

(1) Ego–development is characterized by a process whereby an original state of infantile dependence based upon primary identification with the object is abandoned in favour of a state of adult or mature dependence based upon differentiation of the object from the self;

(2) The process of ego–development may thus be regarded as having three stages, viz.

(*a*) A stage of infantile dependence (corresponding to Abraham's 'oral phases');

(*b*) A transitional stage; and

(*c*) A stage of adult or mature dependence (corresponding to Abraham's 'genital phase');

(3) Schizophrenia and depression are etiologically related to disturbances of development during the stage of infantile dependence—schizophrenia being related to difficulties arising in object–relationships over sucking (loving), and depression being related to difficulties arising in object–relationships over biting (hating);

(4) Obsessional, paranoid, hysterical and phobic symptoms derive their etiological significance from the fact that they reflect the operation of four specific techniques employed by the ego in an attempt to deal with difficulties arising over object–relationships during the *transitional* stage on the basis of the endopsychic situations which have resulted from the internalization of objects with which the ego has had relationships during the stage of infantile dependence;

(5) The four transitional techniques operate functionally as defences against the emergence of schizoid and depressive tendencies originating during the first stage of ego–development;

(6) Whilst the characteristic affect of depressive states is, of course, depression, the characteristic affect of schizoid states is a sense of futility;

(7) The persistence of a preponderating schizoid or depressive ten-

dency arising during the stage of infantile dependence is reflected in the emergence of two contrasting types of individual—(*a*) the schizoid (c.f. 'introvert) and (*b*) the depressive (c.f. 'extravert').

In 1943 (*The Repression and the Return of Bad Objects—with Special Reference to the War Neuroses*) I drew attention to the anomaly arising out of the fact that Freud's later researches upon the nature and growth of the ego had been superimposed upon the psychology of impulse, which had emerged from his earlier researches, without any attempt to revise this psychology of impulse in the light of his subsequent structural concepts. At the same time I expressed the view that it was only on the basis of a psychology of object-relationships, in which relationships between the ego and internalized as well as external objects were taken into account, that any integration between the concepts of impulse and ego-structure could be achieved. I recalled my previous conclusion (1941) that libido is essentially object-seeking, and proceeded to consider its implications for the theory of repression. I also recalled Freud's statement to the effect that, whilst the super-ego is 'a deposit left by the earliest object-choices of the id', it also represents 'an energetic reaction-formation against those choices'. Considered in terms of object-relationship psychology, this statement seemed to me to imply that, whilst the super-ego is obviously an internalized object with which the ego has a relationship involving some measure of identification, repression must be directed primarily against other internalized objects with which the ego has similar relationships. I accordingly gave explicit formulation to the view that repression represents a defensive reaction on the part of the ego, not primarily against intolerably unpleasant memories (as in Freud's earlier view), or against intolerably guilty impulses (as in Freud's later view), but against internalized objects which appear intolerably bad to the ego. This conclusion was supported by observations on the reactions of children who had been sexually assaulted. Another set of observations on the reactions of children with unsatisfactory homes was introduced in support of the view that the internalization of bad objects represents an attempt on the part of the child to make the objects in his environment 'good' by taking upon himself the burden of their apparent 'badness', and thus to make his environment more tolerable. This defensive attempt to establish outer security is purchased at the price of inner insecurity, since it leaves the ego at the mercy of internal persecutors; and it is

as a defence against such inner insecurity that the repression of internalized bad objects arises. Having thus described (1) the internalization of bad objects, and (2) their repression after internalization,
as two defensive techniques employed by the ego to meet difficulties encountered in object-relationships, I then drew attention to
the significance of (3) a further defensive technique which I described
as 'the moral defence', but which is equivalent to 'the defence of the
super-ego'. I pointed out that the bad objects described so far were
'unconditionally' (viz. libidinally), and not 'conditionally' (viz.
morally) bad, and that, in so far as the child's ego was identified with
these objects, he himself felt unconditionally bad. The aim of the
moral defence is to ameliorate this intolerable situation by presenting
the child with the possibilities of conditional (moral) goodness and
badness; and this aim is effected by the internalization of compensatory good objects, which thereupon assume a super-ego role. The
resulting position is one in which conditional goodness depends upon
a preponderating identification with good internalized objects, and
conditional badness upon a preponderating identification with bad
internalized objects; and either of these alternatives presents itself as
preferable to unconditional badness, since even conditional badness
leaves room for hope owing to the possibilities of repentance and
forgiveness. Such considerations lead inevitably to the conclusion
that repression and the moral defence (the defence of the super-ego)
are separate defensive techniques, although, of course, interaction
occurs between them. This explains the fact that analytical interpretations which mitigate guilt may actually have the effect of intensifying repression. In so far as the resistance due to repression is overcome, however, the result is a 'return' of repressed bad objects to the
conscious field. The threat of this is largely responsible for the transference neurosis; but it is therapeutically necessary in order to provide
an opportunity for the cathexes of internalized bad objects to be dissolved. The dissolution of such cathexes assumes special therapeutic
importance in view of a further conclusion arising out of the standpoint
now adopted, viz. that, where repressed bad objects are concerned,
the object-cathexis itself operates as a resistance. This conclusion is, of
course, in contradiction of Freud's view that 'the repressed' itself
offers no resistance to curative efforts; but it follows inevitably from
the view that libido is object-seeking, and that repression is directed
primarily against internalized objects (not impulses). It is in this direction that an explanation of the negative therapeutic reaction is

largely to be found; for, in so far as internalized and repressed bad objects are cathected, the libidinal aim is in conflict with the therapeutic aim. It must be recognized, of course, that the return of repressed bad objects is not in itself therapeutic. Indeed it is really a threatened return of such objects, combined with the effects of the ego's defences against it, that produces the symptoms which drive the patient to seek analytical aid. One of the defences open to the ego is, of course, the paranoid technique, which consists in the active projection of repressed bad objects (as against 'repressed impulses'); but this is different from the spontaneous return of repressed bad objects, which is a phenomenon, not of projection, but of transference. The patient is not slow to sense that the therapeutic endeavour threatens to reproduce the situation against which his defences are mobilized; and it is only by means of a working through of the analytical transference situation in the setting of an actual 'good object' relationship with the analyst that the return of repressed bad objects can be made to serve a therapeutic aim. So far as the spontaneous return of repressed bad objects is concerned, traumatic situations play an important part as precipitating factors; and it is in this direction that we must look for an understanding of the war neuroses. It is also to a massive return of repressed bad objects that we must largely look for the explanation of the phenomenon which Freud described as 'the repetition compulsion'—a concept which loses much of its explanatory value once it is recognized that it is not so much a case of compulsively repeating traumatic situations as of being haunted by bad objects against the return of which all defences have broken down, and from which there is no longer any escape (except in death). Freud's concept of the 'death instincts' would also appear to become superfluous once all the implications of a libidinal cathexis of internalized bad objects is appreciated; for, whilst the cathexis of such objects inevitably calls into operation a dynamic anti-libidinal factor, this factor can now be accounted for in terms of object-relationships without recourse to any theory of specific 'death instincts'. So far as the war neuroses are concerned, two further conclusions remain to be added: (1) In the case of individuals in whom there has persisted an undue state of infantile dependence (characterized as this is by a tendency to identification), military service in itself represents a traumatic situation liable to favour the return of internalized bad objects, since it involves a special degree of separation from familiar, and relatively good, objects with whom an identification has been established in reality (and, in conformity with this fact, separation-anxiety is the most distinctive feature of breakdowns among military personnel); and (2) The failure of repression associated with the return of internalized bad objects is accompanied by a failure of the moral defence, with the result that the authority of the super-ego upon which, as Freud has shown, the morale of a group depends, ceases to function, and, through a dissolution of the libidinal cathexis binding the soldier to the military group, he ceases to be a soldier in spirit.

In 1944 (*Endopsychic Structure considered in terms of Object-Relationships*) I drew special attention to the fact that (as in the case of Freud's conception of the ego) the whole conception of internalized objects, no less than the more limited conception of the super-ego out of which it sprang, had been developed without any significant modification of the psychology of impulse originally adopted by Freud. I also drew attention to the practical limitations inherent in impulse-psychology in respect of its inability to throw any real light on the problem of the disposal of hypothetical 'impulses' released in analytical therapy. I then pointed out that the disposal of 'impulses' is essentially a problem of object-relationships, and that, whilst it is also a problem of the personality, problems of the personality are themselves bound up with the relationships of ego-structures to internalized objects. I went on to express the view that, whilst 'impulses' necessarily involve object-relationships, they cannot be considered apart from ego-structures, since it is only ego-structures that can seek relationships with objects. 'Impulses' must accordingly be regarded as representing simply the dynamic aspect of ego-structures; and there consequently arises a necessity for the replacement of the old impulse-psychology by a new *psychology of dynamic structure*—a step which obviously involves a critical examination of Freud's description of the mental apparatus in terms of id, ego and super-ego. Such an examination immediately reveals an inherent incompatibility between any psychology of dynamic structure and Freud's conceptions of (*a*) the id as a reservoir of instinctive impulses, and (*b*) the ego as a structure which develops on the surface of the id for the regulation of id-impulses in relation to outer reality; for the principle of dynamic structure can only be maintained if the ego is regarded as an original structure which is itself the source of impulse-tension. At the same time, impulse-tension in the ego must be regarded as inherently orientated towards objects in outer reality, and thus determined by the reality principle from the first. Initially, of course, the reality principle is immature; but this immaturity is due largely to lack of experience. Under conditions favourable to adaptation it matures as experience expands. In so far, however, as conditions are unfavourable to adaptation, it is liable to give place to the pleasure principle as a secondary and deteriorative (not regressive) principle of behaviour calculated to relieve tension and provide compensatory satisfactions. The principle of dynamic structure also involves a revision of the view of repression which I advanced in 1943, to the effect that repression was exercised primarily against internalized objects which present themselves as bad; and it becomes necessary to adopt the view that repression is exercised not only against internalized objects (which incidentally are only meaningful when regarded in the light of endopsychic structures), but also against ego-structures which seek relationships with these internal objects. This view implies that there must be a splitting of the ego to account for repression. Freud found it necessary, of course, to postulate the existence of a *structure* capable of instigating repression, viz. the super-ego; and it is really only a step in the same direction to postulate the existence of structures which are repressed, and to envisage the repression of one part of the dynamic ego by another part of the dynamic ego. Such a conception would throw light not only upon the phenomena of multiple personality and hysterical dissociation, but also upon the practical difficulties experienced over the process described as 'sublimation' in impulse-psychology (the 'impulses' to be 'sublimated' being no longer regarded as separate from ego-structure). The view that repression implies a splitting of the ego should not prove difficult to accept for those familiar with the problems presented by schizoid patients; but here we are confronted with the limitations imposed upon psychoanalytical theory in its later developments by a preoccupation with melancholia. It was on a study of melancholia that Freud's theory of the mental apparatus was largely based; and, in conformity with this fact, the 'depressive position' is accorded a central place in the views of Melanie Klein. However, it was upon a study of hysteria that Freud originally based the concept of repression; and it was only when he turned his attention from the nature of the repressed to that of the agency of repression that he became preoccupied with melancholia. In my opinion it is a matter for regret that he did not pursue his study of the agency of repression within the same field as his study of the repressed, and thus did not make the phenomena of hysteria the basis of his theory of the mental apparatus. Had he done so, I feel convinced that his conception of repression would have been based, not upon what Melanie Klein subsequently described as 'the depressive position', but upon what may be described as 'the schizoid position', viz. that his conception would have been based upon recognition of the fact that repression implies a splitting of the ego. Here it is apposite to draw attention to the anomaly that, whereas Freud conceived the Œdipus situation, to which he looked for the rationale of repression, as a genital situation, his account of the origin of the super-ego, which he described as the instigator of repression, is conceived in terms of an oral, i.e. pregenital, situation. Melanie Klein's attempt to resolve the difficulty by ante-dating the Œdipus situation to infancy provides no real solution, if only because it leaves out of account any possibility of repression occurring before the super-ego is formed. The solution seems to lie in looking for the source of repression not only beyond the genital attitude, but also beyond the Œdipus situation, and even beyond the level at which the super-ego is established. This solution is in conformity with my view, recorded in 1943, that repression originates primarily as a defence against internalized bad objects, and that the establishment of the super-ego represents an additional and later defence ('the moral defence') corresponding to the attainment of a new level of structural organization, beneath which the old level persists. Thus, in my opinion, beneath the level at which a 'central ego' finds itself confronted with the super-ego as an internal object of moral significance there lies a level at which split off parts of the ego find themselves confronted with internal objects which are not only devoid of moral significance, but also unconditionally (viz. libidinally) bad from the standpoint of the central ego—internal objects which function equally as internal persecutors whether they present themselves (*a*) as exciting objects, or (*b*) as frustrating objects. Whilst, therefore, the main phenomena of melancholia receive a relatively satisfactory explanation at the super-ego level, the paranoid, hypochrondrical and obsessional features which so often accompany them represent an orientation towards internal bad objects. The phenomena of hysteria are equally incapable of being satisfactorily explained at an exclusively super-ego level. Freud's theory of repression involves the further anomaly that, whereas he describes both the agent and the instigator of repression (viz. the ego and the super-ego) as structures, he describes the repressed as consisting of impulses. The extent of this anomaly is best appreciated in the light of the fact that the super-ego is conceived by Freud as largely unconscious—a fact which raises the question whether the super-ego itself is not repressed. Freud himself was sufficiently aware of this problem to envisage the possibility of the super-ego being subject to some measure of repression (e.g. in hysteria), thus implying recognition of the principle that an endopsychic structure may be repressed. In the light of considerations already advanced, it is necessary to conclude that what is repressed is invariably and inherently structural. At this point it becomes relevant to record certain previous, but unpublished conclusions of mine regarding the nature of dreams. These conclusions resulted from a train of thought initiated during the treatment of a patient whose dreams included many which could not be brought into conformity with the wish-fulfilment principle and were described by her spontaneously as 'state of affairs' dreams. The ,sue of this train of thought was that, under the influence of Melanie Klein's conceptions of psychic reality and internal objects, I came to regard dreams, and for that matter waking phantasies also, as essentially dramatizations of endopsychic situations involving both (*a*) relationships between ego-structures and internalized objects, and (*b*) inter-relationships between ego-structures themselves. Subsequently another patient produced a dream involving problems of interpretation which provided me with the occasion to formulate the concept of a *basic endopsychic situation* involving such relationships, and to crystallize my views regarding the basic endopsychic structures involved. The resulting theory hinges upon the conception of a split in the internalized bad object. The view that the internalization of bad libidinal objects is a primary defence was recorded in 1943; but it now becomes important to recognize that such objects have two aspects—an exciting aspect and a rejecting aspect. This duality of aspects forms the basis of a split of the internalized bad object into (*a*) an *exciting object*, and (*b*) a *rejecting object*. When the defence of repression comes into operation, both these objects are repressed by the original ego; but, since this original ego is attached to both objects by a libidinal cathexis involving a high degree of identification, their repression involves a splitting off and repression of parts of the ego which remain closely bound to each object. Repression of the exciting object is thus accompanied by repression of a portion of the ego which I describe as the *libidinal ego* on the part of the central portion of the ego; and repression of the rejecting object is accompanied by a similar repression of another portion of the ego which I describe as the *internal saboteur*. It will be seen that the resulting differentiation of ego-structure corresponds roughly to Freud's account of the mental apparatus—the central ego corresponding to Freud's 'ego', the libidinal ego to Freud's 'id' and the internal saboteur to Freud's 'super-ego'. It is integral to my conception, however, that the three structures just described are all dynamic ego-structures assuming a dynamic pattern in relation to one another, whereas Freud's 'id' is conceived as a source of energy without structure, and his 'ego' and 'super-ego' as structures without energy except such as they derive from the 'id'— the 'ego' alone being a true ego-structure, since the 'super-ego' is conceived as largely an internalized object. It is also integral to my conception that this dynamic pattern of ego-structures underlies the level at which the super-ego, as I conceive it, is established as an internalized object cathected by the central ego; and it is at this underlying level that, in my opinion, the ultimate origin of all psychopathological states is to be sought. Further features of my conception are (1) that the differentiation of ego-structure which I envisage is the result of repression originally directed against internalized bad objects, and (2) that the dynamic of repression is aggression directed by the central ego not only against internalized bad objects, but also against the subsidiary egos by which these objects are cathected, viz. the libidinal ego and the internal saboteur. Aggression does not remain exclusively at the disposal of the central ego, however. It plays a part in the attitude adopted by the subsidiary egos not only towards the central ego, but also towards one another—and it plays a part of particular importance where the attitude of the internal saboteur towards the libidinal ego is concerned. The uncompromisingly aggressive attitude of the internal saboteur towards the libidinal ego is based on the latter's cathexis of the exciting object and its own cathexis of the rejecting object; and it is thus a reflection of the original ambivalence of the individual towards his libidinal objects. According to my view, ambivalence is not itself a primal state, but one which arises as a reaction to deprivation and frustration. Thus I do not consider that in the absence of frustration the infant would direct aggression spontaneously towards his libidinal object. Accordingly, whilst I regard aggression as a primary dynamic factor in that it does not appear capable of being resolved into libido, I also regard it as ultimately subordinate to libido and essentially representing a reaction on the part of the infant to deprivation and frustration in his libidinal relationships—and more particularly to the trauma of separation from his mother. It is thus the experience of libidinal deprivation and frustration that originally calls forth the infant's aggression towards his libidinal object and so gives rise to ambivalence. At this point the subjective aspect of ambivalence becomes important; for to the ambivalent infant the situation presents itself as one in which his mother functions as an ambivalent object. To ameliorate this intolerable situation, he splits the figure of his mother into two objects—a *satisfying* ('good') object and an *unsatisfying* ('bad') object; and, with a view to controlling the unsatisfying object, he employs the defensive process of internalization to remove it from outer reality, where it eludes his control, to the sphere of inner reality, where it offers prospects of being more amenable to control in the role of internal object. The trouble about such an internal object is that, after internalization, it continues not only to be unsatisfying, but also to be desired (cathected). It thus presents a duality of aspects which constitutes as great a difficulty in the inner world as that formerly constituted by the ambivalence of objects in the outer world. This duality of aspects has already been referred to as providing the basis for a split of the internalized bad object into (a) an exciting object, and (b) a rejecting object—a split which is now seen to be effected by the original ego in an attempt to deal with the difficulties ensuing upon the internalization of bad objects. It is in pursuance of further defensive aims on the part of the ego that the exciting and rejecting internal objects are both repressed, and that the repression of each is accompanied by a splitting off and repression of a corresponding part of the ego itself. It is thus that the libidinal ego and the internal saboteur become established as subsidiary ego-structures independent of the central ego and subject to repression on its part. The aggressive attitude adopted by the internal saboteur towards the libidinal ego remains, however, in need of further explanation; for it is not sufficient to say simply that it is a reflection of early ambivalence. So far as this ambivalence is concerned, the position would appear to be that the child experiences considerable anxiety over expressing not only aggressive, but also libidinal feelings towards his mother in the role of a rejecting object. The risk involved in his expressing aggressive feelings towards her is that it will make her reject him more and love him less, i.e. will make her seem more real for him as a bad object and less real as a good object. This is the risk (loss of the good object) which, as I concluded in 1941, tends to provoke the affect of depression. On the other hand, the risk involved for the child in expressing libidinal feelings towards his mother as a rejecting object is that this is equivalent in his mind to discharging libido into an emotional vacuum and gives rise to a sense of inferiority and worthlessness. This is the risk (loss of libido) which, as I concluded in 1941, tends to provoke the schizoid affect of futility. With the aim of averting both these risks the child supplements the defensive measures already described by a technique akin to the 'Divide et impera' principle. He employs a maximum of his aggression to subdue a maximum of his libidinal need. In conformity with the principle of dynamic structure, this defence is effected by a process whereby the excess of his aggression is taken over by the internal saboteur and directed against his libidinal ego, which in turn takes over the excess of his libido and directs it towards the exciting object. The attack of the internal saboteur upon the libidinal ego must obviously function as an extremely powerful factor in furthering the aims of repression; and it would appear to be on this phenomenon that Freud's concept of the super-ego and its repressive function is largely based. In terms of the concepts which I myself have formulated, however, repression originates as an attack by the undivided ego on both the exciting and the rejecting objects; and this process, which I describe as *primary direct repression*, is accompanied by a process of *secondary direct repression* whereby the ego splits off and subdues two parts of itself (the libidinal ego and the internal saboteur) which respectively maintain cathexes of the two repressed internal objects. The cathexis of the exciting object by the libidinal ego also constitutes a formidable source of resistance to therapy; and this phenomenon conforms to an observation which I recorded in 1943 before I had developed the concept of dynamic structure. However, since the cathexis in question is libidinal, it cannot be regarded as itself a repressive phenomenon. It is otherwise, however, with the attack of the internal saboteur on the libidinal ego; for this not only functions as a resistance, but actively contributes to the repression of the libidinal ego by the central ego. I accordingly describe this process as one of *indirect repression*. When the processes of direct and indirect repression are both taken into account, it becomes obvious that libidinal components in the psyche are subjected to a much greater measure of repression than aggressive components. It may therefore be concluded that, whereas the disposal of excess libido is governed chiefly by the *principle of repression*, the disposal of *excess aggression* is governed chiefly by the principle of *topographical distribution*. My conception of indirect repression brings to a focus the divergence of my views from those of Freud as regards repression in general. According to Freud, repression originates as a means of reducing the expression of libido towards the parent of opposite sex and that of aggression towards the parent of a similar sex in the setting of the Œdipus situation. According to my view, however, both direct and indirect repression originate in infancy before the emergence of the Œdipus situation; and indirect repression is a special technique adopted by the child to reduce the expression of both libido and aggression towards his mother at a stage when she is his only significant object and he is almost wholly dependent upon her. In my view, therefore, the phenomenon of infantile dependence assumes the role ascribed by Freud to the Œdipus situation in the genesis of repression. The Œdipus situation thus ceases to function as an explanatory concept, and assumes the status of a derivatory situation which the child is called upon to meet only after differentiation of endopsychic structure has already taken place and repression has originated. It thus becomes a phenomenon to be explained in terms of an endopsychic situation which has already developed. The chief novelty introduced into the child's world by the emergence of the external Œdipus situation is that he is now confronted with two distinct parental objects instead of only one. Since his relationship with his father as a new object involves problems of adjustment similar to those already experienced in his relationship with his mother, he naturally employs similar techniques—with the result that two internalized figures of his father, as (*a*) exciting object, and (*b*) rejecting object, become established. These would appear to be partly superimposed upon, and partly fused with the corresponding figures of his mother. The adjustment which the child requires to make to his father differs, however, from that which he originally required to make to his mother in that it has to be made upon an almost exclusively emotional plane. This follows from the fact that the experience of feeding at the breast is necessarily precluded from his relationship with his father. Indeed it is chiefly as a parent without breasts that the child would appear to regard his father in the first instance; and it is only later that he comes to appreciate the genital difference between his parents. As the appreciation of this difference dawns upon him and his own libidinal need comes to manifest itself increasingly

174

through genital channels, his needs for his mother and father come to include physical needs for their respective genitals. The strength of these physical needs varies in inverse proportion to the satisfaction of his emotional needs; but, since they are not satisfied, some measure of ambivalence develops towards both his mother's vagina and his father's penis. This is reflected in sadistic conceptions of the primal scene. By this time, however, the relationship between his parents has become important to him; and jealousy of each parent in relation to the other develops. The chief incidence of this jealousy is determined not only by the biological sex of the child, but also by the state of his emotional relationships with his respective parents. However, he is called upon to adjust to two ambivalent situations at the same time; and, in his attempt to do so, he again employs the series of techniques already described, with the result that bad genital figures of both parents come to be embodied, in varying proportions, in both of the already existing internal bad objects (the exciting object and the rejecting object). These internal objects are thus seen to assume the form of complex composite structures, built up partly on a basis of layering and partly on a basis of fusion. The extent to which layering or fusion predominates, in conjunction with the proportioning of component objects, would appear not only to play an important part in determining the psychosexual attitude of the individual, but also to be the chief determinant in the ætiology of sexual perversions. The constitution of the exciting and the rejecting objects is also (biological sex apart) the main factor in determining the nature of the Œdipus situation which develops. This is obvious in the case of inverted and mixed Œdipus situations; but it also applies in the case of the positive situation. Indeed the possibility of inverted and mixed Œdipus situations goes to show that even the positive Œdipus situation is essentially an internal situation—albeit it is transferred in varying degrees to the actual external situation. Once this fact is envisaged, it is easy to see, as indeed deep analysis reveals, that the Œdipus situation is essentially built up around the internalized figures of the exciting mother and the rejecting mother. However, in his attempt to adjust to two ambivalent relationships at the same time, the child seeks to simplify a complex situation by concentrating on the exciting aspect of one parent and the rejecting aspect of the other, and by modifying the nature of the exciting and the rejecting objects accordingly; and in so doing the child really constitutes the Œdipus situation for himself.

It cannot escape observation that the general scheme which I have outlined represents a considerable departure from the views of Freud, although there is a recognizable analogy at all points. This combination of analogy with divergence can only be explained in terms of a difference in basic theoretic principles; and it is not difficult to localize two central points of difference. In the first place, although Freud's whole system of thought was concerned with object-relationships, he adhered theoretically to the principle that libido is primarily pleasure-seeking, viz. is directionless. By contrast, I adhere to the principle that libido is primarily object-seeking, viz. has direction. For that matter, I regard aggression as having direction also, whilst, by implication at any rate, Freud regarded aggression as, like libido, directionless. In the second place, Freud regarded impulse (psychical energy) as theoretically distinct from structure, whereas I do not accept this distinction as valid and adhere to the principle of dynamic structure. Of these two central points of difference, the latter is the more fundamental; and indeed the former arises out of the latter. Thus Freud's view that libido is pleasure-seeking follows directly from his divorce of energy from structure; for, once energy is divorced from structure, the only psychical change which can be envisaged as pleasurable (i.e. as other than disturbing) is one which makes for the establishment of an equilibrium of forces, viz. a directionless change. By contrast, once we conceive of energy as inseparable from structure, the only changes which are intelligible are changes in structural relationships and relationships between structures; and such changes are essentially directional. Freud's divorce of energy from structure must be regarded as a reflection of the general scientific background of the nineteenth century, dominated as this was by the Helmholtzian conception of the physical universe; and it thus constitutes a limitation imposed by outside influences upon his thought. In the twentieth century atomic physics has revolutionized the scientific conception of the physical universe and has introduced the conception of dynamic structure; and the views which I have outlined represent an attempt to reformulate psychoanalytical theory in terms of this conception. The psychology of dynamic structure which I envisage has the special advantage of providing a more satisfactory basis for the explanation of *group* phenomena than any other type of psychology; but it also has the advantage of enabling psychopathological phenomena to be explained directly in terms of structural conformations, and thus doing justice to the unquestionable fact that symptoms are expressions of the personality as a whole. The basic endopsychic situation which I have described appears to be relatively immutable from a topographic standpoint; but from an economic standpoint it must be regarded as capable of extensive modification, whether therapeutic or otherwise. I am convinced that the economic pattern which I have described is that which prevails in hysterical states; and I also believe that this is characteristically the original pattern. In conformity with this belief I interpret the earliest symptoms manifested by the child (e.g. crying fits) as hysterical; and, if this is correct, Freud showed remarkable insight in choosing hysterical phenomena as the material out of which to build the foundations of psychoanalysis. Amends must now be made for an apparent inconsistency in my exposition of the principle of dynamic structure. Although I have spoken of internalized objects as structures, I have treated them simply as objects of dynamic ego-structures, and not as themselves dynamic. I have done so partly in order to avoid too complicated an exposition, but mainly in order to focus attention on the activity of the ego-structures—which is, after all, the most important thing, especially since the internalization of objects is itself a product of this activity. In the interests of consistency, however, I must draw the logical conclusion of my theory and acknowledge that, since internal objects are endopsychic structures, they must be themselves in some measure dynamic; and it should be added that they must derive their dynamic quality from their cathexis by ego-structures. Such a conclusion would appear to be in conformity not only with demonological phenomena, but also with the phenomena observed in the case of dreams and paranoid states.

Quite recently, viz. in 1951, I have found it necessary to introduce a further modification into my theoretical position in an attempt to eliminate an unresolved contradiction between the views which I formulated in 1941 and those which I subsequently formulated. My classification of the four 'transitional' defensive techniques in 1941 depended upon a distinction between two internalized objects which I described as 'accepted' and 'rejected' respectively; and the distinctive features of each technique were related to a characteristic method adopted by the ego in dealing with these two objects according as they were treated, separately or together, as internal or external. The assumption underlying this classification was that ambivalence towards the external object led at an early stage to internalization of both a good and a bad object. In the views which I formulated in 1944, however, my main concern was with relationships between differentiated ego-structures and internalized *bad* objects, and with the resulting endopsychic situation; and this formulation was based upon the conclusion (already reached in 1943) that the object to be internalized in the first instance is the *bad or unsatisfying* object. The internalization of the unsatisfying object was regarded as a defensive technique designed to control the traumatic element in a situation involving the cathexis of an object which was unsatisfying; and there appeared to be no motivè for internalizing a completely satisfying object in the first instance. It was thus considered that good or satisfying objects were only internalized at a later stage to allay anxiety arising out of the presence of bad or unsatisfying objects in the inner world after their internalization. The underlying assumption remained, as in 1941, to the effect that ambivalence was a state arising originally in relation to the external object, and that the external object was split, so far as mental representations were concerned, into a good object and a bad object before any question of the internalization of the bad object arose. This is an assumption which I now (in 1951) feel it necessary to revise in favour of a view which I previously adopted in my earlier paper, 'Schizoid Factors in the Personality' (1940)—a view to the effect that the first object to be internalized is the *pre-ambivalent object* of the early oral phase. From this point of view, ambivalence must be regarded as a state first arising in the original unsplit ego in relation to the *internalized* pre-ambivalent object; and the motive determining the internalization of the pre-ambivalent object in the first instance will be provided by the fact that this object presents itself as in some measure unsatisfying as well as in some measure satisfying. The establishment of ambivalence, once this has been accomplished, leads to an inner situation in which the unsplit ego is confronted with an *internalized ambivalent object*. The next step envisaged is the splitting of this object, not into two objects (good and bad), but into *three* objects; and this result is attributed to action on the part of the ego whereby both the *over-exciting* and the *over-frustrating* elements in the internal object are split off from it and repressed in such a way as to give rise to *the exciting object* and the *rejecting object* (in a manner similar to that which I described in 1944). It follows from this conception that, when the exciting and rejecting objects are split off, there remains a *nucleus of the original object* shorn of its over-exciting and over-frustrating elements; and this nucleus then assumes the status of a desexualized and idealized object which is cathected and retained for itself by the central ego after it (the central ego) has divested itself of those parts of itself which cathect the exciting and rejecting objects, and which I have described respectively as 'the libidinal ego' and 'the internal saboteur.' It will be noticed that the nuclear object in question is an accepted object for the central ego, and is thus not subjected to repression. This is the object which I now regard as providing the nucleus round which the super-ego, as I have come to conceive it, is built up; but, in view of its nature, it would appear appropriate to revive the term 'ego-ideal' for its designation. It corresponds, of course, to what I described as 'the accepted object' in my account of the 'transitional' defensive techniques in 1941; and it is significant that this is the sort of object into which the hysterical patient seeks to convert the analyst. So far as concerns what I have described as 'the rejected object' in my account of the 'transitional' techniques in 1941, it will now be necessary to regard this concept as including both 'the exciting object' and 'the rejecting object', since, according to my later view, both these objects are rejected by the central ego. Accordingly, the term 'rejected objects' (in the plural) will require to be substituted for the term 'rejected object' (in the singular) in my account of the 'transitional' techniques. This change would appear to be justified, since reflection suggests that both the 'exciting' and the 'rejecting' objects are similarly treated by the central ego in the case of each of the transitional techniques. Thus, for example, it would appear that they are both treated as external in the paranoid and phobic techniques, and both treated as internal in the obsessional and hysterical techniques. By contrast, 'the accepted object' is treated as external in the phobic and hysterical techniques, and as internal in the paranoid and obsessional techniques.

PART TWO

Clinical Papers

CHAPTER I

Notes on the Religious Phantasies of a Female Patient (1927)[1]

IN what follows I propose to describe some features in the case of a woman whose experiences included some remarkable phantasies of a religious nature. My account is based upon data obtained during a short course of analytical treatment undertaken with a view to mitigating the severity of the symptoms from which she suffered. These symptoms presented in the main a hysterical complexion; but there was also evidence of a more profound disturbance of a definitely schizoid nature. In this connection it is perhaps interesting to record that, when on one occasion I showed two separate specimens of her handwriting, mixed with other specimens of handwriting from different sources, to the distinguished graphologist Robert Saudek, he diagnosed one specimen as characteristically hysterical, and the other as characteristically schizophrenic. Significantly enough, the 'hysterical' specimen belonged to the period of analytical treatment, whereas the 'schizophrenic' specimen dated from the time of a breakdown ten years earlier.

The patient, to whom I shall refer throughout this account as X, was thirty-one years of age when she came under my observation. She was unmarried, and was the youngest child of a large family consisting of one son and a number of daughters. Her mother had died when she was nineteen. Her father was alive; but she did not recall ever having seen him, as he had lived apart from the family from the time of her birth. He was of alcoholic habits; and his wife left him, taking her family with her, as soon as was practicable after the birth of X. X left school at the age of sixteen; and at seventeen she began to train for the post of art teacher. In spite of the interruptions

[1] A paper read before the Scottish Branch of the British Psychological Society on 5th November 1927.

entailed by a series of nervous breakdowns, which began when she was twenty-one, she eventually completed her training; and at the age of twenty-five she obtained a good post, which she held with apparent success for five years, until a further breakdown finally compelled her to resign.

When I first saw her, she gave a history of a series of nervous breakdowns extending over a period of ten years. These breakdowns had been characterized chiefly by nervous prostration, sleeplessness, disturbing dreams, and inability to face the demands of life. These symptoms she attributed retrospectively to difficulties centring round questions of sex; but she stated that at the time of her first breakdown she was completely innocent of all sexual knowledge, although she frequently experienced unsophisticated cravings for male attentions. It was only two years subsequently that her medical attendant, perceiving the dangers of her ignorance, enlightened her to some extent. Shortly thereafter she began to indulge in masturbation. The commencement of this practice would appear to have dated from a medical examination performed by a strange doctor on the occasion of a sudden illness at a holiday resort. Her masturbatory habits, once acquired, began to cause her considerable mental distress; and eventually she came to regard them as the chief factor in aggravating her nervous state. To this source she, doubtless correctly, traced the exacerbation of a sense of conflict between spirit and body which had already for some time troubled her at nights. Her condition throughout was complicated by the fact that she was subject to visions and phantasies of an absorbing character. The *visions*, which she herself usually described as 'images', were almost invariably disturbing, and were sometimes of such a character as to fill her with disgust. Frequently they assumed a phallic form, in spite of her lack of conscious sexual knowledge; but, when this happened, the visionary genitals would appear to have been infantile. She had been annoyed by such images previous to her breakdown—and even in childhood. As regards her *phantasies*, some of these were distressing, whereas others again were beatific in character. Among the various 'images' and phantasies which she described were many which had a religious colouring; and it is to this group that I desire to direct attention.

Among the earliest of the *religious 'images' or visions* which she remembered having seen was one which appeared at the age of seven. She was convalescent after an illness at the time; and one night she seemed to see the Devil standing at the foot of her bed. She was terrified by the apparition, and felt that he had come to carry her away. She realized that the apparition was immaterial; but she explained this to herself on the grounds that the visitant came from the spiritual world. It may be noted here that, in childhood, her mind was frequently occupied with thoughts about God and Christ, and about Right and Wrong. These thoughts were accompanied by considerable apprehension on her part; and she recorded that ideas about Christ had always caused her anxiety and depression in her childhood. It would seem that the idea of God which was imparted to her was that of a stern Jehovah, rather than that of a loving Father. This conception was largely influenced by religious instruction which she had received at the age of four from an evangelical Sunday School teacher whose ardour outweighed his discretion, and whose lurid descriptions of the raising of Lazarus from the dead were recalled during the analysis with painful emotion. At the age of twenty-two (in the second year of her breakdown) she began to have what she described as 'visions from the spiritual side'. The usual subject of these visions was the Crucifixion of Christ; and it was quite common for her to witness Christ's body being pulled down from the Cross and to see the nails tearing His flesh. It is significant that, in describing such spectacles, she would say, 'I experienced myself some of the agony of spirit which He must have felt.'

Having indicated the nature of the patient's visions, I shall pass to the description of her *religious phantasies*. The most important of these revolved round the themes of Virgin Birth, Crucifixion and Resurrection; and, unlike her visions, such phantasies only commenced to occur after she had received some sexual enlightenment. They are best described in her own words so far as these are reflected in notes which I was able to take at the time. Here is one of her accounts:

'Twice I've thought . . . that I was going to have a baby, without connection, in a spiritual way. I felt I wasn't going to be unwell for nine months, and was going to have a baby because I was filled with a greater will than my own. I thought that, if I did turn unwell that time, it would happen next time. *Now*, of course, I know it to have been a part of my abnormal state of mind. The first time I am aware of anything like that happening, I was home for the week-end. I was in bed all Sunday. The physical feeling was bad; and I was dreaming wild-horse dreams about that time. I was expecting my period that day. The physical feeling came; and it was followed by a terrible misery—as if a devil was there, making me think all sorts of bad words and striking out against God. Then peace came; and I thought I would never be unwell again. I did not think about a baby that time. I thought I wasn't going to be a woman in a physical sense any more. Then the period came on; and I was miserably unhappy.'

Here is another of her accounts:

'I was often depressed between thirteen and fourteen, and had various fears. One was that I was going to come to a bad end and be executed. I remember dimly that my greatest girl friend at school was standing one day with a piece of string in her hand. She showed it to me and said I would be hung some day by the neck. I am still afraid about that. It gets mingled with the idea that I am going to be crucified. That Sunday when it came about me going to have a baby, I had been reading a British-Israel Society book dealing with prophecies. Just after that, the feeling began about the baby. I was recently rejected for life insurance which was to have become due in ten years. I said to myself, "My little son will be ten then". I thought it would fulfil the text, "A little child shall lead them", because he had not been born in the usual way. I thought I would be crucified or hung. I felt I would be willing to make the sacrifice; but I thought nowadays they don't crucify people as they did Christ. Then I thought, with the war on, Bolsheviks would torture me, and it would come that way. I felt it was inevitable and unescapable. A French lady once told me I had a mystic cross in my hand. Everything fitted in. I felt willing not to be married, because of the greater thing . . . I had a sort of trance when I was in a nursing home; and I thought I was being filled with spiritual power. Then came a terror of being buried alive. I believed that, when I was crucified, I would rise again from the dead. But before that, I believed, I would be able to heal people. A few days ago it came that, at the end of ten years, I would be tortured and put to death, but would rise again, and Christ would come back to earth, and that we would be married and have a little baby. That all seemed real to me, until I saw an image of myself beside Christ with a crown on my head. Then I knew that it wasn't in keeping with the humility of the real thing. Then this—whatever it is—began to fade away.'

Another quotation:

'In the nursing home, I had a climax about the ideas of spiritual power—and the power of spiritual healing. One day my body seemed possessed by some spirit for half an hour. I wasn't conscious of my body, except that the heart was fluttering and no more. I thought I was having an influx of spiritual power, which would enable me to heal. When I came to, there were red marks on my arm; and the word "stigmata" came . . . There were times when I felt I was not going to be a woman any more, and that a baby would come—not an ordinary baby, but a second Christ. Also I felt I was going to be a second Messiah, and was going to be crucified. It was very real then, and has not quite gone yet. . . . This sort of delusion I lived in seemed reality, until my brother told me that I had always believed myself to be everything and almost all-powerful. He said I always ordered my sister about, whereas I had always thought she wasn't kind to me.'

The phantasies described in these accounts may be classified into three groups:

(1) *Phantasies of Identification with the Mother of Christ.* Into this group fall those elements in X's phantasy life which embody the themes of the Annunciation and the Virgin Birth. The personal significance of these themes for her appears to lie, not so much in the idea of being the Mother of Christ as in what this implies, viz. the idea of being the Woman upon whom the Holy Ghost descends, the Woman whom the Father chooses to be the Mother of His Son. The Child is to be born 'in a spiritual way'; and some store is placed upon the feeling of 'being filled with a spiritual power', 'being filled with a greater will than my own'.

(2) *Phantasies of Identification with Christ Himself.* Under this heading come those elements in X's phantasy life which embody the themes of Crucifixion, Resurrection and Glorification, and also that of the Messiahship. The personal significance of this group of phantasies is more complex than that of the Madonna group; but it seems possible to isolate two factors determining it. The first of these factors is to be found in the influence of the analogy of the Sonship of Christ. As Christ is the Son of God, so she feels herself to be the Daughter of the Father in a special sense—not in the sense in which all men are the sons of God, but in that in which Christ is *The* Son of God. This is made plain by the fact that she regards herself as a second Messiah; for this title implies a special Sonship—for her, presumably, Daughterhood. The second factor underlying her identification with Christ is her adoption, in a very personal sense, of that system of ideas which embraces Guilt, Sacrifice and Propitiation.

(3) *Phantasies of Identification with the Bride of Christ.* The status of the *Bride* of Christ is, of course, one accorded to the Church in Christian theology; but its personal significance for X would seem to lie in the fact that, for her in her self-adopted role of the Daughter of God, the only possible Bridegroom worthy of her station would be the Son Himself.

When the nature of these phantasies is considered, it is plain that we are not here dealing with the normal religious experience of the devout person orientated in reality, but with experiences of an unusual and grandiose character, in which the imagination has been exalted at the expense of the facts of real life. It is not a case of the ordinary Christian experience of union with God achieved through participation by the sinner in Christ's Sacrifice, but of an actual dramatization within the individual psyche of the themes underlying the religious experience. Thus in her phantasies X is not content to play the part of mere worshipper or even initiate, but feels herself to be the principal figure in the religious mysteries. This feature of her experience must be attributed to the presence of the schizoid disturbance in her personality, to which reference has already been made; for failure to discriminate adequately between phantasy and reality is a distinctive feature of markedly schizoid states.

So far as the psychology of religion is concerned, the characteristic standpoint of the psychoanalytical school is to look for the sources of the religious need in the dynamic unconscious of the individual. It is, of course, in the same direction that this school of psychological thought looks for the source of artistic inspiration and of all the achievements of human culture in general—the guiding principle being that cultural phenomena represent the symbolic and sublimated expression of repressed wishes of a primal character. The phenomena of human culture in general are not, of course, our present concern; but it must be recognized that the influence of religion has played a much greater and more important part than any other influence in the development of culture and the advance of civilization. Where the psychological sources of the religious need are concerned, there are two factors in the dynamic unconscious to which special importance is attached by the psychoanalytical school. These are: (1) persistence of the original attitude towards parents prevailing during early childhood, and displacement of this attitude towards supernatural beings from its attachment to human parents under the influence of disillusionment regarding their powers and their capacity to provide unlimited support; and (2) the persistent influence of a repressed Œdipus situation accompanied by conflict, and an inner need to obtain relief from the attendant guilt. Personally I am very far from being one of those who considers that higher values can be accounted for wholly in terms of their psychological origins; and indeed, if it were so, it would be a poor outlook for human culture. Nevertheless, psychological origins provide a legitimate field for investigation on the part of psychological science. Consequently, it becomes a matter of interest to determine how far the two factors to which psychoanalytical thought attaches importance as sources of the religious need are found to be present in such an extreme case as that of the woman under consideration, characterized as she was by religious phantasies of an almost delusional quality.

(1) *The patient's emotional attitude towards her parents.* X's attitude towards her parents must necessarily have been influenced to a profound degree by the fact that they lived apart, and that she had never known her father as a member of the household. Let us consider in the first place her attitude towards her father. It may be presumed that, after she first learned the facts of the situation as presented to her, her sympathies would lie, on the conscious plane at least, with her mother. What were the actual rights and wrongs of the dispute between X's parents it is difficult to determine in the absence of data which it is now impossible to obtain; but, since her mother had separated from her father owing to his drunken habits, which had ruined his business and brought misfortune to the home, it would seem natural that her mother should be the object of sympathy. We must remember, however, that it was only comparatively late in life that X became familiar with the facts concerning her father. In her early days this subject was taboo; and, of course, it is in early childhood that the fundamental attitude of a child to a parent is formed. In the present case, X would not require to be very old to become conscious of the difference of her home circumstances from those of other children. Other children had fathers; but she appeared to have none. Even those children who had lost their fathers seemed at liberty to talk about them; but in her family circle her father was a forbidden topic of conversation. She came to learn that a father did exist somewhere in the background; but the whole subject was surrounded by an air of complete mystery. It would thus be difficult to imagine a situation more calculated to encourage the development of phantasy. A father she had; but he was unseen. Although unseen, he was evi-

dently a person of considerable influence and importance, as was constantly borne out by the marked reaction provoked in the family by the mere mention of his name, and the still greater reaction which followed any threat of his reappearance. The ordinary infantile idea of the father as an all-powerful, awe-inspiring figure was thus powerfully reinforced in the case of X by the mystery surrounding an almost mythical figure. To her childish mind her unseen father became an infinitely greater power than any visible father; and, further, the conception of him which X formed was uncorrected, as she grew up, by any gradual perception of his human limitations. It may thus be readily appreciated that her conception of the father-figure as a god became confirmed rather than corrected with the advancing years.

Let us now pass to the consideration of X's attitude to her mother. This is more difficult to assess than her attitude to her father—one reason being that the analysis provided fewer data for determining the exact nature of this emotional relationship. A considerable amount of material was, however, produced with reference to her eldest sister, who, after her mother's death, undoubtedly became a mother-substitute, and who, even during her mother's life-time, appears to have assumed the function of a mother-figure towards her. This sister was considerably older than X, and always appears to have dominated her; but after her mother's death this domination became particularly evident. The result is that her mother's death had the effect of rendering her home life particularly unhappy; and her first breakdown occurred two years after this event. Her sister treated her, even after she had attained her majority, as if she had been a mere child; and, although she was undoubtedly childish, this domination appears to have confirmed her childish attitude. Apparently she was not allowed to invite her friends to the house, and was hardly allowed to visit them in their own homes. There can be no doubt that her sister was genuinely interested in her welfare; but her sister's dominating attitude kept her in subjection and roused her hostility. This hostile attitude to the functioning mother-figure gave rise, after X's breakdown, to an obsessing fear lest she should kill or injure her sister. It is, therefore, plain that the fundamental attitude of X to the mother-figure was one of veiled hatred towards a despotic and inauspicious power possessing in her eyes all the attributes of a malevolent goddess.

(2) *The influence of the Œdipus situation.* Let us now consider the

importance of the part played in X's life by the Œdipus situation—
the second of the two factors to which, as we have seen, psychoanalytical thought attaches special importance as unconscious sources
of the religious need. We have already seen that, owing to the circumstances of her early life, her absent father must have come to be
regarded by her with feelings of awe and wonder appropriate towards a god. It is difficult, however, for frail humanity to sustain the
worship of an unseen and spiritual power in the absence of a visible
intermediary and representative. Hence, perhaps, the decay of
Quakerism, which probably represents the most exclusively spiritual
interpretation of Christian belief. The tendency always exists to seek
an earthly representative of spiritual powers. In X's case, therefore,
we would expect to find a significant father-figure in her life,
assuming that the Œdipus situation plays any dominant role in it.
Actually what we find is not one father-figure indeed, but many.
Typical father-substitutes are usually found to belong to one of two
classes of persons—(1) Brothers, male cousins and uncles—individuals in the case of whom the transference of emotion is made easy
by familial ties; and (2) Persons such as rulers, clergymen, doctors
and schoolmasters, who exercise over others authority analogous to
parental authority. What then do we find in the case of X? First of
all we find, incorporated in a phantasy which I have not quoted,
the idea that, if she did not marry Christ, a royal person would be
the most suitable substitute. Further, we find that she had woven
erotic phantasies round the figures of almost all of the many doctors,
under whose care she came in the course of her long illness. These
phantasies were most marked in the case of seven doctors. She had
also woven erotic phantasies round the figures of two clergymen,
two schoolmasters, and at least one male cousin. The most marked
evidence of her fixation in the Œdipus situation is to be found, however, in her attitude to her brother, who incidentally had suffered
from melancholic, and even suicidal tendencies. She recorded incidents of early childhood which strongly suggested the possibility of
physical intimacy between them; and, although few details remained
available to her conscious memory, she had a feeling that something
of this nature might have occurred. Later, at the age of fifteen, she
began to have strong desires to be held and fondled by him. When,
after her first breakdown, she lived in his house for a time, she was
evidently very jealous of his wife; and at this time she frequently
asked him to let her sit on his knee, and longed for him to kiss her. In

strong contrast to her attitude to father-figures was her attitude to young men of her own age—for whom she experienced a feeling of distaste mingled with apprehension; and on this account she avoided dances, and found any excuse good enough to justify her in refusing invitations to any social engagements of such a nature. The importance of the part played by the Œdipus situation in X's life is, however, perhaps most clearly revealed by the fact that one morning during the course of analysis she awoke from a dream with the sentence, 'Perhaps I shall be married to Father,' in her ears. This sentence was made the subject of free association; and from the material provided I quote the following:

'I had a feeling it was strange that Father did not stay with us. My mother left him just after I was born. I was sensitive as a child when asked questions about who my father was. At school a form had to be filled in; and the father's name had to be given. My mother told me not to give it. This worried me very much. . . . I thought it dreadful for him to be cut off from us all; and sometimes I thought of going to look after him. What worries me is that I still care for my brother. I don't want to hold him physically now; but there is no other man who takes his place. It makes me afraid sometimes. I know it isn't a healthy feeling.'

This quotation reveals in brief outline how she felt consciously towards her father as a child; and it indicates not only the close association of her brother with the father-figure in her mind, but also the conflict to which the persistence of the Œdipus attachment gave rise. Included among the other associations to which this dream-fragment led were erotic phantasies woven round the figures of five doctors, a minister, a retired sea-captain, an old man at the head of a business, a male cousin and the fiancé of a sister—all father-figures for her. There were also recorded hostile thoughts towards the sister who, as already stated, had been a mother-figure to her even before her actual mother's death. There were also descriptions of a struggle, of which she was frequently conscious within her personality, between the forces of good and evil, and between spirit and body. These descriptions were accompanied by ambivalent thoughts about God, and an account of her visions of the Devil. The nature of these associations, taken in relation to the facts of her life, can leave little doubt as to the presence, in a quite exceptional degree, of the Œdipus situation and the conflict engendered by it.

Having obtained evidence of the presence in X both of a markedly

infantile attitude towards the figures of her parents and of an unresolved Œdipus situation of exaggerated proportions, we are now in
a position to appreciate the dynamic of her religious phantasies. As
we have already seen, the group of phantasies in which she identifies
herself with the Mother of Christ derives its personal significance
from the fact that the Mother of Christ is the Woman upon whom
the Spirit of the Father descends. These phantasies thus represent a
symbolic fulfilment of her Œdipus wishes towards her own father as
a figure to whom she attributed divine attributes. A similar significance must be attributed to the group of phantasies in which she
identifies herself with Christ as the Son of God. Whereas, however,
in the former group of phantasies she identifies herself with her
mother in a unique relationship with her father, in the latter group
she represents herself as enjoying a unique relationship with him
while still herself retaining the status of child. The special significance
of the third group of phantasies, in which she identifies herself with
the Bride of Christ, also becomes clear; for we can now see that these
represent a symbolic fulfilment of her libidinal wishes towards her
brother, who functioned in her mind as a father-substitute.

SUPPLEMENTARY NOTE—(1951)

In the light of subsequent events, I feel it desirable to add a brief
note regarding the fate of the patient whose religious phantasies
formed the subject of the preceding paper. At the outset of the paper
I stated that my account was based upon 'data obtained during a
short course of analytical treatment undertaken with a view to mitigating the severity of the symptoms from which she suffered.' As I
have learned from experience since I undertook the treatment of this
patient in 1926, and as analysts in general have for long recognized,
it is extremely rash to embark upon the analytical treatment of a case
in the hope of effecting a mitigation of symptoms within a short
time. Accordingly, it will come as no great surprise to the reader to
learn that, in the case of this particular patient, what promised to be a
'short course of analytical treatment' in anticipation later proved to
be not so short in retrospect. In actual fact, the treatment was subject
to repeated interruptions owing to various vicissitudes, which need
not be detailed. However, subject to this qualification, continuity of
treatment was maintained for rather more than two years. By this

time clinical improvement was sufficiently marked to justify the conclusion that the aim which I had set myself at the outset had been
achieved; and treatment was accordingly terminated. During a period
of two years following the termination of treatment the patient
undertook a series of jobs, each of which she proved unable to hold
for any length of time; and during this period she consulted me
occasionally about problems which arose. By the end of this two
years' period, however, it became evident that her mental condition
had relapsed; and, at her request, I resumed treating her for another
three months, although economic difficulties stood in the way of
treatment. After a further interval of six months, treatment was again
resumed at her request for about a year in spite of continuing
economic difficulties; but, as always happened in this case, interruptions of extraneous origin were of frequent occurrence. Thereafter,
for more than a year, she was out of touch with me altogether. During the next fifteen months, however, I did see her from time to time;
and in the course of these fifteen months she spent a few weeks as a
voluntary patient in a mental hospital.

This rather protracted and somewhat disheartening account of the
patient's vicissitudes can only be justified as a background for the
final dénouement, which I am now about to relate. During the last-
mentioned period of fifteen months the patient's condition slowly
deteriorated; but the deterioration assumed for the most part an
apparently physical form, being characterized chiefly by increasing
physical weakness and exhaustion, which eventually rendered her
completely bed-ridden. No organic disease could be found to
account for this weakness and exhaustion; and I think there can be no
doubt that it was of a 'neurasthenic' nature, and that it was associated
with her intensive practice of masturbation. This practice dated from
her first nervous breakdown at the age of twenty-one; and she had no
conscious memory of any previous autoerotic indulgence. The
occasion which served to introduce her to masturbatory practices was
one on which she awoke from sleep to find her hand pressed against
her genital organs and herself experiencing what she described as 'a
hideous sensation with pain shooting up into my stomach and flash-
ing before my eyes'. This, incidentally, was at a time when she was
having 'visions from the spiritual side'. Shortly after the experience
just recorded, the doctor who was attending her during her breakdown asked her if anything was worrying her; and she told him of
the distress which she was experiencing on account of visions of

Notes on the Religious Phantasies of a Female Patient

Christ being pulled down from the Cross. According to her account, the doctor began 'kindly' stroking her neck as he listened to her confidences; and, when she had finished, he bent down and kissed her. Thereafter she began to experience an overwhelming desire to be held in a man's arms. Subsequently, she began to experience a strong desire to touch her genital organs during the visits of another doctor. Somewhat later she had occasion to call in yet another doctor at a country resort to which she had gone to recuperate from her breakdown. She explained to this doctor some of the details of her illness; and, according to her statement, he slipped his hand down to her sex-organs during the course of the consultation. That night she indulged quite overtly in masturbation; and, as she did so, she felt that her spirit was leaving her body; From that time forth she became a complete devotee of masturbation; and the experience accompanying the act was described by her as 'exquisite beyond belief'.

Having digressed by giving some account of the development of the patient's masturbatory practices, I must now return to the final dénouement which I had begun to relate before the digression. I had mentioned the state of extreme weakness and exhaustion to which she had become reduced, and which had rendered her bed-ridden; and I had recorded the opinion that her debilitation was of an essentially 'neurasthenic' nature. By this time she was lying in bed at home under the care of the sister who had always seemed to her such a tyrant. It was her sister who informed me by telephone of the state to which she had become reduced, and who at the same time asked me as a special favour to come and see her. When I went to the house, I found her in the state of extreme weakness which I have already described; and, although neither her own doctor nor a consultant physician who had examined her could find any evidence of organic disease, it was obvious that she had not long to live. During the next few days I visited her fairly regularly; and my last visit was on the day before she finally faded away and died. I thus had the opportunity to see her upon her death-bed. I have no record and no very clear memory of the details of the death-bed scene. Also her voice was weak; and she found it a great effort to speak. So I was not able to learn a great deal about the experiences through which she was passing. I remember, however, that she was perfectly rational and perfectly orientated in time and space. I can also remember that she was experiencing no ecstatic or horrifying visions; but, unless my memory deceives me, she was definitely entertaining sexual phantasies. Be that as it may, it is quite certain that she was in a state of extreme sexual desire; and, when I left her moribund on the occasion of my final visit, almost her last words were, 'I want a man.' The actual cause of death must remain a matter of speculation. Can she be said to have died of unsatisfied sexual desire? Or did she die of masturbation? Or did she kill herself by means of repression? In the light of the total facts, these would appear to be the only available alternatives; but which provides the correct answer is almost anybody's guess.

CHAPTER II

Features in the Analysis of a Patient with a Physical Genital Abnormality[1] (1931)

THE purpose of this paper is to give some account of a case which presents features of special interest, and which in one respect is perhaps unique in psychoanalytical practice; for, although the patient in question had always been presumed to be female, she had an organic genital defect such as to raise some doubt as to the sex to which she properly belonged. On this account alone the case appears to merit recording; for the question naturally arises how far the neurotic symptoms occurring in an individual with such an organic defect were found in the course of psychoanalytical treatment to follow the pattern of familiar psychopathological processes.

The patient was referred to me for psychoanalytical treatment by her family doctor on account of symptoms which will shortly be described. Meanwhile, it seems desirable to give some preliminary account of the nature of her physical abnormality so far as this could be determined. It was originally described by her family doctor as follows:

'She appeared to be a perfectly normal child until she reached the age of puberty. She began then to grow unduly tall, did not menstruate, but kept perfectly well. When she was about twenty, I was consulted and made an examination. I found a complete absence of all genital organs with only a pin head opening as a vagina which led nowhere. As she felt perfectly well, nothing further was done.'

In accepting the patient for psychoanalytical treatment on account of her neurotic symptoms, I also accepted her doctor's account of her genital abnormality as substantially accurate; but, as treatment proceeded, I began to entertain some doubts regarding the complete

[1] An abbreviated version of this paper was read before the British Psycho-Analytical Society on 21st January 1931.

accuracy of his account. These doubts were eventually confirmed by the results of a special gynecological examination which took place some considerable time after the commencement of analysis. This examination was conducted by a distinguished gynecologist who was also well versed in genetics, and who reported in the following terms:

'The general development is strongly masculine, the chest is very broad but the mammary development is, if anything, more suggestive of a female type in that the tissue is soft and slightly dependent. The pubic hair is normal in its distribution for the female and the more superficial external organs are quite definitely female, namely, labia, mons, clitoris, vestibule and urethra. The hymen is completely closed, and is represented by a series of small bands crossing the site of the normal depression. Rectal examination was not easy but I was able to determine quite definitely that the pelvis varies from the ordinary female pelvis in the fact that no cervix or uterine body was made out. These, under ordinary circumstances, are usually made out with perfect ease by this route. At the same time the examination was not sufficiently complete to exclude the presence of an imperfectly developed organ. The general impression which I have formed is that we are dealing with a condition of essential masculinity with the presence of male gonads accompanied by secondary characters of a female type, that is, which usually goes by the name of "male pseudo-hermaphroditism".'

In the opinion of the examining gynecologist, accordingly, the patient had male gonads and was essentially male, although possessing external genitals which were characteristically female. Doubts were subsequently thrown upon this opinion, however, when a specimen of the patient's urine was examined for oestrin and gonadotropic content by a professional geneticist, who reported as follows:

'With reference to the urine sample . . . the findings are as follows: Oestrin—at least 20 mouse units per 24 hours. Gonadotropic hormones—less than 100 mouse units of follicular maturation hormone per 24 hours. These excretion results are similar to those usually obtained in a normal female subject, and the oestrin excretion is higher than would be expected in a male. The results suggest the presence of female secretory gonads.'

The verdicts of the experts were thus in conflict; but the verdict of the professional geneticist must be regarded as carrying greater weight, since it was based upon objective data revealed in laboratory tests, and was not just a matter of opinion as was the verdict of the gynecologist. In the circumstances, the original presumption that the patient was really female in sex must remain undisturbed; and it was never thought wise to impart to her any information which would shake her own conviction to this effect.[1]

It is of some interest to record that the patient was not the only member of her family to be affected in the manner described, and that her genital abnormality was shared by more than one of her numerous sisters. The full extent of this abnormality could only have been determined by exploratory abdominal section. Such deliberate interference would, however, have been difficult to justify; and, as it happened, none of the sisters in question had ever required an abdominal operation, which, had it been performed, might have incidentally revealed the state of the internal genital organs. At the same time, it seems improbable on purely clinical grounds that the uterus can have been represented except in the most rudimentary form; for there had never been any signs of hæmatometra in any of the affected sisters—and it is difficult to believe that, if a functioning uterus had been present, imprisonment of the menses would not have occurred and given rise to the appropriate symptoms. As regards the question of the gonads, the conclusion that these were female may be presumed to apply not only to the patient, but also to those of her sisters who shared her defect. Where she herself is concerned, one fact in favour of the presence of functioning ovaries is that during adolescence she was subject to rectal haemorrhages which lent themselves to interpretation in terms of vicarious menstruation; and indeed these haemorrhages were actually mistaken for proper menstrual periods before her abnormality was discovered. Periodical bouts of epistaxis, to which she became subsequently liable, were also highly suggestive of vicarious menstruation. Whatever doubts may exist, however, regarding her physical and physiological femininity, psychosexually at any rate she certainly conveyed the impression of being a woman; and she had a considerable attraction for heterosexual men. Her own libidinal orientation was conspicuously towards the male sex; and, although she did possess certain masculine character-traits, these were quite consistent with a 'female castration complex' in the psychoanalytical (as against the biological) sense.

The patient was already well into middle age when she was

---

[1]The data contained in the specialists' reports were not available when the present paper was originally written, and have been subsequently incorporated in it.

recommended to me for psychoanalytical treatment; and, fortunately in the circumstances, she had never taken advantage of any opportunity to marry. She was a teacher by profession; but, when she first came to me, she had been off work for more than a year on account of a nervous breakdown. Her parents were both alive; and she was the eldest of a large family, out of which there were many sisters, but only one brother, surviving. She herself was the only member of the family who had developed nervous symptoms; and in this respect she was less fortunate than the sisters who shared her physical abnormality.

Until the age of puberty she had been a gay, irresponsible child, for whom games and play provided the absorbing interests of life. After puberty, however, her energy became diverted into earnest and strenuous preparation for a teacher's career; and she spent every available minute upon her studies. In these, she developed a degree of conscientiousness sufficient to raise the suspicion that the influence of a tyrannical super-ego was already operative in a big way. When eventually she became aware of her physical disability towards the end of her training period, the effect upon her was to increase her enthusiasm for her work. She welcomed the news that it was her fortune to escape the burdens of womanhood; and she dismissed the whole subject of sex and marriage from the conscious field with a sigh of relief. She felt she was now free to devote herself without hindrance to her career. As things turned out, however, her expectations were to be bitterly disappointed. In her very first post after qualification she began to find teaching a considerable strain. She was unduly conscientious about her duties and set herself a standard of perfection which it was impossible for her to realize in practice. The consequence was that from the outset she worried unduly about her work. The question of discipline occasioned her special anxiety. She could not tolerate the least inattention or insubordination on the part of the children in her class. In order to command the complete attention of the children, she taught with an intensity which left her limp at the end of the day; and after school hours she would wear herself out still further by endless preparation. The natural result of these misguided efforts after perfection was to impair her efficiency as a teacher and to antagonize the schoolchildren, who then became more difficult to teach. Thus, instead of rising, her standard of teaching fell. She was not slow to appreciate this fact herself; but the effect was to make her redouble her already over-strenuous efforts. The more she strove after efficiency, however, the less efficient she became; and the less efficient she became, the more she strove. A vicious circle was thus established; and during the passage of the school term her failure was progressive. This progressive failure was accompanied, as one would expect, by progressive feelings of self-reproach. And so by the end of each term she would find her powers of endurance almost at the breaking-point. The holidays, when they came round, provided a period of welcome recuperation; but at the beginning of each term the whirligig began again.

It was some years before an actual breakdown occurred. As a matter of fact, the first breakdown was physical in character; for at the age of twenty-five she contracted an illness which resulted in her being off work for more than a year. During this illness she appears to have been free from all anxiety—a feature presumably due to a narcissistic investment of libido. Reinforcement of her narcissism doubtless favoured her recovery, which was complete; but it led to an increase in her difficulties when she resumed work. It was from this illness, accordingly, that her doctor dated the beginning of her nervous symptoms. When she resumed teaching, her old anxieties reasserted themselves in aggravated form; and in due course she found herself unable to survive the school term without throwing in her hand. An individual of weaker character (i.e. an individual with a less firmly organized ego) would have given in more easily than she did. The organization of her ego was, however, remarkably stable; and her ego-ideal was also powerfully represented in consciousness in the form of a tremendous sense of duty. Consequently, she put up a better fight than might otherwise have been expected. Eventually, however, the forces at work in her unconscious levied too great a tax upon her undoubted capacity for voluntary effort. As the school term wore on, she would find her memory playing her curious tricks in the class-room, would discover herself at a loss for common words, would utter incoherent sentences, or would suddenly find her mind a blank in the middle of a lesson. Problems of discipline would also begin to cause her torments. The slightest inattention or insubordination on the part of a child would cause her to boil with fury which she struggled to master by heroic efforts of self-control. She felt as if she could almost kill a disobedient child; but any severity on her part gave rise to terrible heart-searchings. Her sleep would become disturbed by teaching dreams (analogous to the war-dreams of the soldier). Later in the term sleep would become quite impossible;

and she would walk about for hours during the night. Eventually tension and anxiety would reach such a pitch as to render her completely incapable of teaching. She would then abandon herself to despair and ask to be relieved of her duties. As soon as she was relieved of professional responsibilities, however, a striking transformation scene was commonly enacted. Her anxiety and depression would then vanish as if by magic; and she would return home to prove the life and soul of the family—a fact which not unnaturally gave rise to some unfavourable comment among her friends. To the psychopathologist, however, these sudden transitions from anxious melancholy to mild elation will provide evidence of a manic-depressive process at work. In actual fact, the patient's depressed and elated phases were not always in sequence; and, even when they were, it sometimes, although not usually, happened that the depressed phase followed the elated phase. In general, periods of depression were much more frequent than periods of elation; but an interesting feature of both types of phase was the general shortness of their duration. A still more interesting feature was, however, that the events precipitating the phases, both depressed and elated, proved exceptionally easy to isolate. This holds true particularly of the phases which developed during analysis. As analysis proceeded, some of the phases which appeared had only a few hours' or even a few minutes' duration; and the patient acquired sufficient insight to isolate the precipitating events without much difficulty. It thus became possible to observe the manic-depressive process at work, as it were, under the microscope.

It says something for the patient's tenacity of purpose and for the strength of her professional interest, that, in spite of repeated breakdowns, she did not finally abandon teaching until a year before she embarked upon analytical treatment. The periods of slight elation which followed her various breakdowns at work were comparatively short; and, after she had been at home for a week or two, her ego-ideal would begin to make fresh demands upon her. She would begin to accuse herself of leading an idle and useless life, and of becoming a parasite upon her parents. Her strong sense of independence would assert itself; and she would fling herself into the maelstrom once again. Once, indeed, she made an excursion outside the educational field; for at one stage she embarked upon a secretarial training under the impression that a change of occupation might mitigate her difficulties. This hope proved short-lived; and it was not long before she found the old anxieties attaching themselves to her secretarial work. Within two years, therefore, we find her teaching again—this time in sole charge of a small school in a remote country district. In such a sheltered environment, far from the usual beat of the dreaded inspector and with no supervision except that imposed by her own ego-ideal, she felt that she could create an educational paradise in which the lion of scholastic efficiency could lie down with the lamb of mental peace. Even in this Garden of Eden, however, she soon discovered both the serpent and the avenging angel. The old anxieties returned; and breakdowns followed in their wake. She sought peace in a succession of posts in remote districts; but all in vain. So eventually she gave up teaching in despair and went home to try the effects of a prolonged period of rest.

On her return home, her symptoms began to assume a somewhat different form. She now began to suffer every few weeks from short periods of depression. The periodicity of these attacks was a striking feature; and it was perhaps significant in the light of her sexual abnormality that she always spoke of them as 'being unwell', and that she also spoke of sometimes 'missing a turn'. As such periods of depression approached, she experienced a sense of struggling against some nameless force in herself that threatened to overwhelm her. The nature of this force was a mystery to her, although to the psychoanalyst it bears the unmistakable mark of the super-ego. The struggle would gradually increase in intensity and would eventually reduce her to a state of acute misery, in which thoughts of self-destruction were never far distant. In the end she would find herself completely overwhelmed in her vain struggle against the unseen foe. She would then fling herself down upon the bed or upon the nearest chair, and burst into a flood of tears. This emotional crisis would be followed by sudden relief from tension and anxiety; but she was always left with a sense of having been utterly humiliated and utterly crushed. She would then retire to bed and lie for several days spending her time thinking, reading and sleeping. While in this regressive state, she would allow no one to enter her room except her mother— to whose control she abandoned herself at these times without reserve, and who supplied her every want. The super-ego had conquered; but, in submitting to its victory, she gained temporary entrance to that paradise which she had vainly sought in remotely situated schools. By surrendering herself unconditionally to her mother she regained that state of primal innocence which she had lost in childhood through her first disobedience. She re-entered as a passing visitor that lost paradise where, in return for complete obedience, she could have every infantile want satisfied.

Analytical procedure soon revealed the importance of the Œdipus situation in the development of the condition from which the patient suffered. Her actual father proved, however, to be a comparatively insignificant figure in the drama. He was not a strong personality; and he played an unobtrusive part in the family circle. The dominant figure in the home was the patient's mother—an energetic and efficient woman, for whom the welfare of her family was all-important. She belonged to the type of good mother who is only too liable to instigate the formation of an exacting super-ego in her children. At any rate, in the case of the patient she played an important part in the formation of a titanic super-ego. The strength of the patient's super-ego would appear to have been increased rather than diminished by the fact that the role of father-figure was largely played by her maternal grandfather. This fact appears to have accentuated her rivalry with her mother and powerfully reinforced unconscious guilt. Her grandfather had been dead for some years when she came for treatment; but in her unconscious he lived on with all the attributes of a benevolent deity. She was his first grandchild; and she had always remained his favourite. His favour found expression in innumerable presents, which must have seemed lavish in view of the comparative economy which her own parents found it necessary to exercise in her childhood. His benevolence thus easily earned for him the status of fairy godfather in her imagination. Apart from the affection and the favours which he bestowed, he opened for her the gates of a child's paradise wherein she spent the happiest moments of her life. His professional duties connected him with the running of a neighbouring estate; and through his agency this estate was thrown open to her as a magnificent playground. Play was a perfect passion with her; and the estate provided her with unrivalled opportunities for indulging this passion. Such restrictions as were naturally enforced by the proprietor seemed to her but pale reflections of those imposed by her mother in the home; but, in so far as they were felt to be irksome, they seem to have been associated in her mind with the proprietor's wife, who frequently appeared in her dreams as a disapproving mother-figure, and who played the role of ogre in the magic garden.

The first feature of note in the analysis was the emergence of countless memories of early childhood concerned mainly with the patient's grandfather and the estate with which he was connected. Memories of this period of her life had been withheld from consciousness during her whole teaching career; but, once the preliminary resistances had been overcome, they poured into consciousness as if flood-gates had been opened. Thus she re-lived in memory endless days of happy play. She re-entered the paradise of her childhood, which had become all the more elysian through the operation of unconscious phantasy during the intervening years. In the background, however, there was always the menacing shadow of a mother-figure. When, as a child, she was playing on the estate, this role was assumed by the owner's wife; but, when her grandfather visited her home, it was her actual mother who seemed to stand like a sinister figure in the background frowning disapproval. In the earliest phase of analysis, however, her super-ego was largely in abeyance. It was the happy memories and phantasies of childhood that predominated. She was re-united to her grandfather in phantasy and played gaily with him in the elysian fields. Repressed emotional experiences of a libidinal nature thus broke through the trammels of years; and she re-discovered what she came to describe as her 'infantile self', which had remained for long repressed in her unconscious. This break-through of repressed emotional experiences was accompanied by the emergence of sexual sensations, which at first appeared to her entirely novel, but which eventually revived memories of sensations experienced on swings and see-saws in her early days. Her description of these sensations clearly indicated that they conformed to the clitoris type. They proved to be closely associated in her mind with dreams about butterflies; and the sensations themselves reminded her of the fluttering of butterflies' wings.

At this time also she began to record experiences with men, which she rather aptly designated as 'adventures'. She required to travel by train when she came for analysis; and these adventures took place characteristically on the journeys to and fro. She began to find that, when her only fellow-traveller was a man, she almost invariably attracted his attention; and incidents in which she was hugged and kissed by chance men in railway carriages became not infrequent. This constituted for her a novel experience, which at first afforded her considerable satisfaction. That the incidents described were not simply products of imagination can hardly remain in doubt; and their occurrence was quite intelligible in view of the sudden release of pent-up libido which analysis had effected. This release of libido may well have rendered her particularly attractive to the other sex, whilst at the same time weakening her own inhibitions. So much appears to have been objective fact; but her accounts of her experiences were undoubtedly coloured by subjective interpretation. To what extent this was the case is difficult to determine. Thus she frequently recorded that men who passed her compartment when the train was drawn up at a platform would turn back and get into the same compartment. This may have been true in part at least; for at this stage she certainly exhaled libido. However, when we find her drawing the conclusion that the release of her infantile self had endowed her with the capacity of 'affecting' other people and even animals, it becomes evident that she had left the ground of solid fact for the phantasy world of infantile omnipotence. She was too rational to believe in magic; but she began to imagine herself the master of new powers, which science had so far failed to fathom—powers which, she felt, were capable of being employed for the benefit of humanity as a whole. It is evident, therefore, that she had now become subject to delusions of grandeur with a Messianic colouring. The fact that this exaltation of thought was accompanied by feverish activity and radiant happiness left no doubt that she had passed into a manic phase.

This manic phase, which developed somewhat rapidly in the first stage of treatment, passed off gradually after reaching a climax. Altogether it may be said to have lasted about three months. Thereafter followed a period of comparative equilibrium, in which the patient reaped the benefit of the release of her libido. The train adventures continued, and sexual sensations were constantly liable to obtrude themselves; but there was an absence of extravagant ideas. The 'infantile self' and its manifestations came to be accepted by the patient as a legitimate part of her psyche, which had hitherto been denied expression, and which had now come to its own. During this period her analytical associations were mainly concerned with details of the Œdipus situation, involving, as it did, her fixation upon her maternal grandfather, her resentment of her mother's authority and her rivalry with her mother for her grandfather's affection. There also began to accumulate evidence of a marked degree of penis-envy.

The situation so far described belongs to the first of three stages which may be distinguished in the analysis up to the time of writing.

The Analysis of a Patient with a Genital Abnormality

During this first stage the analysis did not penetrate to any appreciable extent beneath a genital level. In the second stage, however, the deeper levels of the unconscious made their presence felt. It is doubtless owing to this fact that the patient began again to experience periods of depression. The presence of a strong anal fixation had been inferred from the first in view of her extreme orderliness, her hatred of dirt and her passion for cleanliness. Her history of spastic constipation and the suspicion that her rectal haemorrhages during adolescence represented vicarious menstruation increased the expectation formed. During the second stage, however, anal elements began to manifest themselves more overtly. She began to dream of lavatories, winding passages and buildings characterized by disorder and dirt. Anal birth phantasies also occurred; and she began to experience sensations of a sexual character in her rectum. Penis-envy likewise expressed itself under an anal guise—as when she dreamed of finding a cigarette attached to her anal orifice. In due course, however, oral elements began to dominate the field. She began to dream with great frequency about meals and about sweetmeats which reminded her of her favourite delicacies in childhood. On more than one occasion there occurred dreams suggestive of a trauma in connection with weaning. Her attitude to the penis also began to assume a definitely oral colouring, as became evident from dreams in which objects of phallic significance appeared in the guise of food. Thus in one dream she was presented with a chocolate fish to eat; and in another she found a salamander covered with white sauce on a plate in front of her. As time passed, the importance of her oral fixation became more and more apparent; and eventually the field became almost entirely dominated by an intensely oral-sadistic attitude towards the penis. The extravagance of her penis-envy is of special significance in view of the fact that she possessed no vagina; for it was not upon the possession of the characteristically female vagina that her heart was set, but upon the possession of the characteristically male penis. Here it may be recalled that, when at the age of twenty she was informed of her sexual disability, she received the news with a profound sigh of relief. She was filled with joy by the reflection that she was one of the few living women granted complete exemption from the burden of womanhood, which had acquired particularly unpleasant associations for her when, as a child, she saw the blood upon the sheets which had been used at one of her mother's confinements—unpleasant associations which became reinforced later when she was informed about menstruation. She had thus a horror of the vagina, which was accompanied by an unconscious over-estimation of the clitoris. Prior to analysis, she had been ignorant of the existence of the clitoris; but in her unconscious phantasies it played the role of the penis, and was represented in her dreams by phallic symbols of diminished size.

The oral-sadistic attitude towards the penis, which analysis revealed in the patient, proved to have been the chief factor in the production of her symptoms. Its nature was well illustrated in a dream which depicted her brother entering a room in an undressed state, with a wound upon his penis and a look of horror in his eyes. This look of horror haunted her when she awoke, and left her with a feeling of acute unhappiness. Underneath this unhappiness her associations revealed a definite sense of responsibility for the wound; and on a subsequent occasion the dream was recalled with the sudden intuition that the wound on her brother's penis was of the nature of a bite. This dream proved of considerable interest in the light of actual events; for, not long after its occurrence, her brother met with a violent death in an accident which involved considerable mangling of his body. She was herself present when, to use her own phrase, her 'broken brother' was brought to his father's house; and one can well imagine his corpse producing upon her the impression of a body mauled by a carnivorous animal and stirring her oral sadism to the depths. At any rate, her reaction to her brother's death was particularly significant. The rest of the family behaved in orthodox fashion. The suddenness and the gruesome nature of the tragedy prostrated them with grief. It was otherwise, however, in the case of the patient. In view of her previous breakdowns it was feared by the others that the shock would prove too much for her. As things turned out, however, she proved to be the only member of the family who retained equanimity. Everyone marvelled at the way in which she 'rose to the occasion'. While the others remained helpless with grief, she took complete charge of affairs and made all the arrangements necessitated by the circumstances with an efficiency which roused universal admiration. In thus meeting the demands of the situation she experienced a sense of triumphant power, which stood in forcible contrast to the sense of helplessness which oppressed the others. To the psychoanalytical mind this reaction, which seemed so heroic to the uninitiated, must necessarily seem suspicious in view of the dream which so shortly preceded the fatality. In the dream the patient's oral sadism had to rest content with such illusory satisfaction as could be derived from the image of her brother's bitten penis; but the contemplation of her brother's mangled corpse furnished an oral-sadistic satisfaction in reality far exceeding the dreams of oral avarice. The gratification thus provided gave her a sense of omnipotence which carried her through the crisis a complete master of the situation. While the others succumbed to depression, she thus passed into a phase of elation. But, as in due course the depression of the others began to pass off, so did her elation; and, by the time they had recovered their equanimity, she had passed into a phase of depression. The influence of the super-ego had asserted itself; and she now began to pay the price for her guilty oral-sadistic triumph.

The release of repressed sadistic tendencies, belonging chiefly to an oral level, was the distinguishing feature of the second stage in the patient's analysis. During this stage the train adventures continued; but her attitude towards the men involved in them became more and more detached. It gave her a sense of power to play upon their feelings for a time, and then to waive them aside with an air of indifference—sometimes at her destination, sometimes before she reached it. In this attitude we may discern the operation of a sadistic 'revenge motif' directed against men as possessors of the envied penis. The real significance of this revenge motif manifested itself more clearly when she began to feel that she 'affected' certain married men in the vicinity of her home in the same way as she 'affected' chance men in the train—although in the case of the former no actual 'adventures' occurred. This sense of 'affecting' men attached itself particularly to father-figures; and at times she experienced it in relation to her father himself. As time passed, these 'affectings' (as she called them) increased their range; and situations of a remote kind, such as sitting in the same pew as a man in church or meeting a friend's husband at tea, acquired the emotional significance of 'adventures'. As such experiences increased in frequency, she became increasingly subject to transient attacks of depression—'illnesses' as she called them. At first she was unable to recognize the causal connection between the 'affectings' and the 'illnesses' which followed them—the latter seeming to fall upon her like bolts from the blue. In course of time, however, she began to gain insight into the relation existing between the two groups of phenomena; and eventually she became able to trace in retrospect the events which precipitated most of her 'illnesses'. The insight which she thus gradually acquired had the general effect of reducing both the severity and the duration of her attacks of depression. Sometimes they lasted no longer than a few hours or even a few minutes; and sometimes they were completely abortive in character. More than once their appearance or disappearance occurred during the course of an analytical session. The most striking example of this phenomenon was the sudden disappearance of the marked phase of depression which followed her brother's death. On this occasion the course of the associations was such as to precipitate in the patient a flash of insight into the unconscious significance of her brother's death for her. This flash of insight was followed in the twinkling of an eye by the complete lifting of the cloud of depression which hung over her.

The dawn of insight on the patient's part into the factors precipitating her formerly mysterious 'illnesses' marked the beginning of the third stage of the analysis. The ultimate cause of these attacks of depression was, of course, to be found in the unconscious guilt attached to her sadistic tendencies; and the essential feature of the third stage was the gradual emergence of this unconscious guilt. The first stage, as we have seen, was characterized by a release of repressed libido at a genital level, followed by the emergence of such elements in the structure of the super-ego as were relevant to the Œdipus situation. At this level the super-ego was mainly derived from the figure of the patient's mother, who was her great rival for her grandfather's love. In the second stage of the analysis there occurred a release of repressed sadistic tendencies derived mainly from an oral level. This was accompanied by the transient attacks of depression already noted; but the guilt which occasioned these attacks remained buried in the unconscious. It was only in the third stage that components of the super-ego relevant to anal and oral situations began to emerge. As they did emerge, it became evident that, at these deeper levels, the super-ego was mainly derived from the figure of the patient's grandfather, who was the ultimate object towards whom her sadistic tendencies had come to be largely directed. It was, however, only very gradually and in the face of tremendous resistance that the guilt attached to her sadistic tendencies emerged into consciousness.

The emergence of the unconscious guilt attached to the patient's sadism was heralded, as already indicated, by the dawn of insight on her part into the precipitating causes of her 'illnesses'. In due course, however, guilt began to manifest itself more overtly in a sense of embarrassment and shame experienced in relation to 'adventure' situations. She began to feel uncomfortable and ill at ease when a man entered a railway carriage in which she was seated. Her face would begin to burn; and she would not know where to look for embarrassment. She would then make supreme efforts to conceal her feelings of discomfort, either by keeping her eyes glued to the pages of a book under the pretence of reading or by struggling to adopt an attitude of apparent composure. Such experiences in themselves caused her considerable distress; but this distress became almost intolerable when she began to feel that the men in question, and even other persons in the same carriage, were 'affected' by her state of mind—a feeling supported by the fact that not infrequently the men concerned would leave her carriage at an intermediate station and enter another. Incidents of this nature engendered in her an extreme sense of mortification, and led her to feel that she had become a public nuisance. In consequence, the anxiety which first manifested itself in relation to 'adventure' situations began to attach itself to the very thought of a train journey. As the hour approached for her to leave home for the station, she would experience a rising tide of apprehension. She became embarrassed by the sight of men she chanced to meet on her way between her house and the local station. It became an agony for her to ask the booking-clerk for a ticket; and, once her ticket was purchased, she took refuge in the ladies' waiting-room until the arrival of the train. When the train arrived, she searched anxiously for a compartment reserved for 'ladies only'; and, if none such were available, she tried to select a carriage in which there were no men. Then on the completion of her train journey, if she walked along the crowded thoroughfare which provided the most direct route to my consulting-rooms, she was tortured with self-consciousness; and, in consequence, she adopted the practice of making detours through the more sequestered streets.

It is noteworthy that she was free from all embarrassment in the company of women; but, as time passed, every situation in which she ran the risk of meeting men became a danger-situation for her. It was thus that the guilt attached to her sadistic attitude towards the penis gradually emerged into consciousness. In her unconscious, every man presented a potential penis, just as for the scalp-hunter every enemy represents a potential scalp. It was as if, like a scalp-hunter, she walked about with a belt of trophies round her waist. Her self-consciousness was in part a guilt-reaction to this unconscious exhibitionism; but a much more important factor was lust of the eye.

She looked upon every man to lust after his penis with all the lust of oral sadism. Thus every glance she cast upon a man was a guilty glance; and her eye quailed as it caught his. Her guilt, as it emerged, spread in ever widening circles. Thus she began to feel embarrassment when she was served by a male assistant in a shop, when she looked at the clergyman in church, or when she saw a man approaching her on a country road. In due course it came about that the only places in which she felt relatively safe were the consulting-room and her own home. Even in the home circle, however, her peace of mind was liable to disturbance; for the visit of a brother-in-law was always liable to precipitate anxiety, and at times she became embarrassed from a sense of having 'affected' her father. Another source of anxiety arose out of the fact that, after her brother's death, his wife and little girl came to live in her home. The child was somewhat unruly, and thus readily became not only the symbol of the patient's own sadistic impulses, but also the object of all the fury of her super-ego. The fury of her super-ego was particularly liable to be stirred when, as sometimes happened, the child disturbed the order of the garden, which had been placed under her care, and over which she exercised undisputed sway. Never was her indignation aroused so much as when her niece destroyed flowers which she had planted. On such occasions she experienced a flood of positively murderous impulses; and it was only through a supreme effort of self-control that she avoided inflicting physical injury upon the child. Such violent reactions on the part of her super-ego were complicated by the fact that her niece came to symbolize for her not only her own sadistic tendencies, but also her brother's penis. Her violent reaction thus represented a direct expression of her repressed sadism as well as an expression of her sadistic super-ego.

The patient's attitude to her mischievous niece during the course of analysis throws considerable light upon the symptoms which originally brought her for analytical treatment. Like her niece, the children whom she taught during her school career acquired in her mind the symbolic significance of her own repressed tendencies. She was thus driven by her exacting super-ego to demand from the children absolute obedience, complete attention and perfect industry. In so far as she failed to secure these, she had failed to subdue her own unruly tendencies. Like her niece, too, the schoolchildren had a double significance in her unconscious. They symbolized not only her own sadistic tendencies, but also the envied and hated penis. Her attitude to the children thus represented a compromise between her repressed sadism and the demands of her sadistic super-ego. The omnipotence after which she strove was an omnipotence whereby she might satisfy her sadistic tendencies with her super-ego's approval. This fact suggests that *two types of omnipotence* may be distinguished in the symptomatology of the psychoneuroses and psychoses. On the one hand, there is the omnipotence of unthwarted and untrammelled libidinal wishes, which our patient sought to find in the magic garden of her childhood. On the other hand, there is the type of omnipotence which she sought to establish in her school career, viz. such omnipotence as can be obtained through the satisfaction of repressed sadistic tendencies in a sublimated field of activities wherein the super-ego may be satisfied through the same activities. The former type appears to be represented in the omnipotence of mania and schizophrenia, whereas the latter type seems characteristic of obsessional and paranoid states.

The mention of paranoid states brings us back to the behaviour of the patient under discussion during the third stage of her analysis. Attention has already been drawn to the manner in which deeply repressed guilt over her oral-sadistic wishes gradually emerged in the form of exaggerated self-consciousness. This guilt only emerged, however, in face of a resistance infinitely greater than that offered to the emergence of the repressed wishes themselves. The patient's defensive techniques were mobilized to the uttermost to avert any realization of her oral-sadistic guilt. Once she had brought herself to recognize the presence of powerful oral-sadistic tendencies in her psyche, she adopted towards them a conscious attitude of toleration such as would have been appropriate towards the good-natured pranks of a high-spirited child. Consciously she regarded them as indeed a terrible nuisance, but as natural and innocent. This attitude was, of course, a defence against the guilt attached to them in her unconscious. Such guilt manifested itself in a mitigated form in the self-consciousness and embarrassment which she experienced in the presence of men; but she bitterly resented the fact that she was called upon to undergo these humiliating experiences owing to the presence of tendencies which she had come to regard as childish and innocent. In this attitude we can already discern the operation of paranoid techniques; and such techniques were subsequently exploited to a considerable extent for the rejection of unconscious guilt. It is thus that 'ideas of reference' came to be entertained. She began to notice, for example, that in railway stations men frequently approached the door of her compartment as if to enter, and then, after looking in, went on to another carriage. She also began to attach additional significance to occasions when, as we have seen, men seated in her compartment got out and entered another. Such actions on the part of men she interpreted as due to her presence in the carriage. In certain cases there was possibly some basis for her conclusion. Thus, the release of repressed libido which occurred had an undoubted influence upon her manner and appearance; and the embarrassment which she developed in relation to men can hardly have failed to create reciprocal embarrassment. Some of the incidents which she recorded would thus seem to have been genuine incidents explicable along these lines. She found it difficult to believe, however, that emotional states could express themselves so obviously as to be noticed by others; for she had been so self-centred in the past that all but the crudest expressions of emotion in others had always escaped her notice. Consequently she came to the conclusion that she possessed some malevolent power of 'affecting' men, which science had not yet succeeded in elucidating. She resented the possession of this power on account of the distress which it occasioned; but she was unable to recognize the origin of this distress in the guilt attached to her omnivorous sadism.

That the technique of projection was also adopted as a defence became evident from the appearance of dreams of persecution. In one such dream she was arraigned before a tribunal for stealing fir-cones from a wood belonging to a nobleman. These cones were supposed to be used for the propagation of a special kind of tree, and were regarded as possessing tremendous value. She freely admitted having entered the wood and having played innocently with the cones; but she protested that she had played with such cones all her life, and that she meant no harm thereby. She also indignantly denied the accusation that she had taken some away. She entertained a sense of injury at the injustice of the accusation, but felt that her protestations of innocence were useless before a tribunal which she knew to be narrowly biassed and relentless in the extreme. The cones, of course, represented penises; the wood reminded her of the estate with which her grandfather had been connected, and in which she had played as a child; and the nobleman made her think of her grandfather himself. The tribunal represented her super-ego, which was projected as a defence against inner guilt.

Another dream belonging to this period, but occurring later, may be cited to illustrate her exploitation of projection. In this dream the patient was visiting a college friend in prison. The friend was awaiting trial on an unspecified charge involving her brother as well as herself; and she was sitting in the prison cell on a kind of pedestal—a heroic figure, calm and majestic in demeanour. A small window behind her was so placed that the light entering the cell seemed to shed a halo round her head. The impression created by this figure upon the dreamer was that she had been imprisoned by puritanical authorities for some daring, but not unnatural action committed in conjunction with her brother. To the dreamer she seemed to be a martyr about to suffer for her boldness in defying narrow and out of date conventions held to be almost sacred by a community soaked in narrow superstition. There was the suggestion too that her martyrdom was to have widespread effects upon humanity. Analysis showed that the college friend stood for the dreamer herself, and that the accusation was a projection of her own oral-sadistic guilt in relation to her own brother. The theme was thus similar to that of the preceding dream; but in this case the patient's narcissism achieved a more grandiose expression. The Messianic colouring of the phantasy indicated an attempt to achieve omnipotence of the second order, viz. an omnipotence in which both her repressed sadistic wishes and the demands of her ego-ideal should attain simultaneous satisfaction. The obstacle to this achievement lay, of course, in the intensity of her unconscious guilt; and, as in the case of the earlier dream, the technique of projection was exploited to deal with this obstacle. In the later dream, however, a delusion of grandeur had largely supplanted the delusion of persecution displayed in the earlier dream. The patient's history during this stage of the analysis thus provides a remarkable illustration of the evolution of a paranoid state.

At the date of writing the paranoid phase appears to have passed off. The occurrence of the last-mentioned dream registered a crisis in which the patient was compelled to realize the fact that she had adopted delusional ideas as a defence against guilt. Her recognition of the presence of a delusional element in her mental attitude was only achieved in face of a tremendous resistance, which the technique of rationalization was mobilized to strengthen; but that considerable insight has been achieved would appear to be shown by the fact that her embarrassment with men has almost vanished. There are not wanting signs that the locus of her unconscious guilt is being transferred to the consulting-room, where, it may be hoped, it may be dealt with more in the open.

Before the present account is concluded, it seems important to draw attention to another remarkable feature of the case—viz. the tendency of the patient to personify various aspects of her psyche. This tendency first manifested itself in dreams; but it came to be quite consciously adopted by the patient during analysis. The most striking and the most persistent of these personifications were two figures whom she described respectively as 'the mischievous boy' and 'the critic'. The former figure (which appeared constantly in her dreams) was a pre-adolescent boy, completely irresponsible, and for ever playing pranks and poking fun. This boy was frequently represented as annoying the dreamer by his tricks, or as being chased by more sedate figures, whom he mocked as he escaped. With him were identified certain other similar figures, usually of a facetious nature, such as clowns and music-hall comedians. 'The mischievous boy' was regarded by the patient as representing her own childish self; and endless play seemed to constitute his sole object in life, as was actually the position in her own case during childhood. The selection of a boy to represent her childish self was undoubtedly dependent upon the boy's possession of the penis as a magic talisman calculated, in her eyes, to open all the gates of laughter and to convert life into an endless jollification. The behaviour of this dream-figure was highly suggestive of the behaviour of a mildly maniacal subject; and the patient recognized in retrospect that her behaviour during the initial period of elation was determined by the activity of 'the mischievous boy' in herself.

The personification which the patient described as 'the critic' was a figure of a very different character. 'The critic' was essentially a female figure. Occasionally, however, a headmaster under whom she had once worked or some other male figure of a similar character took over the role of 'critic' in her dreams. When a male figure played this part, he was invariably an authoritative father-figure whose good opinion she was anxious to secure. Nevertheless, 'the critic' was characteristically represented by a serious, formidable, puritanical and aggressive women of middle age. Sometimes this woman was a fanciful individual, who uttered public accusations against the dreamer; but more frequently she was represented by some actual female personage to whose authority the patient had been subject in the past, e.g. the matron of a students' hostel, or a senior teacher. At other times she was represented by the mother of a friend. Thus 'the critic' was characteristically a figure endowed with maternal authority; and not uncommonly the patient's own actual mother played the part without any disguise.

The two figures just described were regarded by the patient as fundamentally antagonistic; and it is interesting to note from their descriptions how closely 'the mischievous boy' and' the critic' correspond to the elements in the psyche described by Freud as 'the id' and 'the super-ego'. It should be added that there occurred dreams in which the 'I' of the dream was herself represented as playing the part of 'the mischievous boy,' and that there were also frequent teaching dreams, in which the 'I' of the dream always played the part of the 'critic'. Usually, however, the dreaming consciousness played the part of an independent onlooker, whose sympathies were sometimes on the one side, sometimes on the other. The dreams in which these personifications figured thus provided the scenes of a moving drama in which the leading actors played parts corresponding significantly to those ascribed by Freud to the ego, the id and the super-ego in the economy of the human mind.

The conformity between the three leading actors in this patient's dreams and Freud's tripartite division of the mind must be regarded as providing striking evidence of the practical validity of Freud's scheme. It must be recorded, however, that the dream-figures so far mentioned by no means exhaust the personifications appearing in this patient's dream life. Thus there eventually emerged another figure whom she came to describe as 'the little girl'. This little girl was depicted with remarkable constancy as of about five years of age. She was a charming little creature, full of the vivacity of childhood, but without the exasperating impishness of 'the mischievous boy'. This figure was interpreted by the patient as representing herself as she would fain have been in childhood—a natural, but innocent self, to whom no exception could have been taken on the part of the super-ego; and it is perhaps not without importance that a girl of the significant age of five or so should have been selected to play such a part. Another personification to make an entry during the third stage of analysis was the figure of 'the martyr' who appeared in dreams to which reference has already been made.

Here attention must be drawn to the fact that, although 'the little girl' and 'the martyr' played relatively subordinate roles, their validity as personifications seemed in no sense inferior to that of 'the critic' and 'the mischievous boy'. This fact raises the question whether Freud's tripartite division of the mind has not led us to regard the ego, the id and the super-ego too much in the light of entities. Such a tendency is an almost inevitable consequence of the topographical method of exposition adopted by Freud in his descrip-tion of the mental apparatus. His topographical description has, of course, provided us with an invaluable working hypothesis; but it is a question whether any topographical representation whatsoever can hope to do justice to all the complexities of mental structure, and whether, so far as psychological theory is concerned, such a mode of representation is not bound eventually to prove misleading. The data provided by the case under discussion seem to leave no doubt about the existence of functioning structural units corresponding to the ego, the id and the super-ego; but the same data seem equally to indicate the impossibility of regarding these functioning structural units as *mental entities*. After all, the general tendency of modern science is to throw suspicion upon entities; and it was under the influence of this tendency that the old 'faculty psychology' perished. Perhaps the arrangement of mental phenomena into functioning structural groups is the most that can be attempted by psychological science. At any rate, it would appear contrary to the spirit of modern science to confer the status of entity upon 'instincts'; and in the light of modern knowledge an instinct seems best regarded as a characteristic dynamic pattern of behaviour. Similar considerations apply to Freud's tripartite division of the mind—which must accordingly be taken to represent a characteristic functional grouping of structural elements in the psyche. That the ego, the id and the super-ego do represent characteristic functioning structural units seems to be indi-cated by the facts of the case before us; but the facts of the case also indicate the possibility of other functioning structural units arising.

Whilst the study of the personifications appearing in this patient's dreams would seem to indicate the undesirability of regarding the mind as composed of separate entities, it would also seem to throw some light upon the phenomenon of multiple personality. The characteristic personifications which have been described all presented the appearance of separate personalities; and this fact suggests the possibility that multiple personality may be merely an advanced product of the same processes that created such personifications in the present case. In *The Ego and the Id* Freud has given expression to the view that multiple personality may have its origin in the various identifications of the ego. The appearance of 'the critic' as a characteristic personification in the dream life of the patient under discussion provides evidence in favour of this possibility; for the figure of 'the critic' is obviously based for the most part upon an identification with the dreamer's mother. The other figures do not, however, seem capable of being explained in a similar way. As a whole, the personifications seem best interpreted as functioning structural units which, for economic reasons, attained a certain independence within the total personality; and it seems reasonable to suppose that the mental processes which give rise to multiple personality only represent a more extreme form of those which produced 'the mischievous boy', 'the critic', 'the little girl' and 'the martyr' in this patient's dreams. Although in her particular case these personifications were confined, in large measure, to the realm of the unconscious as revealed in dreams, there is no reason why in more extreme cases similar personifications should not invade the conscious field in waking life. Indeed, even in her case such invasion of waking life by personifications did actually occur. Thus in the prolonged phase of elation at the outset of her analysis 'the mischievous boy' took almost complete possession of her conscious life; and, on looking back upon this phase, she later volunteered the statement that for the time being she was a totally different person.

In the light of what precedes it would thus appear that the personifications represented in this patient's dreams have something in common, not only with the mental structures described by Freud, but also with the phenomena of multiple personality; and it would also appear that multiple personality is ultimately a product of the same processes of differentiation which lead to the isolation of the ego, the id and the super-ego. Evidence of the differentiation of these structures is found so consistently in analytical work that their presence must be regarded, not only as characteristic, but as compatible with normality. It must be recognized, however, that the differentiation of the id and the super-ego from the ego achieves its maximum expression in abnormal individuals; and the question arises how far these structures would be capable of isolation at all in the theoretical case of a completely integrated personality, whose development had proceeded without any hitch. The facts of the case before us would suggest that phenomena of the nature of multiple personality may sometimes be produced by temporary invasion of the conscious field on the part of the 'super-ego' or 'the id'; but it would equally appear that independent formations may become differentiated in the unconscious, having boundaries which do not conform to those implied in Freud's tripartite division of the mind, and that such independent formations may also invade consciousness in cases of multiple personality. The facts of the present case likewise suggest the possibility that manic states are due to invasion of the conscious field by a formation of the nature of the id. If this be so, mania would then appear to have something in common with multiple personality; but in the case of melancholia the facts are too complex to allow us to regard it as a simple invasion of the conscious field by the super-ego.

The present account may now be concluded with a summary of the chief points of interest in the case which has been described:

(1) Obviously the chief interest of the case lies in the fact that the patient was a woman with a physical genital abnormality apparently involving at least the absence of the vagina and uterus. The presence of an accompanying endocrine disturbance, of which there was evidence, but which, for reasons of discretion, has not been described, would naturally tempt the more pedestrian medical mind to hold this responsible for her nervous symptoms; but the improbability of such an interpretation is shown by the fact that those of her sisters who suffered from an identical abnormality were relatively free of psychopathological disturbance. Moreover, the psychoanalytical treatment of this patient has revealed data indicating that, even in such a case, the development of nervous symptoms can be satisfactorily explained in terms of psychoanalytical concepts. In the case of this particular patient it appears beyond question that her physical abnormality was only implicated in so far as its presence constituted a psychical trauma for her, and in so far as it necessarily precluded the possibility of a normal sexual life.

(2) It is of interest to note the extent to which the absence of a vagina in the case of this woman was accompanied by an over-estimation of the clitoris in her unconscious. The equivalence of the clitoris and the penis in her unconscious is also a matter of interest, confirming as it does that the clitoris is not only the physical, but also the psychical homologue of the penis. In view of the nature of her physical defect it might have been expected that the vagina rather than the penis would have been the object of unconscious envy; but in actual fact penis-envy would appear to have been promoted, rather than otherwise, by the absence of a vagina. It may, accordingly, be inferred that, where a physically normal woman is concerned, the

position is that repression of female sexuality is a prerequisite of penis-envy, rather than that penis-envy is a primary phenomenon favouring repression of female sexuality. If this inference is correct, the classic concept of 'the female castration complex' would appear to be in need of revision.

(3) The case is unusual in view of the frequency and short duration of the patient's phases of depression and elation, also in view of the appearance and disappearance of some of these phases during the course of an analytical session. These features made it possible to study the manic-depressive processes, as it were, under a microscope.

(4) The third stage of the patient's analysis provided an excellent epitome of the evolution of a paranoid state.

(5) It was a highly significant feature of the analysis of this patient that the resistance offered to the emergence of guilt over her repressed oral-sadistic wishes far exceeded that offered to the emergence of the repressed wishes themselves. This fact strongly suggests that the super-ego itself is subject to repression on the part of the ego, and that in certain cases it may be subject to a greater measure of repression than the libidinal components which are ordinarily described as 'the repressed'.

(6) The analysis of this case revealed in a striking fashion the extent to which the structure of the super-ego is built up in layers corresponding to stages in libidinal development. It also revealed that the nucleus of the super-ego is pregenital in origin, belongs to an oral level and must therefore become established during the oral stage.

(7) The case provided data indicating the existence of two orders of omnipotence—(a) the omnipotence of primitive libidinal aims, and (b) omnipotence achieved through 'sublimated activities' which provide simultaneous satisfaction for both primitive libidinal aims and the aims of the super-ego.

(8) The reaction of the patient in question to the death of her brother during the course of analysis was particularly significant in view of the sadistic dream which so shortly preceded the event. Its special interest lies in the fact that it provided experimental evidence in support of inferences based on purely psychoanalytical considerations.

(9) The appearance of stable personifications in the patient's dreams seems to indicate the manner in which the phenomena of multiple personality originate. It suggests that these phenomena result from the invasion of the conscious field by functioning struc-

tural constellations which become differentiated in the unconscious under pressure of economic necessity. It also suggests that Freud's tripartite division of the mind should be regarded as representing a description of characteristic structural constellations of a similar nature rather than as representing an analysis of the mind into component entities.

CHAPTER III

The Effect of a King's Death Upon Patients Undergoing Analysis[1] (1936)

O N the occasion of the recent death of King George V (January 20, 1936), I could not help being impressed by the effect which this event seemed to produce upon three of my patients undergoing analysis at the time. Whilst it is always informative to study the reactions of analytical patients to current events, the reactions of a group of patients to the same event are of particular interest—especially when the event in question is so significant and, at the same time, so infrequent as the death of a king. In the present instance, therefore, it seems worth placing on record the reactions of the three patients to whom I have referred. The patients in question were all characterized by a pronounced strain of oral sadism and a marked tendency to oral incorporation; and this fact would appear to have been in large measure responsible for the extreme nature of their reactions to the King's death.

One of the patients was a youth of eighteen, who was sent to me for analysis from a mental hospital about four months before King George V died. He had been an only child most of his life—before the birth of a brother six years younger than himself and after the death of this brother six years later. His chief symptoms were: (1) Inability to tolerate separation from his mother without intense anxiety; (2) A hypochrondriacal preoccupation with the idea that his heart was diseased; (3) Recurring attacks of violent palpitation accompanied by an overwhelming fear of death.

While the clinical picture was thus dominated by anxiety symptoms, the general demeanour of the patient was nevertheless sug-

[1] Read before the British Psycho-Analytical Society on 19th February 1936, and subsequently published in *The International Journal of Psycho-Analysis* Vol. XVII, Pt. 3.

gestive of a schizoid background. After analysis began, it very soon became apparent that the youth's reluctance to be parted from his mother was largely due to the need for constant reassurance that his mother had not been destroyed by his oral sadism. On the other hand, his cardiac anxiety resolved itself into anxiety lest his internalized mother, upon whom he had projected a considerable charge of oral sadism, should kill him by gnawing away his heart. This fact was well illustrated by a dream in which he saw his heart lying on a plate, and his mother in the act of lifting it with a spoon. During the course of four months' analysis previous to the King's death, his symptoms became mitigated to a very marked degree. When, however, disquieting bulletins regarding the state of the King's heart began to be issued, there was a marked exacerbation of his symptoms. Every time the wireless was turned on, he went into a panic; his sleep became disturbed; and he began to ring me up on the telephone at all hours in the hope of obtaining reassurance. The patient learned of the King's death on the morning after its occurrence; and during the following night he dreamed that he had shot a man representing his father. The dream pictured him as being in a room with his mother, to whom he explained that his reason for shooting the man was not dislike, but a fear for his own life. He also explained that in taking the man's life he had taken his own, and that he expected to be sent to prison for six years. Next, a young woman appeared; and he then felt that this woman was the person whom he had killed. His mother now left the room; and, as she left, he heard shouts from an adjoining room. These shouts seemed to come from the person whom he had killed; but this person now seemed to be his brother (whose actual death had been a burden upon his conscience for six years—the term of his prospective 'imprisonment' in the dream). Since 'the young woman' turned out to symbolize his mother as a sexual object, the dream represented a wholesale destruction of the entire family; and the fact that this dream was followed by another dream, in which his mother warned him against eating a jelly at the bottom of a staircase upon which she herself stood, shows that the act of destruction was really an act of oral-sadistic incorporation—an act, moreover, involving mortal danger to the patient himself. The anxiety symptoms precipitated by the King's death would thus appear to have been mainly due to the dangerous qualities with which the patient had endowed the internalized object.

The second patient was an unmarried man of thirty-one, who had been undergoing analysis for rather more than two and a half years, when the King's death occurred. The symptom which drove him to seek analytical aid in the first instance was an incessant desire to urinate, which was so compelling as to monopolize his whole waking life. He had, however, lived a semi-invalid existence ever since the age of five, when he had nearly died of an empyema. Until the onset of his urinary symptoms his life had been largely dominated by anxiety regarding his chest. This anxiety recurred during the course of analysis after his urinary symptoms had abated. Since he was also subject to a fear of food poisoning, it was not surprising to find that, as analysis proceeded, an intense strain of oral sadism became manifest. The emergence of this oral sadism was accompanied by gastric symptoms, which replaced a more or less constant sense of congestion in the chest. In due course the gastric symptoms disappeared; but shortly before the King's death he had become preoccupied with his throat on the basis of a mild tonsillar infection. The King's death had a very depressing effect upon him, reminding him very strongly, as it did, of his own father's death; and he became irritated by the prominence given to the event in the press and on the wireless. His usual interests flagged, his customary concern over his health was intensified and he became subject to a sense of congestion throughout the body from the waist upwards. Above all he became extremely apprehensive about his own safety. He felt as if a war were being waged inside him and sensed the presence of some antagonistic and dangerous force at work within his body. In the light of data which had already emerged during analysis, it was evident that the war inside him was a war between his own oral-sadistic ego and an internalized father-figure, whom he had endowed with oral-sadistic attributes. The King's death represented a consummation of his oral-sadistic designs against his father, whose incorporation became responsible for his sense of a destructive force within.

This patient's immediate reaction to the King's death had an interesting sequel a fortnight later, when he had a dream about 'the King's cigars'. The dream opened with his discovering that his car had been stolen. After telephoning to the police, he found that his father (who was actually dead) had returned from a long voyage. He was overjoyed by this event and promptly entertained his father to a sumptuous dinner. Suddenly the thief turned up with the car; and the patient rushed in fury at his throat. Subsequently he saw an advertisement offering the King's cigars for sale at £147 each.

This dream, of course, introduces the theme of 'the restitution of the object'. It depicts a restitution of the patient's father, whose death had been a gratification to his oral sadism; and it is significant that he celebrates the occasion by a sumptuous meal. The advertisement of the King's cigars, moreover, is tantamount to a restitution of his father's penis as an object of oral gratification.

The theme of restitution reappeared two nights later in a dream in which the patient seemed to be swimming with King George V in a flooded area outside Buckingham Palace. The King kept putting his head under water and was eventually drowned, in spite of the patient's efforts to save him. In the next scene a number of trunks were being removed from a state coach by policemen, whose demeanour was such as to befit both a funeral and a court of justice. The patient then found himself in a luxurious Pullman coach with the King, whose apparent restoration to life and health filled him with a sense of intense relief.

The restoration of the King in this dream corresponds, of course, to the restoration of the patient's father in the previous dream; but in this instance, it will be noted, the death of the father-figure is ascribed to the effects of a flood—a fact which recalls the patient's original symptom of incessant urination. Having restored the object destroyed by his oral sadism in the first dream, he proceeds in the second dream to restore the object destroyed by his urinary sadism.

The third case is that of a patient about whom I read a paper before the British Psycho-Analytical Society on 21st January, 1931[1], and who is still undergoing analysis at the date of writing (1936). This patient is presumed to be a woman, although the presence of a genital defect raises some uncertainty regarding the sex to which she really belongs. Her age is now fifty; and she is in the ninth year of analysis. A teacher by profession, she had to abandon her calling owing to termly breakdowns characterized by anxiety, depression and suicidal thoughts. The prolongation of her analysis has been due largely to uncertainty regarding her true sex, but also in some measure to the fact that, after an initial manic phase, she began to exploit the mechanism of projection and to substitute paranoid ideas of self-reference in the presence of men for manic-depressive symptoms. Occasional attacks of depression were interpolated, however, from time to time; and during these attacks the paranoid symptoms subsided. During the eighth

[1] This paper is included in the present volume under the title of 'Features in the Analysis of a Patient with a Physical Genital Abnormality'.

year of analysis the activity of the projection mechanism became considerably reduced, with the result that the foreground of the clinical picture became occupied by occasional attacks of mild depression. The disappearance of paranoid symptoms had followed the analysis of very deeply repressed anal-sadistic tendencies; but, in proportion as the projection mechanism weakened, a more basic oral sadism revealed itself as the source from which the attacks of depression arose. It now became possible to establish that these attacks of depression were in all cases precipitated by actual incidents, often of a trivial character; and the King's death provided the occasion of one such attack.

Just before the patient retired to bed on January 20 (the night of the King's death), she heard a wireless bulletin to the effect that he was sinking fast. She did not actually learn of his death until the next morning; but during the night she dreamed, significantly enough, that her own father was dead. Throughout the day of January 21 she felt extremely disturbed and terribly cross. She missed her appointment with me; but her excuse had a reality basis; and she kept her appointment on the following day (January 22). She was then still in a very disturbed state of mind; and from this fact she herself inferred that she must be holding herself responsible for the King's death. On 23rd January she awoke feeling extremely depressed; but her depression vanished mysteriously at 11.30 a.m. Meanwhile, on the night of 21-22nd January she had had a series of distressing dreams, which provided a considerable amount of analytical material.

From this series of dreams the following features may be selected for notice: The first dream consisted almost exclusively in hideous and terrifying affect without specific content. The dreamer just felt possessed by terror, misery and despair. She seemed to be groping about in the dark; but what concerned her was the state of her mind; for she felt utterly and hopelessly mad. She then had a dream in which she was gradually turning cold from the feet up, and felt that, when she became cold through and through, she would be absolutely finished. Later she dreamed that she was living in a beautiful little house of her own, where everything was perfect. She entered one of the rooms with her mother to demonstrate its perfection; but to her horror she saw two enormous weeds growing through a lovely crimson carpet on the floor. She immediately stooped down to tear up the weeds, remarking how difficult they were to eradicate. Her house now seemed to be in a public park; and she was sitting beside the house on a box containing an animal. A woman entered the park with a dog, whereupon a cry arose, 'Put out that dog.' An attempt was made to catch it; but it made its escape in a state of intense excitement and ferocity. The dreamer then heard snarling sounds behind her and realized to her horror that the dog was trying to get at the animal in the box and worry it to death. This thought made her extremely apprehensive regarding her own safety. Later she heard a knock at the door of her house and, on rushing to open it, discovered two policemen standing in the rain and darkness outside. She invited them to come in; and they helped her to light the hanging lamp in the hall. She then noticed that the light was red—red for danger. She became extremely alarmed about this visitation and anxiously debated why it was to her door in particular that it had come. The two policemen then turned into three women, who began to explain the nature of their visit. For a long time she could not understand what they said; but eventually she made out that some dreadful disaster had befallen a man named 'David Little'. She awoke wondering who 'David Little' was, and what he had to do with her.

'David', of course, is the name by which the new King (King Edward VIII) is known in the royal family circle. 'David Little' is 'Little David'; and the disaster which had befallen 'Little David' is his royal father's death. The visitation of the patient's house by superego figures in connection with this disaster implies that it is she herself who has killed the King—an act of patricide, which she disowns in the dream on the grounds that she is ignorant of 'David Little's' identity. The oral-sadistic nature of her crime is represented in the scene in which the ferocious dog is seeking to worry the animal in the box. By sitting on the lid of the box, she is, of course, protecting her internalized father from her oral-sadistic libido at the risk of her own life; but it might be a more accurate description of the situation to say that she is internalizing her father in order to save him as a real person from her oral sadism—which then becomes a menace to her own ego. The theme of internalizing the libidinal object in order to save the real person from being destroyed by oral-sadistic impulses had already emerged in this patient's analysis. One day not so long before the King's death she experienced intense feelings of annoyance with her father for sitting in a chair which she herself desired to occupy. She stifled her anger at the time; but the result was an attack of depression. On several previous occasions too an attack of depression followed the stifling of feelings of resentment towards me. In all such instances

228

the attack of depression was a substitute for an open display of resentment; and the aim of internalizing the object was to save the real person from destruction at the price of exposing her ego to the full fury of the sadism released by frustration. The internalization of the object resulting from the King's death falls into rather a different category. It falls into the same category as that which had already occurred on several previous occasions during this patient's analysis: e.g. when her brother was killed by a motor car, when her father was seriously injured in a motor accident, when on two occasions I had a sudden illness, and when one day she saw the daughter of her old schoolmaster dressed in black and presumed (wrongly as it happened) that he was dead. On each of these occasions an attack of depression ensued; but in such instances the onset of depression was promoted not by frustration, but by an unexpected gratification of repressed sadistic wishes—as may be illustrated by the fact that, when the patient's brother was killed, a short phase of elation preceded the inevitable attack of depression. The internalization of the object characterizing this class of depressive attack cannot, therefore, have as its aim the safeguarding of the external object. In such instances the damage has already been done before the defence of internalization is called into action. Under such circumstances the aim of internalization must be to absorb the flood of sadism released, so to speak, 'by the smell of blood'. Perhaps, however, the truth lies in Melanie Klein's statement[1] that every experience which suggests the loss of the real loved object stimulates the dread of losing the internalized object too.

[1] *International Journal of Psycho-Analysis*, vol. XVI., Pt. 2, p. 150.

PART THREE

Miscellaneous Papers

CHAPTER I

The Sociological Significance of Communism Considered in the Light of Psychoanalysis[1] (1935)

PERHAPS the most significant of the later developments in psychoanalytical thought is to be found in the extension of psychoanalytical modes of interpretation to the field of sociological study. So far as its historical origin is concerned, this development dates from the publication in 1913 of Freud's *Totem and Taboo*. It was, however, only after the appearance of Freud's *Group Psychology and the Analysis of The Ego* in 1921 and his *The Ego and The Id* in 1923 that the psychoanalyst came into possession of explanatory principles which enabled him to do justice to that complex mass of phenomena which constitutes the material of sociology. The two most outstanding contributions to existing knowledge made by Freud in these latter works were: (1) his demonstration of the part played by aggression no less than libido within the economy of the individual mind and consequently in social life generally; (2) his demonstration of the influence upon human conduct of unconsciously accepted ideals, which have their origin in the reactions of the individual to his first social contacts, and which, during individual development, become organized into an internal psychical structure (the 'ego ideal' or 'super-ego') representing external social agencies. The development of psychoanalytical theory resulting from these discoveries has placed in the hands of the psychoanalyst a body of explanatory principles, in the light of which he feels justified in attempting to interpret sociological no less than psychological pheno-

[1] Based on a paper read at a meeting of the Scottish Branch of the British Psychological Society on 1st December 1934, and subsequently published in *The British Journal of Medical Psychology*, Vol. XV, Pt. 3. A lecture of a similar nature entitled 'Communism as an Anthropological Phenomenon' was delivered to the Scottish Anthropological Society on 1st December 1936, and published in the *Edinburgh Medical Journal*, Vol. XLIV, pp. 433-45 (1937).

mena. In consequence, sociological problems are exercising an increasing attraction for contemporary psychoanalytical thought. It is surprising, therefore, that hitherto there has been so comparatively little inclination on the part of psychoanalysts to attempt to interpret the significance of what is undoubtedly the most important sociological development of recent times, viz. the establishment of a Communistic society in Soviet Russia. In what follows the results of psychoanalytical research will be taken into account in an attempt to estimate the sociological significance of Communism.

At the outset it is necessary to anticipate the objection that Communism is essentially an economic system, and that therefore it does not constitute a proper subject for psychoanalytical (or indeed for any form of psychological) interpretation at all. This objection is not calculated to impress the psychoanalyst, since one of the conclusions to which psychoanalytical research leads is precisely that economic factors as such exercise much less influence upon human motivation than is usually supposed by those brought up in the atmosphere of Western civilization. A general survey of the conditions prevailing among primitive communities should be sufficient to convince the impartial observer that human beings are content to acquiesce in extremely low economic standards so long as they are emotionally satisfied in other directions. Confining our attention to Russia itself, we cannot help observing that the establishment of Communism was followed by a lowering of economic standards, which appears to have had the effect of intensifying rather than diminishing enthusiasm for Communist ideals. These ideals, as expounded in Communist propaganda no less than in the Hegelian writings of Lenin, are of such a nature as to indicate clearly that Communism is a philosophy and a religion rather than an economic theory. In general, a study of all great historical movements supplies us with good grounds for believing that it is only when economic factors become harnessed to motives of a different origin that they become socially and historically significant. While, therefore, it would be idle to deny the existence of an economic factor in human motivation, the present paper is concerned exclusively with the *non-economic* motives which lie behind the Communist movement. At the same time it is claimed that, while the economic motives of the movement are the more obvious, the non-economic motives are sociologically the more significant.

It will doubtless be anticipated of any attempt to interpret Communism in the light of psychoanalysis that it will be framed in terms of two familiar concepts: (1) the libido theory, and (2) the concept of the Œdipus situation. While these two concepts by no means exhaust the resources of psychoanalytical interpretation, yet this anticipation will, in general, prove justified so far as the present attempt is concerned. It must be added, however, that both concepts will be understood in the light of Freud's classic theory that the dynamics of human behaviour are constituted by an interplay between libido and aggression. It is implied in this theory that the conflict involved in the Œdipus situation is a characteristic expression of just such an interplay.

In the light of the libido theory thus understood, all sociological developments must be regarded as governed by two fundamental principles:

(1) The cohesion of social groups is a function of libido. It is libido which binds members of a group together; and the cohesion of any given group depends upon the extent to which libido is bound within the group. It is in the light of this principle that we must interpret what may perhaps pardonably be described as 'the Aryan heresy' fostered in Nazi Germany—the great function of this heresy being to bind the libido of the German people within national limits, while directing aggression towards a group arbitrarily described as outside the nation (viz. members of the Jewish race).

(2) The source of social disintegration in all groups is to be found in aggression. It is to the aggression of the individual that we must look for the source of the disruptive forces found in all societies. It is for this reason that the rulers of Nazi Germany took pains to direct the aggression of the nationals against a group declared to be extra-national.

Applying these two principles to the data provided by anthropological research, let us now proceed to review the historical evolution of social groups. For it is only in the light of such a developmental approach that we can hope to appreciate the real significance of the new social order represented by Communism.

(1) *The Family* is the original social group. In conformity with the general principles just enunciated, the cohesion of the family as a group depends upon two factors: (a) upon libido being bound within the family, (b) upon aggression being excluded from family relationships. The great significance of the Œdipus situation lies in the fact that it is the chief source of rivalry within the family circle, and there-

fore the chief portal whereby the disruptive factor of aggression is introduced into the group—although, of course, disruptive forces so introduced are powerfully reinforced by the rivalry of children with one another for parental affection. The significance of the Œdipus situation as a source of social disintegration is reflected in the fact that in primitive patriarchal societies the two great crimes are incest and patricide. Hence arise the stringent taboos placed upon these crimes in primitive societies—taboos which, as psychoanalysis has shown, operate with undiminished intensity in the unconscious of the civilized individual. The taboos upon incest and patricide are undoubtedly the cultural mainstay of the family group and consequently the foundation upon which all the higher forms of social organization and culture rest. They are the first line of defence erected by the family group against the disruptive forces of aggression. The group's second line of defence is the practice of exogamy, in accordance with which marriage within the group is forbidden to the younger generation. The practice of exogamy, however, must be regarded as the chief factor in promoting the union of family groups in a new and more comprehensive social grouping.

(2) *The Clan* is the next social group in the evolutionary series. Though the clan embraces a number of families, it is itself organized as a family group. It is characteristically ruled over by a chief, who represents the father of the clan, and to whom all members of the clan owe the allegiance of children to their father. The social cohesion of the clan is threatened by two dangers of an opposite kind: (*a*) the danger of the individual's libido being too much bound within the narrow limits of the family, (*b*) the danger of the individual's libido finding attachment outside the clan. Either of these eventualities would involve a loss of the binding power of libido to the clan as such. The latter eventuality is combatted by means of religious sanctions such as those involved in totemism and ancestor worship. The former danger (that of libido being bound too narrowly within the family) is guarded against by a reinforcement of the already existing incest taboo. The practice of exogamy, which, as we have seen, was the second line of defence of the family group, is also necessarily carried over into the clan system; for, since the clan is organized as a family, marriage within the clan involves technical incest. The extension of exogamy to the clan carries with it, however, the risk of the individual's libido finding attachment outside the group; and we seem justified in assuming that, just as the practice of exogamy led to

the supersession of the family by the clan, so it led in turn to the supersession of the clan by the tribe, which is the next social grouping in the evolutionary series.

(3) *The Tribe* consists characteristically of a union of clans. Like the clan, it is organized after the family model, being ruled over by a paramount chief (or, in highly organized tribes, by a king), whose authority is supported by religious sanctions. Exogamy is practised between the component clans; and in this way technical incest is avoided, while the necessity for marriage outside the tribe can be dispensed with. By means of this device, the tribe is enabled actually to discourage marriage outside the group and so to bind the individual's libido within itself in a way which was impossible under the family and the clan systems. The result is that the tribe has proved a singularly stable form of social organization.

(4) *The Nation* evolved out of the tribe through a weakening of the influence of the clans comprised in the tribal organization. This weakening of the clan influence within the tribe may be interpreted as due to the success achieved by the tribe in binding the libido of the individual to itself as a social group—a process aided by the establishment of tribal religious cults. The social cohesion of the tribe favours expansion at the expense of less stable communities, promotes the free circulation of an increased population within the tribal area, and tends to enhance the territorial tie at the expense of affiliation by blood. These changes undermine the practice of inter-clan exogamy both by rendering it increasingly difficult to observe and by removing its rationale. The clan thus loses its significance as a unit in the social structure; and the disappearance of the clan within the tribe converts the tribe into a nation. Throughout the whole civilized world of today the nation has supplanted the tribe as a social organization. So far as Great Britain is concerned, the rebellions of 1715 and 1745 were 'the last kick' of the tribal system, although the ghost of the tribe still haunts the annual meetings of 'The Macrae Society' and similar bodies.

Although the emergence of the nation as a social group involves the complete disappearance of the clan and the tribe, it is to be noted that the family as a social group has hitherto resisted extinction during the course of social evolution. The persistence of the kingship in certain civilized countries (including Great Britain) is evidence of the imprint left by the patriarchal family system upon national organization; but still more significant is the persistence of the family itself.

The survival of the family as a social institution shows that the nation has failed to eradicate the family group as it eradicated the clan and the tribe, and has been compelled to make terms with the family by incorporating it into the national organization. Even this task has only been achieved at the expense of significant compromises, as is exemplified by the fact that the years of early childhood have tended to remain almost exclusively within the province of the family. It must be recognized, however, that in recent years the civilized state has made considerable encroachments upon this province. Nevertheless, these encroachments have only been effected in the face of considerable resistance on the part of the family. In spite of all the compromises wrung from both sides, an intense conflict still persists between the family and the state. The extent of this conflict is liable to be obscured by the fact that it is so largely a hidden or, more strictly speaking, *repressed* conflict. According to psychoanalytical findings, of course, a conflict arising out of the Œdipus situation characteristically plays a major role in the genesis of all psychopathological symptoms. It is less generally recognized, however, that the persistence of the Œdipus conflict in the unconscious of the adult involves the presence of two more specific conflicts:

(1) The Œdipus conflict proper, i.e. a conflict arising strictly within the limits of the family system in the years of early childhood, during which the child's social horizon does not extend beyond the family circle.

(2) A conflict arising out of the fact that intra-familial and extra-familial objects compete for the libido of the individual—a conflict arising characteristically during the adolescent period.

It should be noted that, while both these conflicts involve the question of loyalty to the patriarchal father, the latter represents the counterpart in the individual of the sociological conflict, to which reference has just been made, between the family system and more comprehensive social organizations such as the nation.

Inadequate as our review of the evolution of social groups has been, it should serve to indicate the general tendency characterizing this evolutionary process, viz. the tendency for the individual's libido to become increasingly expansive, and for the group to become correspondingly more comprehensive. In the light of this tendency we cannot fail to be impressed by the fact that Communism represents a social system even more comprehensive than the nation. It is true that the Communist régime established in Russia in 1917 still remains at the time of writing (1934) confined within national limits;[1] but the Communist objective was from the first avowedly 'international', although this fact later became obscured by the opportunist policy of Stalin. In reality, the Communist movement is, properly speaking, a *supra-national* movement; for its aims transcend all national boundaries. The sociological significance of Communism now becomes obvious. In the course of social evolution the family, which constituted the original social group, yielded place to the clan, the clan to the tribe, and the tribe to the nation. The rise of Communism as a supra-national movement can thus only represent the beginning of a further evolutionary movement in the direction of the emergence of a world state, which shall supersede the nation as a social group, and to which each individual shall owe unreserved allegiance. If this goal is attained, the individual's libido, which was originally bound within the family, and which later became extended by successive stages to the clan, the tribe and the nation, will eventually be weaned from its national loyalty and become invested in a world state embracing humanity at large.

Even if we assume the correctness of the conclusion just reached, we shall still fail to appreciate the full significance of Communism until we realize that the fulfilment of its universal aims involves the elimination not only of the nation, but also of the family group, which the nation has so far failed to destroy. It is implicit in the Communist philosophy (even when, as in Soviet Russia, its concrete embodiment is disguised by inevitable compromise) that children are to be regarded as belonging, not to the family, but to the Communist state. It is to this fact, rather than to any ostensible economic or political considerations, that we must look for the real explanation of the Communist's hatred of the bourgeoisie; for the bourgeoisie is essentially a stronghold of the family system. The Soviet persecution of the Kulaks, or peasant proprietors, may be similarly explained; for the fact that the Kulaks produced primarily for their own families, and not for the state, constituted them natural enemies of the Communist régime. Even the Soviet drive against capitalism, which appears *prima facie* to be nothing more than an energetic protest

---

[1] Communist régimes have, of course, subsequently been established not only in all the countries of Eastern Europe, but also in the vast territory of China; and the characteristic status of these countries is now that of satellite states of Soviet Russia. However, the effect of such recent developments is only to confirm the argument here presented.

against the exploitation of man by man, would appear to be dictated to some extent by a deep animus against the family system. It must be remembered that the fruits of capitalism are enjoyed less by the capitalist himself than by the members of his family, who not only share his income, but also inherit his wealth. In destroying capitalism, therefore, Communism is really striking a vital blow at the family system.

It is perhaps not wholly superfluous to remark at this point that, in speaking of the aims of Communism, I refer not to the conscious and avowed policy of Communist leaders so much as to the deep, and for the most part *unconscious*, motivation of the Communist movement. The psychoanalyst, whose work familiarizes him with the profound influence of unconscious motivation in the individual mind, will, of course, find little difficulty in appreciating the influence of unconscious motivation in the sociological field. But, psychoanalysis apart, it can hardly be disputed that evolutionary processes occur for the most part independently of conscious direction on the part of the organisms concerned. This holds true even so far as the evolution of human society is concerned. Although we have reason to believe that the means adopted by the evolutionary process to achieve its aims become progressively more conscious as evolution proceeds, yet we must also believe that the direction of the process itself is determined by biological aims which are essentially unconscious. There is, therefore, no reason to suppose that the Communist movement is any more exempt from the influence of unconscious motivation than were the earlier movements which led to the establishment of the family, the clan, the tribe and the nation.

Since it is with the unconscious aims of Communism that we are at present particularly concerned, our conclusions regarding the hostility of Communism to the family group remain unaffected by any criticism based upon the conscious policy of the Communist leaders. There are good grounds for believing that it was no part of Lenin's conscious policy to destroy family life; and it must be recognized that a number of measures have been adopted in Soviet Russia to protect the family from disintegration under the Soviet régime. Recognition of such facts is, however, in no sense incompatible with the view that Communism as a social system is inherently hostile to the institution of the family. Since we have already had occasion to note the persistence of a hidden conflict between the family and the nation, there is every reason to anticipate a similar conflict between the family and the Communist state. The concessions made to the family under the Communist régime must, therefore, be regarded as of a similar character to those secured by the family from the nation. There can be no doubt, however, that the position of the family under Communism is much more precarious than its position within the nation, and that actually under the Soviet régime family life is confined within the narrowest limits. This fact is presumably due in large measure to the universal character of the Communist ideal, which admits no loyalties whatever except loyalty to the world state. The national ideal, on the contrary, necessarily involves the recognition by the nation of other national groups; and the dangers arising out of international rivalry make it inevitable that the nation should make terms with the family in the interests of internal security. It is thus no coincidence that, in recent times, an intensive cult of the family should have been such a distinctive feature of the proverbially nationalist régimes of Nazi Germany and Fascist Italy. No similar stimulus to compromise with the family would operate in the case of the world state envisaged by Communism. In so far, however, as Communism remains confined within national boundaries, the Communist state will necessarily remain subject to national necessities; and this fact, together with the natural resistance of the family group to extinction, must be regarded as accounting for many of the concessions accorded to the family under the Soviet régime. The existence of such concessions is thus in no sense incompatible with the view that hostility to the institution of the family is implicit in Communism as such. We, therefore, seem justified in our conclusion that the Communist goal of a world state, to which each individual shall be libidinally bound, involves among its subsidiary aims not only the disintegration of the nation but also the disintegration of the family group.

The essential antagonism of Communism to the family system (which we have seen to be implicit, where not explicit) may serve to remind us that all sociological problems are ultimately reducible to problems of individual psychology. There are many psychologists, of course, who would prefer to speak of 'group psychology' in this connection; but, unless, with Lévy-Bruhl, we assume the existence of mental processes in groups considered apart from the individuals who compose them, 'group psychology' must be regarded as essentially the psychology of the individual *in a group*. In his work *Group Psychology and the Analysis of the Ego* (1921) Freud points out conclusively that the very existence of a group depends upon the existence of libidinal ties which are necessarily functions of individual libido. Consequently, when the individuals composing a group simultaneously withdraw their libido from it (as occurs when panic overtakes an army in the field), the group ceases to exist; and it is then a case of 'every man for himself'. Freud also points out that the family is the group within which libidinal ties are first established. It is to this fact that he attributes the need for a leader, which is such a marked feature of all stable groups. The significance of the leader lies in the fact that he represents a common ego-ideal for the individuals composing the group; and the origin of the ego-ideal can be traced to the introjection by the child of figures of his parents during early childhood. It thus becomes obvious that the Œdipus situation must exercise a profound influence upon all sociological developments. These considerations would seem to have a bearing on the antagonism of Communism to the family group. They would seem to justify us in seeking an interpretation of this antagonism in terms of the psychology of the individual; and, within this field, they would also seem to justify us in looking to the Œdipus situation for a clue. This being so, it seems legitimate to surmise that the (implicit, where not explicit) attack of Communism upon the family system involves a drastic (if unconscious) attempt to deal with the Œdipus conflict by abolishing the Œdipus situation, out of which this conflict arises. Since the Œdipus situation is inherent in the family system, the only means of eradicating the Œdipus conflict in the individual mind lies in the elimination of the family as a social group. The appeal of Communism to the individual may, therefore, be regarded as depending in no small measure upon the fact that the achievement of its goal would remove the *raison d'être* of those taboos upon incest and patricide which maintain the Œdipus conflict in a state of repression in the unconscious, and which impose such extensive restrictions upon the free disposal of the individual's libido.

The present thesis is now complete; but it is perhaps pardonable to raise one further question—a question which, from the practical point of view, is perhaps the most vital of all, although, strictly speaking, it lies outside the province of the psychologist. What follows is only justified on the assumption that the psychologist is also a human being with a partiality for prophecy and a natural curiosity regarding what the future holds in store. On this assumption and on the further assumption that the present interpretation of Communism as a phenomenon in the evolution of social groups is correct, it is interesting to speculate how far Communism is likely to succeed in eliminating the nation and the family as social groups and in thus establishing its 'brave new world'.

So far as the conflict between the Communist and the national systems is concerned, it is not easy to predict the issue; but it may safely be assumed that, if the Communist ideal of a universal world-state is ever realized, it will not be without a tremendous struggle. In this connection it is significant that the establishment of a Communist régime in Russia has been accompanied by a wave of nationalism in a number of other countries—Nazism in Germany and Fascism in Italy providing outstanding and extreme examples. Whatever be the ultimate issue of the conflict, however, it seems unlikely that the national system will survive indefinitely in its present form. At the same time, it seems equally improbable that the Communist ideal of a universal world-state will ever prove capable of realization; and in that event, we may expect some alternative form of supra-national organization to emerge. It must be recognized, of course, that there does actually exist such an alternative—an alternative rendered possible through the influence exercised upon the national system by the original family organization. It is thus quite possible that the supra-national system of the future may prove to consist of a *family of nations*, just as the tribe consisted in a family of clans. As a matter of fact, this is the ideal which would appear to have inspired the formation of the League of Nations after the Great War of 1914–18. It is true that, up to the time of writing (1934), the League of Nations does not appear to have gone far towards the realization of its ideal; but the largely unrealized ideal of the League of Nations is perhaps less significant than the practical embodiment of the same ideal in the family of nations represented by the British Commonwealth. The ultimate fate of the British Commonwealth is, of course, difficult to predict; but the fact of its having displayed greater cohesion than the League of Nations may reasonably be attributed to its patriarchal basis, modelled as this is upon the family pattern. Its sanction depends upon common loyalty to one father-figure represented by the King; and it may well be that the fate of the British Commonwealth depends upon the fate of the monarchy.[1]

[1] As subsequent events have proved, the British Commonwealth has outlasted the League of Nations; but the establishment of the United Nations Organization to replace the defunct League of Nations is obviously the reflection of a world-

As regards the prospects of success attending the Communist encroachment upon the family group, it is perhaps possible to speak with less uncertainty. It has already been pointed out that, although the family as a social group has been superseded by a series of more comprehensive organizations, it has so far resisted extinction and has insinuated itself into the very texture of the national system. Even the Communist régime, as we have also noted, has been compelled to make some concession to the family system; and the influence of the Communist leaders, particularly Lenin (alive or dead), must be attributed in no small measure to their assuming the mantle of 'benevolent god-father', torn from the shoulders of the Tzar when he assumed the role of 'malevolent devil-father' in the eyes of his people. It would therefore appear that the resistance of the family group to extinction in the course of social evolution is by no means exhausted. This resistance must ultimately be attributed to the profound biological foundations of the family; for, after all, the family is not simply a sociological group; it is also a biological group. Even if the epoch envisaged in Aldous Huxley's brilliant satire, *Brave New World*, ever dawns and the babies of the future are conceived in bottles, it by no means follows that the Œdipus situation will be completely abolished from the unconscious of the individual. After all, even the baby of the future will require to be brought up by others; and those who perform the parental function will inevitably acquire the significance of parent-figures in the child's mind. It may be objected that under such a régime all parent-figures will exercise a function roughly analogous to that of the mother under prevailing conditions, and that, in consequence, the triangular Œdipus situation will cease to be a feature of the child's environment. Matters are not quite so simple as that, however; for it is found by psychoanalysts that the Œdipus conflict develops even in children who are brought up by a single parent, i.e. by the mother (for, if the father is left with the child, a mother-figure is always introduced into the family circle). The author has had the opportunity of analysing several individuals (of both sexes) who have never seen their fathers; and in each case the intensity of the Œdipus conflict was so extreme as to be highly pathogenic. The prospect of a régime which will dispense completely with parenthood as we understand it to-day is, however, too remote

wide need, and is the expression of a movement indicating the possibility that the supra-national organization of the future will assume the form, not of a Communist world-state, but of a family of nations.

to deserve our serious consideration. A study of contemporary tendencies certainly suggests that the influence of the family as a social institution will diminish still further under the pressure of more highly evolved organizations. But the profound biological basis of the family would seem to preclude its ultimate extinction. It seems more than probable, therefore, that, even if Communism succeeds in its campaign against the nation, the Communist state will find itself compelled (as did the nation) to make terms with the family and incorporate it into its own more comprehensive organization. It may be predicted that any attempt on the part of Communism to carry its encroachment upon the family group to its logical conclusion would inevitably have the effect of compromising the success of the Communist movement. We may also anticipate that, so long as man exists upon the earth, the Œdipus conflict will continue to play a significant part not only in influencing the psychological development of the individual, but also in determining the nature of social institutions and defining the path of human culture.

POSTSCRIPT—(1951)

Any attempt to discuss subjects involving political and ideological (no less than religious) issues from a scientific standpoint is always hazardous; and various criticisms of the above paper, which have reached my ears from time to time since its original publication, have only served to confirm this fact (if indeed confirmation were needed). I console myself with the reflection that, if it is difficult for an author to be objective in formulating views upon such subjects, it is no less difficult for critics to be objective in their criticisms; and I can only hope that readers who may feel disposed to be critical of this paper on grounds of objectivity will try to be as objective in their criticisms as I have tried to be in my formulation of the views expressed. In the hope of anticipating such further criticisms as may arise, I feel it desirable to offer some explanation of the circumstances in which the paper came to be written. It was written under the stimulation of a book entitled *At Home with the Savage* (Routledge, 1932) from the pen of J. H. Driberg, who became Lecturer in Ethnology at Cambridge University after serving as District Commmissioner successively in Uganda and the Sudan. The book in question contains an anthropological study of the evolution of social groups in

Africa; and it occurred to me, after I had read this book, that it would be a constructive step to attempt to throw some light upon the evolution of social groups from a psychoanalytical standpoint. The above paper was the result of such an attempt on my part; and, in making this attempt, I saw no valid scientific reason for excluding from my survey the more recent developments in the evolution of social groups. Indeed, I felt that, since my survey was general in scope (and not restricted to the study of developments in any particular area of the world), it would be incomplete unless recent developments were taken into account. It is thus that I came to include the Communist state within the scope of my enquiry and, in view of its evolutionary importance, to concentrate particular attention upon it. I included it, not because it represented a political system inviting approval or disapproval (and no one who is sincere can disclaim personal views on the subject), but because it represented a momentous phenomenon in the evolution of social groups. Among the more general features of this evolutionary process, to which I directed attention, are (1) a tendency towards progressive comprehensiveness in social groupings, and (2) the existence of conflict between the more comprehensive and the less comprehensive groups. It would thus be arbitrary on the part of any critic, e.g. to isolate my discussion of the conflict between the Communist state and other groups such as the family from my discussion of similar conflicts between other groups in the evolutionary series. Where the psychology of the individual is concerned, the conflict between social groups inevitably assumes the form of a conflict between group loyalties; and, since group psychology ultimately reduces itself to the psychology of the individual in a group, it follows that the fruits of psychoanalytical research on the unconscious motivation of the individual must be relevant to the explanation of group phenomena.

CHAPTER II

Psychology as a Prescribed and as a Proscribed Subject[1] (1939)

WHEN I received the invitation to open a discussion at this meeting of the St. Andrews University Philosophical Society with a short controversial paper, it occurred to me that it would be a suitable occasion to raise the question why certain specific systems of psychological thought should be more or less taboo in academic precincts when psychology itself is a subject approved for study in all our universities, and even made compulsory for students of education. The present occasion seemed to me particularly appropriate for this purpose, since it is not so long ago that a meeting of psychologists at St. Andrews University was made the scene of an attempt to deny the status of psychological science to a psychological system in which I happen to be specially interested— viz. psychoanalysis. This particular attempt to discredit psychoanalytical theory is of no significance for our present purpose except in so far as it reflects a widespread tendency in university circles to exclude psychoanalytical theory from the field of academic study. This tendency is not, of course, everywhere equally strong; but, in general, it is sufficiently marked to make it little exaggeration to say that, so far from being a *pre*scribed subject in the psychological curriculum, psychoanalytical theory is actually a *pro*scribed subject. I shall, accordingly, make it my business on this occasion to consider what it is that leads to the inclusion of psychoanalytical psychology in the academic Index Expurgatorius.

Even already enough has been said to enable you to anticipate the reply which we shall receive when we ask the compilers of the academic black list why psychoanalysis should be relegated to the

[1] A paper read to the St. Andrews University Philosophical Society on 9th February 1939.

same invidious status as alchemy and astrology in academic eyes. We shall be told, of course, that psychoanalysis is unscientific. To this charge the psychoanalyst will reply that it is the academic psychologists who are unscientific since, in formulating their theories about human nature, they neglect a vast proportion of the significant facts. Not content with ignoring the extensive realm of mental phenomena to which the psychoanalyst applies the comprehensive designation of 'the unconscious', they even ignore a large proportion of strictly 'conscious' phenomena. Thus they consider they have said all that there is to say about the whole range of human behaviour and experience which is represented by the words 'sex' and 'love' if, in drawing up a list of human 'instincts', they make brief reference to the existence of a sex instinct, or some euphemistic equivalent such as a 'reproductive instinct' or 'mating instinct'. They also turn an almost completely blind eye to that whole group of most significant phenomena to which we make reference when we speak of 'conscience', 'sin', and 'guilt'. Further, as if their amblyopia were not already sufficiently extensive, they ignore so far as possible all the hydra-headed manifestations of human hate and aggression such as war, persecution, oppression, revolution and fanaticism. The academic counterblast to this argument usually takes the form of an attempt to deny the objectivity of such psychoanalytical data as have escaped the observation of the laboratory-trained psychologist. Thereupon the psychoanalyst points out that, whilst some of the data in question could only be missed by an investigator who had emotional reasons for being blind to them, the remainder are only amenable to discovery by means of the standardized analytical technique. The analytical technique itself then becomes the object of the attack launched by academic critics. It is really the technique, they say, that is unscientific; and they claim that the ostensible 'data' obtained by means of the analytical technique are in large measure the product of the technique itself. The psychoanalyst points out, of course, that nothing could be more scientific than the free-association method, upon which the analytical technique is based, in the hands of an observer trained to be strictly impartial. Nevertheless the critics immediately seize upon the fact that in psychoanalytical treatment the material produced by the patient in the course of free-association is subject to interpretation on the part of analyst; and from this it is inferred that subsequent associations become increasingly contaminated by the analyst's preconceptions owing to the analyst's prestige in the patient's eyes. This inference is not accepted by the psychoanalyst, however; for in psychoanalytical treatment what is interpreted is not so much the actual material produced by the patient as the stubborn resistance which he characteristically offers to the production of material and his reactions to the analytical situation in general. In so far as this resistance is overcome, the material speaks largely for itself. There are times, it is true, when the analyst finds it necessary to interpret the actual material; but, in so doing, he is only following the recognized scientific procedure of applying knowledge already acquired for the elucidation of further facts. It should be added that the various manifestations of the resistance itself must be regarded as among the most impressive data elicited by the analytical technique. They thus constitute significant phenomena demanding explanation; and it is upon the observation of these phenomena that the fundamental psychoanalytical theory of repression is based.

After all the accusations levelled against psychoanalysis by academic critics on scientific grounds have been ventilated and disputed, there always emerges yet another line of criticism, which would appear to represent the real objection to the inclusion of psychoanalytical theory in the academic curriculum. This criticism is really just a modern edition of the charge levelled against Socrates when he was accused of corrupting the youth of Athens. So far as Socrates is concerned, it turned out to be, literally, as much as his life was worth to advocate the principle of γνῶθι σεαυτόν ('know thyself'). So perhaps the psychoanalyst is really rather lucky to get away with a whole skin when he invites human beings to inspect their own motives.

As a matter of fact, there is really quite a good case for excluding psychoanalytical theory from undergraduate courses in psychology —particularly if psychoanalytical theory happens to be true. According to psychoanalytical findings, there lie hidden in the depths of human nature dark and dangerous forces, against which there have been erected a number of somewhat precarious defences, partly internal and individual, partly external and social. In view of the precariousness of these defences and the turbulent nature of the forces against which they have been erected, it becomes a matter for legitimate doubt how far it is safe to entrust human beings with the truth about themselves. Among the various changes in outlook which characterize our contemporary world, not the least significant perhaps is a weakening, even in scientific circles, of that Victorian and post-Victorian optimism, which regarded the growth of modern science as the herald of a Golden Age, towards which, with the aid of science, the human race was destined to pursue a path of uninterrupted progress. Contemporary events in the world at large (1939) are bringing home to us with increasing conviction that scientific knowledge is anything but an unmixed blessing to mankind. Thus we can now hardly take up our newspapers without reading of some fresh menace to human happiness and welfare, and indeed to civilization itself, resulting from the possession by human beings of the knowledge derived from recent advances in the sciences of Physics and Chemistry.[1]

It is to be noted, however, that the real danger attached to the possession of such knowledge by human beings arises out of the presence in human nature of those turbulent and destructive forces which are shown by psychoanalytical investigation to play so great a part in the economy of the unconscious mind of the individual—so vastly greater a part than is ordinarily apparent, or than the veneer of culture would lead us to believe. It is thus not so much the knowledge conferred by the advance of the physical sciences that is dangerous as the increased effectiveness which the possession of such knowledge confers upon the destructive tendencies present in human nature. In the case of such psychological knowledge as psychoanalytical investigation claims to provide, the position is rather different; for here it is not a case of increasing the effectiveness of man's destructive tendencies but of unmasking these destructive tendencies themselves. What really alarms people about psychoanalysis is thus the nature of the facts which it discloses. Psychoanalysis itself is felt to be dangerous because it reveals the presence in human nature of dangerous forces which the individual is only too anxious to disclaim. In the earlier days of psychoanalysis, when repression of sexual wishes was the phenomenon upon which attention was almost exclusively focused, it appeared as if it were the presence of repressed sexual tendencies that man sought above all to deny. In the light of further investigation, however, it has become evident that what man seeks to deny more unreservedly is the intensity of his own aggression, and that his

[1] This was written early in 1939, at a time when, although gas-masks had been issued to the population of Great Britain, the Second World War was as yet only a threat and the full horrors of totalitarian aggression had yet to be revealed; but it has even greater point at the present day (1951), when the menace of the atomic bomb is an inescapable reality and is perhaps only the herald of greater menaces to come.

attempts to deny the extent of his own sexuality is in no small measure due to the association of his sexual tendencies with aggressive attitudes on his part. It would thus appear that the exclusion of psychoanalytical theory from the academic curriculum represents an attempt to keep the veil drawn over a side of human nature which is the occasion, not only of guilt in the individual, but also of a taboo on the part of society.

It is interesting to reflect that, in drawing aside the veil which conceals the more primitive side of human nature, psychoanalysis is only performing within the scientific field a task which has been performed repeatedly outside that field by moral and religious reformers throughout the ages. Thus, in his *Epistle to Titus*, St. Paul writes, 'For we ourselves also were sometimes foolish, disobedient, deceived, serving divers lusts and pleasures, living in malice and envy, hateful, and hating one another'. It is, of course, the invariable lot of moral and religious reformers to encounter the most strenuous opposition on the part of the established order; but it would be grossly inadequate to attribute this opposition simply to the presence of an unexplained strain of innate conservatism in the human race. The fact is that all new gospels have the effect of undermining existing cultures, which themselves function as social defences against the primitive forces in human nature. The resistance encountered by new gospels is thus essentially a defence of existing cultural defences; and the social resistance encountered by psychoanalysis is of a precisely similar nature.

It is characteristic of moral and religious reformers, of course, that, not content with simply drawing aside the veil which conceals man's more primitive tendencies, they make it their aim to show up the weaknesses of existing cultural defences. Thus it is not enough for the apostle of a new creed to convince his potential converts of their own wickedness; he also seeks to convince them that any creed which they have hitherto embraced is a mass of ignorant superstition. In doing this, of course, he is himself supported by the conviction that, in destroying existing cultural defences, he is in a position to substitute better ones in their place. By contrast, the psychoanalyst as a scientist has no new gospel to offer; but neither does he seek to destroy existing cultural defences. At the same time, in following his own particular path of scientific enquiry, he has been unable to escape the necessity of formulating a theory regarding the psychological nature and origin of such defences; and, in virtue of this fact, he is regarded as having broken the taboo which guards the sanctity of human institutions just as much as of he had laid violent hands upon them.

We are thus in a position to appreciate the true nature of the objections to psychoanalysis. These are (1) that psychoanalysis reveals the presence in human nature of primitive and destructive forces which human nature would fain disclaim, and (2) that it gives an account of the nature and origin of the psychological defences erected by human beings as a protection against such forces in themselves. These objections appear to acquire special cogency when any question arises of teaching psychoanalytical theory to university undergraduates, of whom the majority have not yet emerged from the impressionable and unsettled phase of adolescence—a phase proverbially characterized by a tendency to question accepted cultural values.

At this point it will be profitable for us to remind ourselves that psychoanalytical theory is not the only scientific theory which has the misfortune, in one part of the world or another, to find its name upon an academic black list. Indeed in Nazi Germany (1939) the academic black list has assumed quite formidable dimensions. It is virtually impossible, for example, for any anthropological or ethnological theory which conflicts with the official Nazi doctrine of the 'Aryan Race' to obtain a hearing in any German University. Academic circles in Great Britain are, of course, unanimous in their protests against the imposition of such restrictions upon freedom of thought; but it is only fair to recognize that, if psychoanalytical theory is excluded from the academic curriculum in a country like Great Britain because it is regarded as culturally disruptive, it is for a precisely similar reason that various anthropological and ethnological theories which are freely expounded in British universities have been banned from the academic curriculum in Germany. The only difference here is that, whereas in the one case the culture which is being protected is the traditional Classico-Christian culture of Western Europe, in the other case it is the Nazi ideology consisting, as it essentially does, in a revival of the old pagan Teutonic culture in modern dress.[1]

[1] The illustration chosen in this paragraph (written early in 1939) has, of course, been rendered out of date by subsequent events. Unfortunately, however, the same cannot be said about the phenomenon illustrated; and there would be little difficulty in drawing equally apposite illustrations from conditions prevailing under totalitarian régimes today (1951).

Psychology as a Prescribed and as a Proscribed Subject

We must not judge the social group too harshly for seeking to protect its cultural integrity by limiting free enquiry. Whatever we may think of totalitarian ideologies, there can be no doubt that the integrity of such an ideology is essential to the cohesion of the group organized under the régime which imposes the ideology; and it is safe to assume that the cohesion of every group is bound up with some ideology or other, however inexplicitly this may be formulated and however tolerantly it may be maintained. It seems inevitable, therefore, that some limit should always be imposed upon free enquiry by any social group which seeks to survive. It has ever been the wisdom of the Catholic Church that there are some things which it is better for the average man not to know; and it is a very real psychological question how far human nature, in its present form, is capable of tolerating the truth, the whole truth and nothing but the truth.

We are told that a little knowledge is a dangerous thing; but the fact remains that a lot of knowledge may be much more dangerous. In accordance with this fact, it seems quite possible that recent advances in the physical sciences may lead to the complete destruction of the human race. Interestingly enough, although almost complete freedom of thought and enquiry is now permitted in the chemistry departments of our universities, there are other academic departments in which thought is no less limited than enquiry. Thus, although, in general, religious tests have been abolished in British universities, it remains impossible for a Roman Catholic, however distinguished as a scholar, to be appointed Professor of Hebrew in a Scottish university. It is almost equally difficult to envisage the appointment of an avowed surrealist to a university chair in Fine Art. *The fact is that, the higher the cultural value of a subject in the university curriculum, the less freedom of thought and enquiry is permitted.*

In the light of these various reflections we find ourselves inevitably confronted with the question, 'What is the proper function of a university?' There are three possible functions which a university may perform in the community: (1) that of a centre for the promotion of culture, (2) that of a technical school, and (3) that of an institution for the promotion of free and unrestricted scientific enquiry. The actual situation at the present day represents a compromise, in accordance with which our universities attempt to perform all three functions in part, whilst avoiding the performance of any one function exclusively. It must be recognized, however, that each of these functions represents a different aim, and that the aims in question are not easily reconcilable. In particular, it is difficult to see how an institution which still accepts its historical role as the guardian of a definite traditional culture can be expected to function simultaneously as a place of free and unrestricted scientific enquiry; for the study of history permits of no reasonable doubt that every significant advance in scientific knowledge has had a disintegrating effect upon the prevalent culture.

In view of the rapid advances of modern science, accordingly, our universities are now placed in a position in which a choice of functions is rapidly being forced upon them. If it be decided that a university should above all remain a guardian of culture, we shall expect to find the academic list of *prescribed* subjects accompanied by an academic list of *proscribed* subjects; and, of course, it may very well be that there are certain subjects and certain scientific theories which it is better for young people as a whole not to study. On the other hand, if it be decided that a university should function, above all, as an institution for the furtherance of scientific truth, it will be inconsistent to maintain an academic censorship of scientific subjects or scientific theories; and in such a university one would expect to find psychoanalytical theory occupying a very prominent position on the syllabus of the student of psychology. In this latter event, perhaps the result will not be so very disastrous to culture after all; for it is now time for us to remind ourselves that, if knowledge may be used destructively, it may also be used constructively. Thus the same chemical knowledge which enables men to manufacture lethal gases for use in war enables them to devise means of protection, not only against such man-made agents of destruction, but also against the onslaughts of bacterial enemies. Similarly, if psychoanalysis may appear dangerous both because it unmasks the hidden disruptive and destructive forces in human nature and because it subjects to scientific scrutiny the character of the defences erected to control these forces, yet at the same time it provides us with a knowledge of the conditions under which the disruptive and destructive elements are fostered and the conditions under which their influence is most likely to be reduced. It would be difficult to exaggerate the importance of such knowledge; for knowledge of the conditions under which phenomena occur is the first step towards mastery of the problems created by the phenomena in question and towards effective influence over the phenomena themselves. After all, psychoanalysis originated as a form of psychotherapy; and, if modern psychoanalytical theory is capable of ameliorative clinical application in the case of psychological disorders, it is also capable of ameliorative clinical application in the case of sociological disorders, which are only psychological disorders writ large. It seems possible, therefore, that psychoanalysis may actually have an important contribution to make towards the furtherance of the very aims for which culture stands; and this is more than can be said for most of the more academic forms of psychology.

CHAPTER III

The War Neuroses— Their Nature and Significance[1] *(1943)*

IN what follows I propose to record some conclusions which I have reached regarding the nature of the so-called 'War Neuroses'. These conclusions are based in no small measure upon my experience of psychopathological conditions among military personnel while I was acting in the capacity of Visiting Psychiatrist to a special hospital in the Emergency Medical Service during the war which broke out in 1939; and I am indebted to the Department of Health for Scotland for permission to publish this paper in so far as it is based on this experience. Needless to say, the Department accepts no responsibility for any of the views expressed.

THE TRAUMATIC FACTOR

The term 'war neuroses' is an omnibus term covering a great variety of clinical conditions; and there is now fairly general agreement among psychiatrists that, so far as symptomatology is concerned, the war neuroses possess no distinctive features differentiating them sharply from the various psychoneurotic and psychotic states which prevail in time of peace. It has been proposed by some psychiatrists, accordingly, that it would be more accurate to speak of 'the neuroses in wartime' than to speak of 'the war neuroses'. On the other hand, there are psychiatrists who maintain that, where cases among military personnel are concerned, a distinction must be drawn between (1) a group of psychopathological states which appear to be precipitated by active warfare, and (2) familiar psycho-pathological states which chance to occur during the course of mili-

[1] A much abbreviated version of this paper was published in the *British Medical Journal*, 13 February 1943.

tary service, but which might equally well have occurred in civilian life. This attempted distinction appears to be based upon the observation that in a certain proportion, albeit only in a certain proportion, of military cases a psychopathological state is found to have supervened upon some traumatic experience associated with active warfare (e.g. a near shell-burst or bomb-explosion). In contrast to this observation it is to be noted that 'traumatic neuroses' are by no means unknown in time of peace; and here it must be kept in mind that, if such neuroses are less common in peacetime than in wartime, so also are violent traumatic experiences themselves. Actually it is not uncommon to find that a soldier suffering from a traumatic neurosis acquired in war has a previous history of a traumatic neurosis acquired in civilian life. In a considerable percentage of military cases also the trauma upon which a 'war neurosis' has supervened is found to be one (e.g. a motor accident) which is only incidentally associated with conditions of war. It is impossible, however, to dismiss the question of the part played by traumatic experiences in the precipitation of war neuroses without pausing to consider what constitutes a traumatic experience.

It is all too often assumed that a traumatic experience is one which produces a psychopathological state *de novo*. Yet, when investigation is sufficiently painstaking, it is rare to find a case in which evidence of pre-existing psychopathological characteristics cannot be detected in the previous history. It is reasonable to conclude, accordingly, that a traumatic experience is one which serves to precipitate a psychopathological reaction through the activation of pre-existing, but hitherto latent, psychopathological factors. The correctness of this conclusion is confirmed by the fact that in certain cases it is possible to detect a very high degree of specificity in the traumatic experience. In illustration of this point I may cite the following case.

Case 1. Gunner W. I.; R.A.; aged twenty-seven; single.

This soldier developed an acute anxiety state accompanied by incapacitating phobic symptoms after an oil-tanker in which he was serving as a maritime gunner was sunk by aerial attack. The vessel was hit by bombs and was almost immediately converted into a raging inferno owing to the inflammable nature of the cargo. He thought at first that he was going to be trapped in the burning vessel; but he managed to make his way to a boat, which proved to be the only one successfully launched. There was some delay in the casting off of the boat, however; and, anticipating (quite correctly as it turned out) that the boat would also catch fire, he plunged into the water and swam away from the ship. It was fortunate for him that he did so, since the other occupants of the boat were burned to death; but, as he swam, he was pursued by burning oil which spread outwards from the ship on the surface of the water, with the result that he had a race for his life before he was picked up. During the course of the incident he was thus faced with a whole series of dangerous situations—being bombed, being trapped in the burning ship, finding his most promising hope of escape (the boat) to be but an additional menace to his life, being pursued by burning oil as he swam, and finally facing the risk of being drowned. On the surface it would appear that any one of these situations might in itself have served to constitute a traumatic experience; but in the case of this soldier none of them actually did so. It must now be added that, just as he felt that he was making some headway in his race against the pursuing flames, he found himself grasped and pulled down by a drowning Chinaman who was a member of the ship's crew. In a desperate effort of self-preservation he gave the Chinaman a blow on the head and saw him sink back into a watery grave; and it was this quite specific situation that constituted for him the traumatic experience. It functioned as a traumatic experience because, as investigation revealed, it brought to a focus in an act of 'murder' an intense and long-standing hatred of his father, which in the past had been deeply repressed owing to the anxiety and guilt attendant upon it. The experience thus acquired for him all the emotional significance of patricide; and it precipitated all the latent anxiety and guilt attached to his repressed hatred of his father, as well as activating various psychopathological defences which had already been prepared in his mind to deal with patricidal contingencies.

It is by no means always so easy to demonstrate the specificity of a traumatic experience as in the case quoted; but this fact in itself may not be without its significance, once the principle of specificity has been established. It is also not without significance that in many cases it is far from obvious why a situation precipitating a psychopathological state should possess any traumatic quality at all, even when it is a situation which has been repeatedly experienced and may be presumed to have acquired a cumulative effect; for many experiences which prove to be traumatic appear comparatively trivial in themselves. Investigation reveals a remarkable range of traumatic experiences, as may be illustrated by the following examples chosen more or less at random from cases which have come under my notice: being blown up by a bomb, being trapped in the cabin of a torpedoed ship, seeing civilian refugees massacred, having to throttle a German sentry in self-defence, being let down by an officer in a tight corner, being accused of homosexuality by another soldier, being refused compassionate leave to go home for a wife's confinement, and even being shouted at by the sergeant-major. When we consider the wide range of such a series, the question may well occur to us whether in many cases the traumatic experience which precipitates a war neurosis may not be constituted by military service itself.

THE FACTOR OF INFANTILE DEPENDENCE

On the basis of data collected in the course of private psychotherapeutic practice I have gradually found myself driven to the conclusion that all psychopathological developments in the adult are ultimately based upon a persistence into later life of an exaggerated degree of that emotional dependence which is characteristic of childhood, and more particularly of infancy.[1] The all-round dependence which distinguishes childhood requires little emphasis. It is a biological fact bound up with the extreme helplessness of the human infant at birth, and embedded in the very structure of human society. It is a fact of which the institution of the law takes special cognizance; and it provides the rationale of that most basic of all social institutions, the family. In conformity with the fact that the family constitutes the primal social group, the dependence of the child is focused essentially upon his parents. It is upon his parents that he depends for the satisfaction of his psychological, no less than his physical, needs. It is to them that he looks for moral, no less than for physical, support; and it is upon them that he largely relies for the regulation of his behaviour and the control of his wayward desires. In particular, it is round his parents that his emotional life revolves; for his parents are not only his original love-objects, but also the original objects of his hate and the objects to whom his earliest fears and anxieties are attached. In the ordinary course of development the individual's

[1] The various considerations upon which this conclusion is based have already been recorded in my paper, *A Revised Psychopathology of the Psychoses and Psychoneuroses* (included in the present volume).

dependence upon his parents (and upon parental figures who come to deputize for them) undergoes a progressive decrease throughout the phases of childhood and adolescence until the comparative independence of maturity is reached. It is uncommon, however, for the process of emotional emancipation to prove a smooth passage; for, even under the most favourable of conditions, there is always a certain conflict between (1) a progressive urge to abandon the state of infantile dependence on account of the many limitations which it imposes, and (2) a regressive urge to cling to it on account of the many advantages which it confers. Where conditions are unfavourable, this conflict assumes exaggerated proportions, is accompanied by marked anxiety and gives rise to exaggerated reactions. Whatever adjustments and compromises may issue from an acute conflict of this nature, its most significant consequence is the perpetuation of an attitude of infantile dependence in the emotional sphere—an attitude which is none the less present at deep levels of the psyche even when at more superficial levels it is over-compensated by an attitude of quasi-independence representing nothing more than a denial of the dependence which persists at a deeper level. It is the undue persistence of such an attitude of infantile dependence that I have come to regard as the ultimate factor predisposing to all psychopathological developments; and, in conformity with this view, all psychoneurotic and psychotic symptoms must be interpreted as essentially either (1) effects of, or (2) defences against the conflicts attendant upon a persistent state of infantile dependence.

At the time when war broke out in 1939 I was already approaching the point of view which has just been indicated; and I was well on the way towards formulating my conclusions when it became one of my duties to investigate cases of 'psychoneurosis' among military personnel on a considerable scale. I was thus most conveniently presented at the appropriate moment with a unique opportunity to test the validity of my emergent views. My views were originally based upon an intensive study of a comparatively small number of patients living in their normal environment; but I was now placed in a position to check up these views by means of a comprehensive survey of a large number of patients who had been suddenly removed from their normal environment, separated from their love-objects and isolated from all the accustomed props and supports upon which a dependent person would ordinarily rely. It was almost as if a laboratory experiment under controlled conditions had been gratuitously provided for the testing of my conclusions. The result of this experiment was to confirm those conclusions in a most striking manner, as may perhaps be most conveniently illustrated by the description of a case in which dependence assumed such exaggerated proportions as to leave no room for doubt regarding its etiological significance.

Case 2. Gunner A. M.; R.A.; aged twenty-four; married for eighteen months.

This soldier had a small one-man business in civilian life; and his calling-up papers were deferred for three months on business grounds. When he reported for duty at the end of this period of deferment, he insisted upon his wife accompanying him to the barracks, which were situated about 250 miles from his home. He also insisted upon her remaining in the town in which the barracks were situated until, at the end of six weeks, circumstances necessitated her returning home. The prospect of her departure alarmed him so much that he applied for week-end leave with a view to accompanying her. He was successful in his application and was thus able to postpone the date of separation by several days. During his leave he never left the house; and it was with great difficulty that he tore himself away from his wife when his leave came to an end. After his return to duty he made frantic efforts to keep in touch with her by telephone, putting through a trunk call to her every day unless circumstances rendered this quite impossible. Interestingly enough, his preoccupation with thoughts about his wife was such as to render him quite unable to mobilize sufficient power of concentration to write letters to her. Inability to concentrate also resulted in his being the only man who failed to pass the prescribed test at the end of a course of instruction in gunnery; and owing to this failure, combined with a fear of guns which he displayed, he was allocated to routine telephone duties. Throughout the day his mind was constantly preoccupied with thoughts about his wife and about the distance which separated him from her; and at night he found difficulty in sleeping owing to the pressure of similar thoughts. He was very self-conscious and felt 'different' from the other men. He tended to feel that his company was not wanted; and he made no friends in the Army with the exception of one man fifteen years older than himself. He had felt 'depressed' from the day that he entered the Army; and, in the absence of his wife, he felt completely 'alone'. It seemed to him that everything was against him; and he felt that his only hold on life resided in the hope of seeing his wife again—a fact in explanation of which he volunteered the remarks, 'She is like a mother to me', and 'She is all I have'.

This soldier was admitted to hospital within three months of entering military service, having reported sick ten days previous to his admission on account of two fainting attacks, which occurred on successive days, and the first of which came on while he was sitting in the confined space of the telephone exchange. It emerged that he had been subject to such attacks for a period of nine years—ever since an occasion when, at the age of fifteen, he had seen a woman collapse in the street. This spectacle precipitated in him a state of acute anxiety, which persisted throughout the remainder of the day until, in the evening, his first fainting attack occurred. Similar attacks occurred with great frequency for a period of several months, during which he was kept off school and was not allowed to go out of sight of his home unescorted. When his condition had improved sufficiently to enable him to resume attendance at school, he was afraid to go to school alone and always required to be accompanied. Even after leaving school at the age of sixteen, he remained afraid to go out alone in case an attack should occur when he was at any distance from his home. When he did venture to go out alone, he adopted the expedient of going on a bicycle in order that he might reach home with a minimum of delay if he felt an attack coming on. His bicycle thus came to assume for him the significance of a link with home. It became like an umbilical cord connecting him with the doting maternal grandmother who had performed all the functions of a mother for him since the age of three, when his actual mother had died.

His dependence upon his grandmother was very great. An only child, he had gone to live with his maternal grandparents when his mother died; and he saw very little of his father, towards whom he displayed an unnatural, and almost complete, absence of feeling. After his first fainting attack he 'slept between' his grandparents until the death of his grandfather, which took place a few months later; and after his grandfather's death he occupied the same room as his grandmother until, when he was eighteen years of age, she also died. As his grandmother's health declined and the prospect of his losing her began to dawn upon him, he spent more and more of his time in her company, receiving no little encouragement to do so from the old lady herself. His devotion to her was tempered, however, by considerable concern regarding the state of isolation and loneliness, into which his impending bereavement threatened to plunge him. He had made no male friends; and he had never taken up with any girl. Consequently he felt faced with the appalling prospect of finding himself completely alone in the world when an inexorable fate deprived him of the person upon whom he had hitherto depended for everything. His anxiety over this prospect was, however, considerably relieved through the agency of a *deus ex machina* in the form of the bicycle upon which he had relied so much in the past as a means of allaying his separation-anxiety; for one day, as he was hurrying back to his grandmother's bedside from a necessary expedition on his bicycle, he was fortunate enough to bump into a young woman who was crossing the street. His bicycle thus proved to justify more than all the confidence which he had placed in it as an umbilical cord. It provided him with another point of attachment, another woman upon whom he could depend; for this was the woman who eventually became his wife. Discreetly enough, he did not disturb the peace of his grandmother's last days by informing her of the new attachment which he had contracted. His attentions to his grandmother were not allowed to suffer; but, with an eye to his own future security, he did make a point of arranging frequent surreptitious meetings with the girl. He persuaded her to come to the door for him when they went out together, and often to see him well on his way home when the time came for him to return. She gradually came to be the means of conferring upon him the only confidence that he had in himself. What sense of security he derived from her friendship did not, however, prevent his being plunged into the depths of desolation by the death of his grandmother, when this event occurred. His sense of desolation was certainly mitigated by his friendship with the girl; and indeed it was only this attachment that reconciled him to the prospect of continued life. Nevertheless, the fact that his financial position was too precarious to permit of his marrying her proved a perpetual source of anxiety to him. Refusing his father's offer of a home, he went to live with an aunt, hoping all the time that something would turn up to place him in a position to marry. Meanwhile he constantly 'went about in a trance waiting for the girl'. Providence again turned out to be kind, however; for, besides coming into some money which his grandfather had left, he achieved some remarkable success in football pools. The result was that he accumulated enough money to buy a small 'gent's outfitter' business; and on the strength of this he was able to marry. Marriage in itself did not, however, provide an adequate solution of his problems; and indeed his clamouring need for safeguards against separation-anxiety tended to become whetted, rather than allayed. The fact that his shop was a one-man business proved a special stumbling-block; for, whilst he found himself unable to bear being alone in the shop, the demands of housekeeping made it impossible for his wife to be at his side constantly during business hours. He attempted to strike a compromise by engaging a boy as an assistant; but the boy proved such an inadequate deputy for his wife that this compromise was not a success. He then sought to support a waning faith in the umbilical virtues of his bicycle by installing telephones in his shop and in his house, thus establishing a means of almost immediate, if somewhat ethereal, contact with his wife. Finally he took advantage of another smile on the part of fortune and secured the lease of a flat above his shop, with the result that at last he was able to achieve his ambition to have his wife constantly at his side. Once this ambition had been achieved, however, fortune provided him with some evidence of her proverbial fickleness; for, with the inexorability of a cruel fate, his final calling-up notice duly arrived to set at nought all his efforts to meet the demands of his dependence and safeguard himself against the distress of separation-anxiety. Although he made a desperate attempt to maintain the closest contact with his wife compatible with the conditions of military service after his call-up, the extent to which this attempt failed to satisfy his emotional needs may be judged from the disabling nature of the symptoms which he was not slow to develop. At the same time the development of these very symptoms served the purpose of enabling him to achieve what, without them, he would have failed to achieve, viz. a discharge from the obligations of military service and a return to the wife, who, by a sort of apostolic succession through his grandmother, had acquired for him all the virtues of a mother towards whom, in death as in life, he had always retained an attitude of infantile dependence.

The above case may appear to represent such an extreme degree of dependence that it should be regarded as constituting an isolated instance rather than a paradigm of the endopsychic situation which characteristically underlies the development of a war neurosis. It would be quite possible, however, to quote numerous instances in which the relationship of a war neurosis to a persistence of infantile dependence from days of childhood would be almost equally obvious; and, once such a relationship has been recognized to exist, it may be detected in every case, if only investigation is sufficiently thorough and is pursued to a sufficient depth of psychic level. If the relationship in question is not equally obvious in all cases, this is due partly to the fact that the persistence of infantile dependence is subject, in common with all characteristics, to an infinite degree of variation, but chiefly to the fact that the anxieties to which the state of dependence exposes the individual call into operation, in varying degrees and combinations, a number of mental defences which have the effect of concealing the real position. From these facts it follows (1) that the amount of stress required to produce a breakdown varies from individual to individual, and (2) that the incidence of the war neuroses is determined not only by the degree to which infantile dependence has persisted in the individual, but also by the nature and strength of the mental defences which he has erected to control its disturbing effects. In most cases it is only after such defences have been worn down that the underlying dependence becomes apparent; and it is seldom that they are quite so precarious as in the last-mentioned case. Appreciation of the relationship existing between the development of a war neurosis and an underlying state of infantile dependence is to some extent obscured by the fact that a number of psychopathological symptoms themselves constitute desperate forms of defence against the conflicts attendant upon infantile dependence; and this would appear to apply particularly to phobic, hysterical, paranoid and obsessional symptoms. There are, however, other classes of symptom which must be regarded as products of a fundamental attitude of infantile dependence rather than as defences against its effects. Depressive and schizoid states would appear to come essentially under this heading; but the most obvious and significant symptom belonging to this category is unquestionably separation-anxiety. Not only is separation-anxiety invariably present in war neurotics, but it is the only single symptom which is universally present. This symptom must, accordingly, be regarded as the greatest common measure of all forms of war neurosis.

SEPARATION-ANXIETY

Separation-anxiety is so universal a feature of the war neuroses that it is difficult to believe that its prevalence can have escaped observation hitherto; and indeed the literature of the war neuroses does contain various passing references not only to this phenomenon, but also to the occurrence of an exaggerated degree of dependence among neurotic soldiers. To the best of my knowledge, however, the universality and the real significance of these phenomena (separation-anxiety and exaggerated dependence) have never been properly appreciated, even by those who have not been oblivious to their existence. The commonest interpretation placed upon them is to the effect that, like many a physically disabled soldier, the neurotic soldier wants to go home because he is ill. Even on this assumption, however, it should be remembered that the effect of illness of any kind is to produce a state of helplessness, which tends to revive an attitude of infantile dependence; but, so far as the neurotic soldier is concerned, the truth would appear to be, not so much that he craves to go home because he is ill as that he becomes ill because he craves to go home. It is impossible, therefore, to draw any fundamental distinction between the war neuroses and the neurotic state popularly described as 'homesickness'.[1] Indeed the term 'homesick' could quite appropriately be applied to the neurotic soldier in view of the outstanding part played by separation-anxiety amongst his symptoms and the compulsive nature of his urge to return home at all costs.

Another common, and misleading, interpretation of the phenomenon of separation-anxiety is that it is really secondary to anxiety over situations of danger, and that it is therefore a by-product of the so-called 'self-preservative' tendency. This point of view would appear to ignore the prevalence of suicidal thoughts and impulses among neurotic soldiers—a fact which is difficult to explain in terms of self-preservation. It would also appear to ignore the frequency with which breakdowns occur under military conditions involving little prospect of personal danger, e.g. among troops stationed in the Shetlands, where isolation, rather than danger, is the predominant feature of the soldier's life. It may be argued, however, that the wounded, no less than the neurotic, soldier is often found to exploit, if not actually to welcome, his disability as a means of escape from the dangers of the battlefield, and that the hope of receiving a 'blighty' (to use the terminology of the 1914–18 war) is not far from the con-

---

[1] I had not been long engaged in the study of the war neuroses when I was vividly reminded of a homesick Welsh student with whom I was brought into contact at Strasbourg University in my younger days. I could not avoid being impressed in retrospect by the essential similarity of the picture presented by this student and the characteristic picture presented by the soldier suffering from a war neurosis.

scious thoughts of many a good soldier in the face of the enemy. It would be idle, of course, to deny the strength of self-preservative motives or the influence of personal danger in provoking a state of anxiety; but it still remains to be explained why some soldiers should break down in face of danger, whilst others should not. The explanation would appear to be that the capacity to endure danger varies with the extent to which the individual has outgrown the stage of infantile dependence; and this explanation is in conformity with the notorious proneness to anxiety which characterizes the child as compared to the mature adult.

In military circles soldiers have been traditionally classified as falling into three groups according to their attitude to military service: (1) those who like it, (2) those who don't like it, but stick it, and (3) those who don't like it and don't stick it. Where the conditions of modern warfare are concerned, those who 'don't like it, but stick it' would appear to represent the average individual who has been relatively successful in outgrowing the stage of infantile dependence, whereas those who 'don't like it and don't stick it' would appear to represent the neurotic individual who has, relatively speaking, failed to take this momentous step in emotional development. As for the group of those who 'like it', this would appear to include a considerable proportion of psychopaths who have developed a denial of infantile dependence into such a fine art that callousness and indifference to ordinary human relationships have become embodied in the very structure of their personalities.

PSEUDO-INDEPENDENCE

The category of soldiers who 'like it' is not without its significance for the problem of the war neuroses; for it by no means follows from the fact that they 'like it' that they are necessarily able to 'stick it'. Accordingly, it is quite a common experience for the psychiatrist to find himself called upon to deal with individuals of this class. In some cases they become psychiatric problems because, in an attempted denial of infantile dependence amounting to the adoption of an attitude of pseudo-independence, they react in an exaggerated way against such dependence as is necessarily involved in membership of a military organization. In other cases they become psychiatric problems because they are unable to prevent the deep underlying state of infantile dependence, which is concealed by their superficial pseudo-independence, from reasserting itself under military conditions. They are thus liable either (1) to present aberrations of behaviour upon which disciplinary action has little influence, or (2) to develop symptoms in just the same way as do those individuals who 'don't like it and don't stick it'; and indeed quite commonly both disciplinary difficulties and symptoms are found to arise in conjunction in such cases. In the following case it can hardly be said that disciplinary difficulties actually arose during military service; but there was a previous history of trouble with the police. It may also be presumed with some confidence that disciplinary difficulties would have arisen very shortly if the exacerbation of a pre-existing symptom, which might almost be described as an unconscious manifestation of indiscipline, had not occurred in time to save the situation before disciplinary measures became inevitable.

Case 3. Driver J.T.; R.A.S.C.; aged twenty-five; single.

This soldier had suffered from nocturnal enuresis since childhood. His father had been a seafaring man; and during the period of six years immediately previous to his entering military service he himself had spent a total of three years at sea. The seafaring life provided him with an occupation in which his enuresis was a minimal disability, both because the system of four hour watches ensured that he was frequently wakened, and because the habit of merchant seamen either to ignore the peculiarities of their fellows or else to treat them as a joke ensured that he 'was never made to feel a nuisance'. In spite of these favourable circumstances, however, he could never bring himself to settle down to a permanently seafaring life; and he was in the habit of taking various shore jobs between voyages. When war broke out in 1939, as it happened, he was driving a bus; and, having joined the Supplementary Reserve on the day before war was declared, he was duly called up and employed as a driver. He was sent to France in September 1939. During the earlier part of his service he was comparatively immune from enuretic 'incidents'; and, while in France, he remained quite pleased with himself and quite contented. His maternal grandfather had been a regular soldier; and his 'idea of wartime was to be in the Army'. He had volunteered 'in good faith'; and it gave him particular satisfaction to serve in France—a country which had always exercised a special fascination for him, largely because his father and one of his uncles had held it in special esteem and were always talking about it in his childhood.

After the German attack was launched in the spring of 1940, he remained in good spirits; and he felt 'perfectly in order' during the retreat to Dunkirk. During the passage from Dunkirk to Dover, however, he began to experience 'a feeling of displacement quite apart from the Dunkirk affair'. He found 'seeing sailors go to fetch soldiers' much more impressive than 'military operations'; and the old call of the sea reasserted itself in strength. This fact, as he himself came to feel in retrospect, had a great deal to do with the circumstances which eventually led him to report sick, viz. circumstances attending a marked exacerbation of his nocturnal enuresis. This exacerbation caused him considerable embarrassment when quartered in a room with several others; and the situation developed in such a way that, after a stormy scene with the N.C.O. in charge of his room, he reported sick on his own initiative in order to avoid being reported by the N.C.O. for bed-wetting. Meanwhile, since his return from France, he had become definitely 'homesick for the sea' and had suffered from a 'displacement and general depression', which became progressively worse until he reported sick. After his admission to hospital, he adopted an extremely reserved attitude towards members of the medical staff; but, on occasions on which this reserve was to some extent overcome, he admitted that he had a definite tendency to regard others as hostile, that he nursed grudges, that he often felt himself to be an enemy of society and that he sometimes experienced a strong temptation to commit crimes. In a moment of unwonted frankness he also disclosed the carefully guarded secret that, at the age of thirteen, he had written a story in the first person about a boy of his own age, who lost both parents and ran away to sea. Having made this disclosure, he immediately volunteered that 'this was a cruel idea' (referring to his having represented the boy as losing both parents), and admitted that he himself had entertained death wishes towards his parents during childhood.

An only child, he had been extremely unhappy in his early life, which had been characterized by an atmosphere of great insecurity. His father drank, his mother was nervous, and there were constant quarrels between his parents. At the age of four he had seen his father knock his mother down, with the result that she fell with her head in the grate; and he recalled many subsequent incidents of a similar character—incidents which would appear to have been always followed by nocturnal enuresis. The police were constantly being called in to deal with domestic disturbances; and, on account of his father's violence, his mother often took him out of the house about midnight to spend the rest of the night with her in a hotel. The family never remained long in one house; and, wherever the household went, there were rows with the neighbours. Eventually his father left home never to return; and, on his own return from his first voyage, he learned that his father had been killed in a motor accident. Once he had tasted life at sea, he lost all 'fancy' for being at home. Nevertheless, from time to time he experienced an overwhelming compulsion to go to stay with his mother between voyages. He was always overjoyed to see her on his arrival; but they invariably got on one another's nerves after a few days, with the result that it became as much as he could manage to remain at home for so long as a fortnight. In addition, he often wished quite frankly that his mother were dead.

This case is especially interesting and informative as an example of the way in which a deeply repressed attitude of infantile dependence may persist underneath, and be masked by, a more superficial attitude of exaggerated independence or pseudo-independence. In his early childhood—a period of life in which it is not only natural to be childishly dependent, but necessary for satisfactory development to be able to depend safely—his soldier was exposed to conditions which made it impossible for him to depend with any confidence upon either of his parents. He had no security of tenure even in his home itself, since the family was constantly moving from one house to another; and, owing to his father's bouts of drunkenness and his mother's anxiety, he never knew, when he went to bed, where he would find himself in the morning. He was thus brought up in an atmosphere of the greatest insecurity. His method of dealing with this situation resolved itself into an attempt to convert his liabilities into assets at the expense of turning himself into a psychopathic personality. He capitalized his insecurity and his inability to depend safely by renouncing all intimacy of social contact and all but the more remote of group bonds. The consequence was that he never made friends, and that he could reconcile himself to no discipline except such as prevails on board a merchant ship—discipline characterized by the principle that 'so long as you do your job, no one interferes with you'. At the same time he placed a premium on his own insecurity by developing a continued 'Wanderlust' and an incapacity to sustain any continuity of employment. By the adoption of a paranoid attitude he also sought to safeguard himself against the risks of that insecurity which dependence of any kind seemed to him to involve. Nevertheless, in spite of all the measures which he adopted to establish himself on a basis of exaggerated independence (pseudo-independence), traces of an underlying state of infantile dependence could be detected in his behaviour. Although, as the story which he wrote in his early adolescence bears witness, he was prompted to go to sea by hatred of his parents and a desire to be independent of them, yet he never remained free tor long from a compulsion to go back to stay with his mother. The situation was complicated by the fact that the sea itself came to represent for him the mother upon whom, in his childhood, he had longed to depend, but upon whom he found it impossible to depend safely; and it was for this reason that he became 'homesick for the sea' after a period of separation from it, whilst at the same time he found it impossible to reconcile himself to a permanently seafaring life. He was thus reduced, at the deeper mental levels, to the position of a child tossed to and fro between two mother-figures, neither of whom he could trust, and neither of whom he could do without. The case of this psychopathic personality serves to illustrate the extent to which a deep attitude of infantile dependence may be seen to underlie a superficial attitude of pseudo-independence, which, by its very exaggeration, reveals itself as but a defence against the infantile dependence underlying it.

THE COMPULSION TO RETURN HOME

The significance of the part played by infantile dependence in the etiology, and by separation-anxiety in the symptomatology, of the war neuroses may perhaps best be judged by the compulsiveness of the desire to return home, which is such a marked feature in all cases, and which manifested itself even in the case of the pseudo-independent psychopath just quoted. In cases in which the general symptomatology assumes a psychoneurotic form, this compulsion, although experienced, is seldom so urgent as to give rise to marked disturbances of behaviour. In cases in which the general symptomatology assumes a psychotic form, however, the situation is otherwise; and in such cases it is not uncommon for the compulsion in question to manifest itself either in a fugue or in a consciously executed flight such as to constitute, from a disciplinary point of view, either absence without leave or desertion, or else, where the individual's sense of duty is sufficiently strong, in an attempt at suicide. The compulsiveness of the desire to return home is typically illustrated in the following case of an N.C.O. in whom separation-anxiety assumed a psychotic complexion.

Case 4. Cpl. J. F., K.O.S.B.; aged twenty-six; married.

This N.C.O. was admitted to hospital in a state of depression accompanied by a certain degree of agitation, as well as by various phobic and obsessional symptoms (e.g. a fear of enclosed spaces and a compulsion to go back to make sure that he had extinguished cigarette ends). He was extremely tense and anxious in his appearance; and he experienced a constant sense of separation-anxiety. During the day his attention was constantly preoccupied with thoughts about his wife and about returning home; and dreams about being back at home were a regular feature of such sleep as he was able to obtain.

He had first begun to 'feel queer' in September 1938, while serving with the Regular Army in India. He had enlisted in 1932 and had married just a few weeks before his departure for India in 1934. Since he was not old enough to be on the married strength, his wife was unable to accompany him; and he felt the parting acutely. However, throughout the whole of his service in India he was buoyed up by thoughts of the day on which his time would expire and he would become free to settle down in a home of his own with his wife. He 'got on all right in the Army' because he knew he 'had to'; but his heart was really at home all the time. He found it a great consolation in the loneliness which he often experienced to make plans for the golden age of home life, to which he looked forward with increasing anticipation, particularly after learning that his wife had given birth to a child; and, as the term of his unexpired service became shorter, he built more and more upon the prospect of his discharge from regular service. However, this prospect was doomed to be blighted just when it appeared to be on the point of realization; for, owing to the international crisis of September 1938, the sailing of the troopship, upon which he was due to return to the U.K. for discharge, was suddenly cancelled. It was the resulting postponement of his discharge and the accompanying interference with his carefully laid plans that precipitated the first onset of recognizable symptoms. He felt that the ground had been taken from under his feet; and he was instantly plunged into a state of extreme despair, in explanation of which he volunteered the remark, 'The separation from my wife got on top of me'. In conformity with this statement, he experienced an intense degree of separation-anxiety, which was accompanied by a number of other symptoms (e.g. headache, loss of appetite and suicidal impulses) clearly indicating that he was suffering from an attack of acute depression. When the crisis passed and the prospect of war receded, the cloud which had descended upon his hopes of discharge began to lift; and, as the cloud lifted, his depression lifted with it. When he eventually obtained his discharge (actually a transfer to the Reserve) in April 1939, it would appear that he passed into a hypomanic state; for, after he had been reunited to his wife and had obtained a Post Office job in his native town of Z, he felt 'on top of the world' and 'got on rare' at his work. As it turned out, his newly found happiness was short-lived; for he had not been at home for many weeks when, as a Reservist, he received instructions from the War Office to report at his Depot on 15 June 1939 for employment in the instruction of recruits under the Military Training Act. Upon receipt of these instructions he immediately became preoccupied with thoughts about the impending separation; and he again began to suffer from separation-anxiety, accompanied by loss of appetite and severe headaches. Having received an assurance, however, that his services would only be required for two months, he reconciled himself to the situation and duly reported at the Depot. Here his anxiety was further mitigated by the fact that he was permitted to go home for each week-end (a fact, incidentally, which did not free him of the necessity to write to his wife twice a day during the week); and it was an intense relief to him when his services were dispensed with on 26 August 1939. On this occasion, however, his relief was even more short-lived than before; for the country was already on the eve of war and on 27 August 1939 he learned from a wireless announcement that, as a Reservist, he was required to report at his Depot without delay. This he duly did on the following day, but not without fainting in the lobby as he was about to leave home. On his return to the Depot he was immediately absorbed into the establishment as an Instructor; but the fact that this reduced his prospects of being sent abroad to a minimum did little to prevent him once again becoming the prey of intense separation-anxiety. Having taken advantage of every opportunity of short leave which he could obtain in the meantime, he was granted compassionate leave in December 1939, to be present at a confinement which his wife was expecting. The confinement proving a difficult one, he obtained a two days' extension of leave on the grounds of his wife's illness; but, in spite of this, he over-stayed his leave and thus, for the first time in his military history, committed a breach of discipline at the instance of his separation-anxiety. The offence was overlooked in view of his good record for conduct; but his symptoms now assumed a proportion which com-promised his efficiency. In particular, his efficiency was compromised by a failure of concentration, in consequence of which he often found himself unable to remember what he was talking about while in pro-cess of instructing a squad. The one thing that obsessed his mind con-stantly was his need for his wife. Nothing else mattered to him; and his whole attitude was summed up in the remark, 'I just wanted to be beside my wife, war or nothing'. In March 1940 he received a letter from his wife to say that his baby was about to have an operation for hernia; and he obtained compassionate leave to enable him to be at home at the time of the operation. As it happened, the operation was postponed. Being unable to obtain an extension of leave until after it should take place, he set out for the Depot; but the tug of home proved too much for him during the journey. He accordingly turned back and remained at home until the operation was safely over. Thereupon he again set out for the Depot; but again he turned back. This time, however, he did not proceed to his home on his arrival at the railway station of his home town. Instead, he went to a chemist's, bought a bottle of lysol, returned to the station and drank the con-tents of the bottle. The conflict between his sense of duty and his compulsion to return home had proved too much for him; and he sought what to him seemed the only solution. As it happened, his attempt at suicide was a failure; and, instead of finding his way to death, he found his way to hospital.

His early life had been unhappy; and he retained many painful memories of quarrels between his parents—particularly of one quarrel which led to his mother leaving home for four days. Her departure left him desolate. He had no hope that she would ever return; and he felt that 'the light had gone out of life' for him. He was very much attached to his mother and very dependent upon her; and he often sat for hours talking to her. She died when he was six-teen years of age; and, on learning of her death, he became speechless for twenty minutes and remained off work for seven days. He was employed in a butcher's shop at this time; and he imagined himself under the circular saw in the shop. After his mother's death his father broke up the home; and he went to live with an aunt. He missed his mother so badly, however, that he was miserable at his aunt's; and it was under the influence of this misery that he enlisted in an impulsive moment.

EMOTIONAL IDENTIFICATION

The compulsion to return home, which assumed such exaggerated proportions in Case 4, is a characteristic accompaniment of separation-anxiety; and it is in no sense robbed of its characteristic quality by the fact that in certain cases it may assume the restricted form of an insatiable longing. The presence of such a compulsion in association with separation-anxiety is of special significance on account of the light which it sheds upon the psychology of infantile dependence; for it serves to direct our attention to the mental process which constitutes the distinctive psychological feature of this state. The process in question is that of *identification*—a process in virtue of which the individual fails to differentiate himself from, and thus spontaneously identifies himself emotionally with those upon whom he depends. So intimate is the connection between identification and infantile dependence that, psychologically speaking, they may be treated as the same phenomenon. So far as we can conceive the mental state of the child before birth, we must regard it as characterized by a degree of primary identification so absolute as to preclude his entertaining any thought of differentiation from the maternal body, which constitutes his whole environment and the whole world of his experience. The process of identification which subsequently characterizes the emotional relationships of childhood would thus appear to represent the persistence into extra-uterine life of an emotional attitude existing before birth. So far as it influences behaviour, it would also appear to represent an attempt to restore emotionally an original state of security which was rudely disturbed by the experience of birth.

It requires little imagination to appreciate that the experience of birth must come as a profound shock to the child accustomed, while *in utero*, to a blissful state of absolute identification; and there is good reason to believe that birth constitutes not only an extremely unpleasant and painful experience, but also one fraught with acute anxiety. It may be presumed, further, that birth provides the occasion of the child's *first* experience of anxiety; and, since birth also represents the child's first experience of separation from his mother, birth-anxiety must be regarded as the prototype of all the separation-anxiety which is subsequently experienced. This being so, it can be readily appreciated that separation-anxiety will always retain the impress of the birth trauma by which it was originally evoked, and that any postnatal experience which provokes separation-anxiety will in some measure assume the emotional significance of the original birth trauma. It is not implied, of course, that any conscious memory of the birth trauma is retained; but that the experience is perpetuated at a deep mental level and is capable of reactivation under certain conditions may be inferred from a number of psychopathological phenomena. As an instance of such phenomena may be cited the common nightmare about going along an underground passage which becomes so narrow that the dreamer feels unable to move and wakes in a state of acute anxiety. A similar significance is attached to the even commoner nightmare about falling from a height—a nightmare which, in my experience, is perhaps the commonest of all nightmares amongst soldiers suffering from a war neurosis. These considerations shed a new light upon the phenomenon of the traumatic experience which is so commonly found to precipitate a war neurosis. It can now be seen that such experiences not only function in the same manner as the birth trauma, but actually precipitate a revival of the birth trauma at the deep mental level at which it lies buried. It can also be understood in a more profound sense why such traumatic experiences should have the characteristic effect of producing a state of acute separation-anxiety.

In the light of what has just been said it can now be stated that separation-anxiety is a characteristic product of the tendency of individuals who have remained in a state of infantile dependence to make identification the basis of their emotional relationships with those upon whom they depend. The figure with whom the dependent individual is originally identified is, of course, his mother; and, whilst it is not long before he begins to identify himself with other figures, particularly his father, the original identification persists underneath all others subsequently made. The extent to which this original identification persists, even in individuals who have relatively outgrown the state of infantile dependence, may be judged from the frequency with which the wounded soldier is known to cry for his mother in his agony. It remains true, nevertheless, that the more emotionally mature an individual becomes, the less his emotional relationships are characterized by identification. In the necessarily dependent phase of early childhood it is, of course, both natural and inevitable that identification should play a predominant role; but, when emotional development is satisfactory, there is a progressive decrease in identification throughout the years of childhood and adolescence until the relative independence of emotional maturity is reached. This progressive decrease in identification is accompanied by the progressive increase of a capacity on the part of the individual to differentiate himself from emotionally significant figures. At the same time the importance of the figures with whom he originally identified himself (parents and parent substitutes) tends to diminish. Emotional maturity is consequently characterized, not only by a capacity to sustain relationships with other individuals on a basis of mutual independence, but also by a capacity to contract fresh relationships. In the case of the individual who fails to outgrow the stage of infantile dependence both of these capacities are deficient. His capacity to sustain relationships with others on an independent basis remains inadequate; and so does his capacity to establish fresh relationships. The relationships which he is best able to sustain are such as conform most to the pattern of his early relationship with his mother; and the only relationships which he is able to establish with any measure of stability are relationships calculated to assume for him, by a process of transference, all or much of the significance of his original relationship. Such then is the condition of the individual who develops a war neurosis. He is an individual who has retained an undue measure of childish dependence upon his home and his loved ones; and he is too closely identified with them to be able to endure any great measure of separation from them. They still tend to constitute for him, as was the case in his childhood, not only his emotional world, but even, in a sense, himself. He tends to feel that he is part of them, and equally that they are part of him. In their absence his very personality tends to be diminished—and, in extreme cases, even his sense of personal identity may be compromised. Such being the case, it is not difficult to understand why a compulsion to return home should be so universal and characteristic a feature of the war neuroses—a feature no less universal and characteristic than the symptom of separation-anxiety, with which it is so intimately associated. The explanation of this compulsion lies in the process of identification as it is found to operate in an individual who has failed to emerge adequately from the state of infantile dependence. Unlike the emotionally mature soldier, such an individual, when placed under military conditions, finds it too difficult a task to establish himself as a separate personality within the framework of the military organization, subordinate himself to the aims of the military group without any surrender of independence, and maintain stable emotional bonds with the group whilst remaining differentiated from it. On the other hand, the dependent individual usually finds great difficulty either in establishing or in maintaining a reliable relationship with the military group on a basis of identification. This is due, of course, to the fact that his identification with his home and his loved ones does not readily admit of a competitor; and it is to the strength of this identification above all that the development of a war neurosis must be attributed.

Actually there is a certain proportion of soldiers who actually do succeed in establishing a relationship with the military group on a basis of identification. It remains true, however, that such a relationship is one which they find it difficult to maintain, especially in face of frustration or stress; and, since frustration and stress are such characteristic features of the soldier's lot, the percentage of those who prove capable of maintaining such a relationship indefinitely is extremely small. A significant feature of this group of soldiers is a tendency on their part to establish such a strong identification with the military group that with them soldiering actually assumes a quality as compulsive as does the desire to return home in dependent individuals who fail to make this identification. Such soldiers are apt to convey the impression of being as keen as mustard; but it by no means follows that they make reliable soldiers. On the contrary, they are usually so consumed with military zeal that they itch impatiently to be in the forefront of the fray, are intolerant of such delays as are involved in training, become irritated by routine duties and soon begin to smart under the imagined failure of the military authorities to reward their devotion with promotion to match what they feel to be their deserts. Paradoxical as it may appear, these keen soldiers are particularly liable to develop a state of acute 'separation-anxiety' —the traumatic 'separation' here being constituted by the apparent rejection which they experience at the hands of the military authorities when, as it seems to them, their enthusiasm is found to meet with so little recognition.

THE FACTOR OF MORALE

It should now be evident that identification, which is such a characteristic feature of the emotional life of the dependent individual, is not only the fundamental process underlying the development of a war neurosis, but also a process imposing serious limitations upon the social adaptability of the potential war neurotic. That the process of identification should prove to be a common factor operating both in the direction of compromising social relationships and in the direction of promoting psychopathological developments in the soldier is a consideration of the greatest significance. It is a consideration in the light of which the whole problem of the war neuroses assumes an aspect which has hitherto suffered from almost complete neglect in medical literature. During the course of the 1914–18 war a remarkable scientific advance was undoubtedly registered by the abandonment of the term 'shell-shock' in favour of the term 'war-neurosis'; for this change of terminology indicated a recognition of the fact that the states to which these terms were successively applied were essentially of psychological, and not of neurological, origin. In spite of this advance, however, the tendency to regard each case as 'individual', which was an inevitable feature of the neurological approach, was in large measure carried over into the newer psychological approach. It is true that during the 1914–18 war there arose a powerful school of psychotherapists who regarded the war neuroses as products of a conflict between the soldier's instinct of self-preservation and his sense of military duty—the symptoms of the war neurotic being interpreted as motivated, albeit quite unconsciously, by a desire to find a means of escape from the danger zone without experiencing the sense of guilt which a deliberate dereliction of duty would involve. This view at any rate had the merit of recognizing the bearing of questions of social responsibility upon the etiology of the war neuroses. Nevertheless, quite apart from what is now seen to be the superficiality of such an interpretation of the war neurotic's symptoms, no real attempt was made to explain the incidence of the war neuroses; and the conflict in which they were held to originate was treated as essentially a problem of individual psychology. In particular, no account was taken of the general character of the war neurotic's social relationships, or of the underlying factors which determine it. Subsequent to the war of 1914–18, attempts were made, particularly under the influence of Freud's conceptions, to obtain a deeper understanding of the war neuroses; but the general tendency was to lay even greater, rather than less, emphasis upon the individual nature of the war neurotic's emotional conflicts. This might have been otherwise if the line of thought pursued by Freud in his *Group Psychology and the Analysis of the Ego* (1921) had received more of the attention which it deserved.

Among the various conclusions recorded by Freud in the work in question is one to the effect that the state of panic notoriously associated with the collapse of an army in the field is essentially due to a breakdown of the emotional bonds which unite members of the military group to one another under common leaders. According to the ordinary view, of course, it is when the situation of 'every man for himself' arises that the group spirit ('esprit de corps') disintegrates. According to Freud, on the contrary, it is when the group spirit becomes weakened that the situation of 'every man for himself' arises, and that panic invades the individual heart. It is thus not a case of the group spirit collapsing because the individuals who compose the group have given way to panic, but of panic assailing these individuals because, owing to the collapse of the group spirit, they have ceased to be members of the military group. The essential feature of the situation is that each *quondam* member of the military group becomes deprived of the support both of his former fellow-soldiers and of the military group as a whole, and is relegated to the status of an isolated individual facing the combined strength of a hostile force without any support. Confronted with such a perilous situation, it is small wonder if the soldier is assailed by panic—panic which, as Freud points out, is not solely due to interests of self-preservation, but is partly conditioned by anxiety over the aggressive impulses which he is now tempted to direct against his former associates and his former leaders. It is, of course, *mass* anxiety that Freud is here discussing; but the reader who has followed the argument of the present paper will have little difficulty in recognizing that the phenomenon of panic to which he refers is essentially one of separation-anxiety affecting all (or nearly all) the members of a military group simultaneously. The panic-stricken condition of soldiers belonging to an army which has collapsed in the field must, accordingly, be regarded as one of transient war neurosis occurring under special conditions in individuals who are preponderantly 'normal'. The difference between the state of such soldiers and that of soldiers suffering from a frank war neurosis is then seen to lie in the fact that, whereas in the case of the 'normal' soldier separation-anxiety only occurs when the bonds uniting the group as a whole are dissolved, in the case of the neurotic soldier separation-anxiety may occur even when the bonds uniting the group as a whole remain intact. This means, of course, that the emotional bonds uniting the neurotic soldier to the military group are unduly slender and precarious. How this comes to be so has already been considered at some length. In a word, it comes to be so because the neurotic soldier has retained from his childhood an excessive degree of infantile dependence and has remained, at any rate at the deeper mental levels, so closely identified with his original love-objects within the family group that he is incapable of establishing any stable emotional relationship with the military group, or of participating adequately in that group spirit which is so indispensable to military efficiency, and which constitutes the essence of 'morale'. It should be added that, in the case of such a soldier, the anxiety which develops over separation from those upon whom he depends in the home environment is accompanied by anxiety over the aggressive impulses which he comes to entertain towards the military group, and which have a disintegrating effect upon such morale as he possesses.

We are now in a position to appreciate that the question of the war neuroses and the question of morale are inseparably bound up with one another. The fact that, as we have seen, even the 'normal' soldier may develop a war neurosis, albeit a transient one, in circumstances in which morale becomes impaired can leave us in no doubt regarding the intimate connection of the two questions. This phenomenon also serves to show that some measure of infantile dependence may be revealed in the case of the most 'normal' individual. The truth is that emotional maturity is never absolute, but always a matter of degree. Infantile dependence is equally a matter of degree, never being entirely absent, but being subject to an infinite degree of variation from individual to individual; and, of course, individuals vary likewise in the degree of stress which they can endure without experiencing anxiety under conditions of separation from their loved ones. In the light of what happens when an army collapses in the field we are further entitled to draw the conclusion that, whilst any high degree of infantile dependence is, in itself, inimical to morale, the existence of a high state of morale within a group can exercise a profound influence in counteracting the ill effects of infantile dependence among its members. In conformity with this fact, it has been strongly maintained by well-informed military opinion that during the war of 1914–18 the incidence of war neurosis varied between units in inverse proportion to the morale of the unit concerned; and this opinion would appear to be capable of statistical verification, even when allowance is made for the idiosyncracies of regimental medical officers.

It has always been the tendency of the military mind, of course, either to interpret a war neurosis as evidence of cowardice or to dismiss it as a sheer case of malingering. So far as cowardice is concerned, it must be admitted that the soldier suffering from a war neurosis does usually, although by no means invariably, tend to behave as a coward in fact of external danger; but this in no way affects the fact that such a soldier does actually suffer from incapacitating symptoms. In any case, it always remains more important to know why he should behave as he does than simply to treat him as a coward; for treating him as a coward will certainly not in itself convert him into an efficient soldier. As regards the question of malingering, my own experience is that, where cases of war neurosis reaching hospital are concerned, not more than 1 per cent. can possibly be regarded as true malingerers, i.e. as failing to present *bona fide* symptoms; and even this small proportion of individuals are usually found, in my experience, to have the characteristic history of a psychopathic personality. It is impossible, nevertheless, to dismiss the traditional military attitude towards the war neuroses as entirely irrelevant from a psychiatric standpoint. It must be insisted, of course, that the neurotic soldier does suffer from genuine symptoms. At the same time, there can be no doubt that, characteristically, his consuming desire is to get out of the Army and back to his home at all costs, war or no war; and this is a fact about which no one can possibly remain a sceptic if he has once witnessed the wave of enthusiasm which sweeps over a body of neurotic soldiers leaving hospital for home on discharge from military service.[1] Whilst, therefore, it is impossible to accept any explanation of the war neuroses couched simply in terms of cowardice and malingering, it must be recognized that the traditional military attitude towards these conditions contains more than a grain of truth. The real truth embodied, however

[1] It may now be stated that, during the course of the 1939–45 war, the earlier practice of granting neurotic soldiers their discharge direct from hospital was abandoned on account of this very phenomenon.

imperfectly, in this attitude is that the incidence of the war neuroses is a criterion of morale; and, as it seems to me, this is a truth which has suffered from sad neglect in the literature of the war neuroses.

Morale is an extremely difficult quality to assess; and it is a quality in respect of which it is particularly difficult to draw comparisons. It would be interesting, if it were possible, to compare the state of morale prevailing in the British Army at the time of writing (1942) with that which prevailed during the corresponding period of the war of 1914–18; but the conditions under which the 1939 war is being waged are so different from those under which the 1914–18 war was waged that it seems impossible to establish a reliable criterion. It may be remarked, however, that, since under war conditions the British Army is essentially a citizen army, its morale cannot be considered apart from the morale of the country as a whole. At this point it therefore becomes pertinent for us to ask ourselves whether the developments which have taken place in national life between the two wars have been calculated to raise, to maintain or to lower national morale. Whatever answer the individual reader may be disposed to give to this question, there can be no doubt, at any rate, as to the verdict reached by the dictators prior to the outbreak of the 1939 war; for 'the degeneracy of the democracies' had for long been one of their favourite slogans. Indeed the estimate of democratic morale embodied in this slogan provided them with one of their chief incentives in precipitating the struggle unleashed in 1939.

In speaking of 'the degeneracy of the democracies' the dictators would appear to have had in mind a certain lack of public spirit which crept insidiously over the British and other similarly constituted nations in response to the disillusionment of hopes, which followed the Armistice of 1918. So far as Great Britain is concerned, this lack of public spirit was reflected in a marked inconclusiveness and ineffectiveness of international policy. It also manifested itself in an obvious reluctance on the part of the individual to make personal sacrifices in the interests of the national group, and in a very 'bourgeois' preoccupation with narrow personal, sectional and familial interests. This development must be regarded as registering a definite deterioration of national morale since 1918; and, in the light of what precedes, it can now be appreciated that this deterioration of morale was accompanied by a regressive resurgence of infantile dependence throughout the community as a whole. Such then is the general background of the national war effort and the recruitment of the British Army following the outbreak of war in 1939. There can, of course, be no denying that the impact of war had the immediate effect of, in some measure, reviving the waning group spirit, and that this revival became markedly intensified after the evacuation from Dunkirk. But, if we are to be frank, we must ask ourselves seriously whether at the time of writing (1942) all the leeway has been made up. I venture to suggest that any attempt to deal radically with the problem of the war neuroses must involve not only the making up of leeway, but an actual making of headway within the field of morale.

If it is difficult to draw any valid comparison between the morale of the British Army in the Second World War and its morale at the corresponding stage of the First World War, it is certainly not easy to make a comparative assessment of the state of morale prevailing in the armies of the various combatant powers. It must be recognized, however, that the cultivation of morale was a leading article of policy with the totalitarian states for many years prior to the outbreak of war in 1939. That this policy met with considerable success both in Germany and Russia is evident from the extent to which the populations of those countries proved as a whole willing to sacrifice both personal and familial interests to the interests of the national group; and there can be little doubt that, even after the outbreak of war in 1939, they showed themselves capable of sacrifices far in excess of any required of the population of Great Britain. The result is that Goering's 'Guns for butter' became much less of a joke than it had seemed in the ostrich-like days of pre-war wishful thinking.

In view of the central thesis of the present paper, the characteristic totalitarian technique for the cultivation of morale is not without its interest; for it is an essential feature of this technique to take all possible steps to wean the individual from family ties and family loyalties. In so far as such steps meet with success, we should expect the soldier who has been brought up under such a régime to be correspondingly less subject to separation-anxiety under conditions of active service. At the same time, it by no means follows that steps taken to wean the prospective soldier from familial bonds will, *ipso facto*, wean him from a state of infantile dependence; for, under the Nazi régime at least, it also became part of the technique deliberately to cultivate dependence upon the State as a substitute for dependence upon familial love-objects—and thus actually to exploit infantile dependence in the national interest. Under conditions of political or military success this technique would appear to achieve its object owing to the sense of security which success engenders; but it may be expected that under conditions of persistent political or military failure the resulting sense of disillusionment regarding the capacity of the State to provide security would lead to a revival of the individual's original infantile attachments, and so to an outbreak of acute separation-anxiety accompanied by a collapse of morale. Indeed, this is what actually occurred in Germany in 1918. It would appear, accordingly, that national failure constitutes the greatest test of totalitarian morale. On the other hand, comparative national success would appear to constitute the greatest test of democratic morale; for, since in a democracy the individual is less dependent upon the State and more dependent upon his familial love-objects for a sense of security, the conditions of national success will tend to promote undue complacency regarding national issues.

Reference has already been made to the view, widely held by psychotherapists during the 1914–18 war, that the war neuroses derived their significance from the fact that their symptoms provided the affected soldier with an unconsciously motivated means of escaping from the dangers of the battlefield with a good conscience. The limitations of this view at once become obvious when we consider that many soldiers contract typical war neuroses without ever having been near a battlefield, and even in the absence of any great prospect of being near one. Actually, it is to the symptom of separation-anxiety, as I have tried to show, that we must look for the real significance of the war neuroses. It is towards a return to his home and his loved ones, rather than towards an escape from the dangers of the battlefield, that the neurotic soldier is orientated. At the same time the older view just mentioned does embody an observation which, when properly interpreted, is certainly of great significance. This is the observation that the neurotic soldier characteristically displays a remarkable absence of guilt over his evasion of military duties. Such an absence of guilt is not invariable; for, when the clinical picture is dominated by depressive and obsessional features, there is often a definite tendency on the part of the soldier to worry over letting his country or his unit down. This feature is particularly liable to be present in the case of senior non-commissioned ranks of the Regular Army—men who characteristically have a reputation for conscientiousness, and into whom a high sense of discipline has been instilled throughout long years of service. Even in such instances, however, one usually gains the impression that, by the time such men reach hospital, they have given up all real effort, and that their apparent scruples amount to little more than lip-service to abandoned standards of the past. Further, in so far as their self-reproach is genuine, it is only in the prodromal stage of the war neurosis that it assumes an acute form, i.e. in the stage at which there is real conflict between the desire to return home and the sense of duty. In such cases this is usually before the individual reports sick; for by the time such individuals report sick (which they only do after a prolonged struggle) the issue of the conflict is already almost invariably decided. With the exception of these cases, however, neurotic soldiers display a remarkable absence of self-reproach over the failure in military duty involved in their neuroses. This holds true not only of conscripts who have perhaps entered military service with reluctance, but also of volunteers who have joined the Army out of patriotic motives. It is evident, accordingly, that the war neuroses are characterized not only by separation-anxiety, but also by a definite deterioration of the sense of duty, i.e. by a definite disintegration of the mental structure of conscience (a collapse of the authority of the super-ego). An unmistakable disturbance of the personality is thus seen to be involved in the development of a war neurosis. This disturbance is part and parcel of the regression involved in that revival of a hidden state of infantile dependence, to which, as we have seen, a war neurosis is to be ultimately ascribed. What happens is that the war neurotic regresses, in greater or lesser degree, to an infantile level corresponding to a stage of development at which the structure of conscience (or super-ego) has not yet been organized upon a stable basis. The neurotic soldier is thus more or less reduced to the emotional state of a child who has not yet reached the stage of accepting his parents as authoritative conscience-figures. At this stage the child is not so much concerned whether his own behaviour is good or bad (morally) in the eyes of his parents as whether his parents appear to love him or not, i.e. whether, from his point of view, they present themselves to him as good (in the sense of 'nice') or bad (in the sense of 'nasty') figures. What happens, therefore, when a soldier develops a war neurosis is that, regressing to an infantile emotional level, he ceases to regard his superiors in rank and the military organization in general as representing authoritative parental figures to whom he is bound by a deep sense of moral obligation, and begins to regard them as 'bad' parental figures who have no love or consideration for him. At the same time he regards those at home as 'good' parental figures who love him, and who will look after him if only he can get back to them (distance often lending no little enchantment to the view). He thus becomes consumed by an overwhelming desire to escape from the insecurity which he experiences at the hands of the 'bad' figures, into whose clutches he feels that military obligations have delivered him, to the security which the 'good' figures at home seem, by contrast, to offer him. That this is a correct interpretation of the situation which develops is confirmed in an interesting manner by two of the stock complaints voiced by hospitalized neurotic soldiers in proof of their inability to 'go back' to the •Army. These are (in all cases almost identically phrased), 'I can't stand being shouted at', and 'I can't eat Army food'—the latter complaint being almost invariably followed, in the case of married men, by the remark, 'But I can eat anything my wife cooks for me'. The inner meaning of these complaints is, of course, that every word of command has become the shout of an angry father, and that every 'greasy' (always 'greasy') meal from the cook-house has become additional evidence of the indifference of a heartless mother. Further evidence that the neurotic soldier feels himself to be in the power of evil figures is provided by the frequency of such symptoms as a sense of being watched, as well as by the frequency of nightmares about being chased or shouted at (not to mention somewhat less common nightmares about being crushed, strangled or visited by ghosts). Such being the situation, it is not difficult to understand why it is that the war neuroses should prove so resistant to psychotherapy—and indeed to any form of remedial treatment in the medical armamentarium. Perhaps it is small wonder too that, after acquiring some disillusioning experience of neurotic servicemen *en masse*, I was driven to remark, 'What these people really need is not a psychotherapist, but an evangelist'. In the light of further experience, I see no reason to think that this remark was greatly in error; for I remain convinced that, from the national standpoint and from the standpoint of military efficiency, the problem presented by the war neuroses is not primarily one of psychotherapy, but one of morale.

CONCLUDING REMARKS

If my conclusions meet with general acceptance, a number of important questions of policy are bound to arise. I do not propose to deal with these questions here; but I cannot refrain from drawing attention to one of them—the question of awarding pensions to individuals who have been discharged from the services on account of a war neurosis. It is not open to question that, from a strictly medical point of view, such an individual must be regarded essentially as a patient. He is suffering from *bona fide* symptoms; and, in so far as his condition is amenable to treatment, he should receive the treatment which he requires. At the same time his social rehabilitation is obviously a matter for national concern; and, in so far as his capacity as a wage-earner is affected, he and his family will require some adequate form of economic assistance from the State. It merits consideration, however, whether, from the point of view of morale, a specifically *war* pension, possibly accompanied by a badge 'for service rendered', is an appropriate award in respect of the special form of disability represented by a war neurosis. The question of pensions for the war neuroses is, of course, one which lends itself all too readily to the influence of backdoor political pressure; but, in view of the intimate association of the problems of war neurosis and morale, it is clearly in the national interest not only that such pressure should be resisted, but that the whole question should be reviewed afresh.

CHAPTER IV

The Treatment and Rehabilitation of Sexual Offenders[1] (1946)

Tʜᴇ Scottish Advisory Council, to whom my evidence is about to be submitted, has been appointed to consider 'the treatment and rehabilitation of offenders'; and I understand that the Council desires me to submit evidence bearing specially on the question of the 'provision of facilities for psychotherapeutic treatment in Scottish prisons with special reference to sexual and unnatural offences'.

To me as a medical psychologist the terms 'treatment' and 'rehabilitation', which appear in the Council's terms of reference, differ from one another in significance to an extent which seems to demand some special consideration. In the medical sense the term 'treatment' signifies such technical assistance of a therapeutic nature as a doctor is able to provide for a patient who consults him, whether in private or in a clinic, in the hope of obtaining relief from a pathological condition which is causing him distress; and psychotherapeutic treatment is a special form of technical assistance appropriate for conditions of a psychopathological origin. Such treatment, if successful, is likely to lead to favourable consequences for society, although this is by no means necessarily the case; but it is essentially something which the individual patient seeks on his own initiative for the relief of his own distress or for his own peace of mind.

'Rehabilitation', on the other hand, is a term which is primarily social in its reference; for it signifies essentially the restoration of the individual's social capacities which have been compromised, and which require to be restored in the interests of society.

The difference between 'treatment' and 'rehabilitation' was

[1] Evidence submitted to the Scottish Advisory Council on the Treatment and Rehabilitation of Offenders on 17th May 1946.

brought home to me with particular insistence during the 1939-45 war in the case of members of the combatant services suffering from psychoneuroses. Many psychiatrists who have been concerned in the treatment of the so-called 'war neuroses' have approached the problem of treating members of the services from the customary standpoint of a medical man practising in civilian life, i.e. they have, quite arbitrarily, carried over and sought to apply within a service group under wartime conditions standards established under peacetime conditions within a civilian group. It is obvious on reflection, however, that the function of a psychiatrist dealing with service cases is, not to cure patients seeking relief from personal distress, but to rehabilitate sailors, soldiers and airmen who have ceased to fulfil the requirements of the group to which they belong. So far as I am personally concerned, it required little experience to discover that the problem of the war neuroses was essentially a problem of morale, i.e. a problem of the relationship of the individual member of a service to that service as a group. Thus it became obvious that the neurotic soldier was an individual who had in varying degree ceased to be a soldier in spirit—if indeed he had ever wholeheartedly accepted allegiance to the military group at all. So much was this the case that one of the commonest remarks made quite spontaneously by the neurotic soldiers whom I have come across in hospital was, 'I can't *go back* to the Army'. The significance of this remark lay, of course, in the fact that, although such soldiers were still theoretically members of the Army group, they had more or less completely dissociated themselves from it. They were unwilling soldiers; and deep down in their minds they had motives which rendered a psychoneurosis preferable to normal participation in the life of the Army group. In conformity with this fact, their attitude was unfavourable to ordinary psychotherapy, since psychotherapy demands a measure of co-operation lacking in those who have a minimum of motives for desiring the results which it is designed to achieve.

I regret to say that, in my experience, very similar considerations apply to those who commit unnatural sexual offences in civilian life. I know that in recent times there has been a widespread movement among psychiatrists towards the point of view that perverse sexual tendencies are 'symptoms' in the same sense as those which characterize the psychoneuroses; but this is a point of view which I cannot see my way to share. It is a point of view which arises out of a general modern tendency to substitute purely scientific standards for the moral standards of the past; but, in my opinion, it represents an interpretation based upon an erroneous psychopathology.

What requires above all to be recognized is, I think, that perverse sexual tendencies are not just unfortunate excrescences which in some mysterious fashion become attached to an otherwise normal personality, but integral components of the structure of the personality itself. Thus homosexuality must be regarded, not simply as a perverse expression of natural sexuality, but as the natural sexual expression of a personality which has become perverse in its essential structure. Here I must admit that, in my opinion, it would be equally true to say that psychoneurotic symptoms represent expressions of the personality itself rather than excrescences upon it. Nevertheless the fact remains that there is a profound difference between perversion and psychoneurosis. This difference was succinctly described by Freud when he spoke of neurosis as the 'negative' of perversion. It is to Freud also that we owe the illuminating conception that psychoneurotic symptoms are essentially defensive in character. By this he means that such symptoms are due to the influence of structural elements in the personality which perform the function of defending the personality as a whole against tendencies which are also part of the psychical structure, but which are unacceptable to the part of the personality responsible for defensive action. In accordance with this conception the psychoneurotic is an individual so constituted that he would rather endure suffering than give natural expression to tendencies conflicting with a part of his personality which not only rejects them, but subjects them to control by means of repression and other defensive techniques with no small measure of success. It is true that such repressive measures may operate against normal as well as against abnormal sexual tendencies; but the fact remains that, when perverse sexual tendencies are present in a psychoneurotic, these are subjected to drastic measures of control at the hands of a powerful part of the personality. It is characteristic of this part of the personality that it will go to almost any lengths rather than permit the offending tendencies to become overt. With the sexual pervert it is otherwise; for what the sexual pervert does is to capitalize his perverse tendencies instead of repressing them, with the consequence that they not only become overt, but assume a dominant position in the structure of his personality. The resulting situation may, to use psychiatric terms, be summarized in the statement that the sexual pervert is not a psychoneurotic, but a psychopath.

It remains true, of course, that there are no hard and fast dividing lines in Nature. It must be recognized, accordingly, that circumstances may arise in which a psychoneurotic displays perverse tendencies in some degree; but, in so far as such a contingency arises, his psychoneurosis has failed in one of its major aims, and to that degree he ceases to be a psychoneurotic. Similarly it may happen that a sexual pervert suffers from psychoneurotic symptoms; but, in so far as this is so, the sexual perversion ends where the psychoneurosis begins. Nevertheless, in the interests of intellectual clarity, it is necessary to preserve the theoretical distinction between a psychoneurosis, which operates as a defence against perversion, and an overt sexual perversion, which represents the capitalization of perverse tendencies in a psychopathic personality. Unless this distinction is recognized, it is impossible to approach the problem of 'the treatment and rehabilitation' of sexual offenders with any hope of fruitful understanding.

In illustration of the contrast which I drew earlier between 'treatment' and 'rehabilitation' I referred to the psychoneurotic soldier as presenting a problem which was essentially one of 'rehabilitation', rather than one of 'treatment' such as would be appropriate in the case of the psychoneurotic civilian. The relevance of this illustration will now become evident when I say that, in my opinion, the problem of the sexual pervert is also one of 'rehabilitation' rather than 'treatment'. At the same time it may be thought that my analogy between the *psychoneurotic* soldier and the sexual *pervert* is inconsistent with the distinction which I have just drawn between psychoneurosis and sexual perversion. There is no real inconsistency, however, since the relevance of my analogy is confined to the relationship of the individual, whether psychoneurotic or perverse, to the social group in which he finds himself placed. As we have seen, the psychoneurotic soldier has resigned his membership of the Army as a social group; and fundamentally he refuses to lead a normal military life within that group, albeit he justifies this refusal by suffering distress in virtue of which he feels unfit to do so. In similar fashion the sexual pervert refuses to lead a normal sexual life within the community and, in so far as sexual life is concerned if in naught else, he refuses to acknowledge allegiance to the standards of Society. In confirmation of the fact that an attitude towards the social group is involved, attention may be drawn to the frequency with which individuals addicted to certain forms of sexual perversion form groups of their own within the community. This is, of course, particularly common in the case of homosexuals; and it is characteristic of such groups that the difference between their standards and those of the community is not necessarily confined to the sexual sphere.

Having drawn an analogy between the sexual pervert and the psychoneurotic soldier in illustration of a principle to which I attach supreme importance, I must now draw attention to the point at which this analogy breaks down. The psychoneurotic soldier buys himself out of the Army at the price of self-imposed personal suffering which at any rate implies some acknowledgement of social obligations; and, in conformity with this fact, a scanning of his service record will usually show that, whilst he is frequently confined to hospital, he is comparatively rarely confined to barracks. By contrast, the sexual pervert pays no such self-imposed personal price for his renunciation of solidarity with the group. Characteristically he regards his perversion as a personal asset, although he may disguise this fact for reasons of expediency; and any distress which he may display, if he falls foul of the Law, consists rather in fear of the forfeiture of social and material advantages than in any genuine guilt or remorse, which, if present at all, is invariably short-lived. Basically, he despises the standards of the community of which he falls foul, and resents the attitude adopted by this community towards him; and what he seeks at the hands of the community is not cure, but *reinstatement*. This desire for reinstatement in the absence of cure is perhaps the most characteristic feature of his attitude once the initial shock of arrest or conviction is over, although he may pay lip-service to the cause of cure until he feels that he is safe.

In my opinion, it is only in the light of the considerations now advanced that the community can profitably approach the problem of dealing with those convicted of sexual and unnatural offences. As has been indicated already, the personalities of such offenders are not such as to lend themselves to effective 'treatment' in the hitherto accepted sense, i.e. they are not readily amenable to individual psychotherapy. I myself have given individual treatment to several persons who had committed and been charged with sexual offences; and I think I may say that I have done so with a reasonable measure of success. So far as I know, at any rate, none of the cases which I have treated have ever been charged with a repetition of their original offences. I feel I should only be deluding myself, however, if I were to claim that I had been the means of effecting any radical change in the personalities of these individuals; and, in any case, they constituted a selected group among the general run of sexual offenders, since their treatment was only undertaken after preliminary investigation had shown them to be specially favourable subjects. At the same time, I think I can justly claim that the results obtained by individual treatment in these cases were very much better than would have been the results of a comparable period of imprisonment without treatment. Further, I consider that the results obtained would have been much less satisfactory if the treatment had been conducted under conditions of imprisonment; for prison life as at present constituted seems to me calculated to compromise still further the already compromised relationship of the offender to the community. Prison life also seems calculated to compromise any good effects which individual psychotherapy might achieve. Imprisonment in the accepted sense involves reducing the group life of the offender to the minimum permitted by modern standards; and it thus appears a curious method to adopt with a view to promoting an improvement in the offender's relationship to the community.

It is now time to consider what constructive conclusions may be drawn from these general principles for the guidance of future policy regarding the 'treatment and rehabilitation' of sexual offenders. I shall content myself with stating two general practical conclusions which appear to me to emerge quite clearly.

In the first place, what is primarily appropriate in the case of the sexual offender is not 'treatment' in the sense of individual psychotherapy, for which his personality is unsuited, but 'rehabilitation' in the sense of psychologically controlled cultivation of his social relationships within a group characterized by an active social life in which he can participate. Ordinary prison life fails to provide the conditions necessary for the effective establishment of such a group. On the other hand, the ordinary social life of the community fails equally to provide the appropriate background—not simply on the grounds of punitive considerations or because the community requires protection, but also because the sexual offender is in certain respects too much out of touch with the group life of the community to be amenable to constructive influences within it. What appears to be required therefore, is the establishment of special communities for offenders—settlements with a group life of their own, in which offenders can participate, and which is psychologically controlled with a view to its gradual approximation to the life of the community at large. Whether such settlements should comprise all classes of offender or sexual offenders only, or alternatively whether the various classes of sexual offender should be segregated in separate settlements, or again whether the settlements should include members of both sexes or members of one sex only—all these and similar questions admit of no *a priori* answer. They can only be answered after careful, and perhaps prolonged experiment. And here it may be noted that the establishment of such settlements would have the advantage of providing a unique opportunity for social experiment in general. It would also provide a unique field for the scientific study of social relationships and the factors which determine the nature of a group.

In the second place, an invaluable lesson can be learned from experience gained in the study of the 'war neuroses' among members of service groups during the 1939–45 war. As I pointed out at an earlier stage, psychoneurotic soldiers have on the whole proved unfavourable subjects for individual psychotherapy; and consequently the therapeutic results achieved by this method during the 1939–45 war were distinctly disappointing. As the war progressed, however, recognition of this fact, together with a realization of the supreme importance of morale, led to interesting developments initiated by certain psychiatrists employed in military hospitals for cases of war neurosis. Relegating individual psychotherapy to a subsidiary role, these psychiatrists concentrated their efforts upon the fostering and consolidation of a group spirit within the hospitals concerned. Not content with this, they made it their special aim to cultivate in their patients a sense of belonging to a group which was specifically military, and thus to restore their relationship to the Army as a group to which they owed special allegiance. Concurrently, certain other Army psychiatrists, of similar outlook but employed on War Office Selection Boards, began to experiment with a technique of leaderless discussion groups as an aid to the selection of candidates for commissions. This technique consisted in taking a small group of candidates and telling them to start an impromptu discussion among themselves. The reaction of the various candidates to one another and to the situation as a whole were then observed, with an eye to evidence for qualities of leadership and mutual adjustment in the various candidates. A somewhat similar technique was subsequently adopted for therapeutic purposes in rehabilitation centres for repatriated prisoners of war; but here, as might be expected, the members of the.

staff made it their aim to exercise a certain guiding influence in a socializing direction upon the mutual reactions of members of the groups. Now that the demobilization of R.A.M.C. personnel is well under way (1946) a few of the psychiatrists concerned in these various developments have begun to experiment with *group psychotherapy* among psychoneurotic patients in civilian life. For this purpose, a group of about eight is favoured; and members of the group are encouraged to discuss with one another whatever problems occur to them to discuss. While the discussion proceeds, the supervising doctor takes the opportunity at appropriate moments to interpret the reactions of the various members to one another, as well as the developments which occur within the group as a whole; and these various reactions and developments themselves become the subject of discussion. The result is that individual members are confronted with the implications of their own behaviour not only towards one another but also towards the group; and the significance of the attitudes which they adopt is in some measure brought home to them both by the reactions of the group towards them and by interpretations of the social situations which develop. Such interpretations also bring home to them the significance of group reactions. Thus a continuous process of social insight and social education is encouraged in a setting of actual social situations.

It must be recognized, of course, that these various experiments only represent a breaking of the ground, and that the whole method is as yet only in its infancy. Yet the results so far obtained appear to be encouraging—sufficiently encouraging at any rate to justify further serious trial of the group method of psychotherapy in various fields. Where sexual offenders in particular are concerned, the method of group psychotherapy seems to me to offer much greater hope of successful application and development than does the method of individual psychotherapy; and it should be added that the method of group psychotherapy partakes more of the nature of 'rehabilitation' than of the nature of 'treatment' in the ordinarily accepted sense.

List of Works to which Reference is made in the Text

BRIERLEY, M.
'Notes on Metapsychology as a Process Theory', *The International Journal of Psycho-Analysis*, Vol. XXV, Pts. 3 and 4 (1944).

DRIBERG, J. H.
At Home with the Savage. London: 1932. George Routledge.

FREUD, S.
Beyond the Pleasure Principle (1920) (Translation). London: 1922. The International Psycho-Analytical Press.

Civilization and its Discontents (1929) (Translation). London: 1930. Hogarth Press and Institute of Psycho-Analysis.

'A Neurosis of Demoniacal Possession in the Seventeenth Century' (1923), *Collected Papers*, Vol. IV (Translation). London: 1925. Hogarth Press and Institute of Psycho-Analysis.

'Mourning and Melancholia' (1917), *Collected Papers*, Vol. IV (Translation). London: 1925. Hogarth Press and Institute of Psycho-Analysis.

'On the History of the Psycho-Analytic Movement' (1914), *Collected Papers*, Vol. I (Translation). London: 1924. The International Psycho-Analytical Press.

Group Psychology and the Analysis of the Ego (1921) (Translation). London: 1922. The International Psycho-Analytical Press.

The Ego and the Id (1923) (Translation). London: 1927. Hogarth Press and Institute of Psycho-Analysis.

Totem and Taboo (1913) (New Translation). London: 1919. Routledge and Kegan Paul.

JUNG, C. G.
Collected Papers on Analytical Psychology (1916) (Translation). London: 1917. Baillière, Tindall and Cox.

KRETSCHMER, E.
Physique and Character (1921) (Translation). London: 1925. Kegan Paul, Trench, Trubner and Co.

MASSERMAN, J. H., and CARMICHAEL, H. T.
'Diagnosis and Prognosis in Psychiatry', *The Journal of Mental Science*, Vol. LXXXIV, No. 353 (November 1938).

STEPHEN, A.
'A Note on Ambivalence', *The International Journal of Psycho-Analysis*, Vol. XXVI, Pts. 1 and 2 (1945).

Index

Abraham, K., 10, 29–36, 59, 92, 124, 143, 147, 155, 162
Acceptance of the object, 36, 38, 47
  hysterical, 44–5
  paranoid, 45
  phobic, 45
  obsessional, 45
Accepted object, *see* Object, accepted
Acrophobia, 42
Activity—
  anal, 138
  artistic, 16, 18
  excretory, 14
  obsessional, 44
  oral, 14
  urinary, 138
Affect—
  expression of, 20, 114
  incongruity of thought and, 20–1
  of depression, *see* Depression, affect of
  of futility, *see* Futility
  repression of, 15, 20–1, 131
Aggression, 44, 49, 53–5, 74, 102–5, 110, 113–16, 118–19, 128, 233, 235, 248, 250–1, 254, 280–1
  anxiety over, 49, 113, 281
  as dynamic of repression, 108, 112, 114, 116, 147, 171
  as socially disruptive factor, 235
  directional nature of, 126, 176
  disposal of excess of, 115, 116, 119
  internal redistribution of, 119
  subordinate to libido, 109, 158, 171
Agoraphobia, 42
Ambivalence, 24, 39, 48, 53, 109–10, 112, 117, 120–2, 124, 135, 146, 171–2, 175, 178
  towards father, 121
Ambivalent object, 110, 121, 124, 172
  internal, 135, 178

Amnesia for early life,
  its absence in schizophrenics, 64, 77
Anaclitic choice, 42
Anal—
  activity, 138
  erotism, 40
  fixation, 207
  phases, *see* Phase(s), anal
  sadism, 227
  techniques, 33, 43
Anal attitude—
  contrasted with genital and oral, 86
Ancestor worship, 236
Animism, 132
Anti-libidinal factor, 129, 166
Anxiety, 103, 107, 260
  and hysterical suffering, 103, 125
  at birth, 110, 275
  cardiac, 224
  conversion of libidinal affect into, 125
  exhibitionistic, 16
  obsessional, 44
  over being emptied, 44, 113
  over destroying, 12, 24
  over emptying the object, 23
  over expressing aggression, 49, 113, 281
  over expressing libidinal need, 113
  over giving, 18
  over identification, 42–3
  over incorporating, 49
  over loss of contents, 18–19
  over loss of libido, 113
  over loss of the object, 113
  over retention, 44
  over separation, *see* Separation-anxiety
  over undischarged libido, 125
  over violent outbursts, 52
  phobic, 43

298

Index

Anxiety—
  state of, 257
Atomism, 139
Autoeroticism, 33–4

Badness—
  conditional and unconditional, 66, 93, 165
Basic endopsychic situation, 106–15, 120, 129–31, 133–5, 147, 160, 170, 177
  and schizoid position, 131
  flexibility and rigidity of, 130
  in hysteria, 130–1, 161, 177
Birth—
  anxiety, 110, 275
  trauma, 276
Biting, 39, 48, 147
Bleuler, E., 10, 108
Brave New World, 244
Breast—
  as internal object, 41
  as libidinal object, 10–11, 46, 89
  as natural part-object, 31, 33, 40–1, 48, 109, 138, 144
  father as parent without a, 122, 174
  fullness and emptiness of, 11, 23–4
Brierley, M., 139, 150
British Commonwealth, 242

Capitalism, 239
Carmichael, H. T., 4
Castration, symbolic, 54
Castration complex, female, 199, 220
Cathexis of internalized objects, 20, 50, 132
  as source of their dynamic nature, 177
Cathexis of repressed (internal) objects, 74, 78–9, 84, 135
  as a resistance, 72–4, 116–17, 165–6, 173
  dissolution of, 69, 74, 165
Cathexis of super-ego by central ego, 159–60
Catholic Church, 253
Central ego, 85, 93, 101, 104–6, 108, 114, 116, 118, 128, 130, 135, 147–8, 159, 169, 170, 172, 179
  cathexis of super-ego by, 159–60

Christ—
  religious phantasies involving figure of, 185–8, 193
Clan, the, 236, 239, 243
Claustrophobia, 42
Clitoris, 198, 205, 208, 220
  unconscious over-valuation of, 208, 220
Communism, 234, 238–46
Communist world-state, 239, 241, 243, 245, 246
Conditional goodness and badness, 66, 93, 165
Conflicts, schizoid and depressive, 49–54
Contents—
  equivalence of bodily and mental, 14–15, 17
  fear of loss of, 18–19
  object treated as, 41
  over-valuation of, 15, 22
Cowardice, 282
Culture, 188, 250, 252–5

Death instincts, 78–9, 84, 166
De-emotionalization of the object-relationship, 14
Defaecation—
  as basis of rejective techniques, 35
  as creation, 14, 36
  as elimination, 14
  as giving, 36
  as symbolic rejection, 35, 138
Defence(s), 249, 254
  against effects of infantile dependence, 265
  cultural, 251–3
  delusions as, 215
  hysterical, *see* Technique, hysterical
  manic, 30
  moral, 65–7, 68, 81, 93, 165, 167, 169
  non-specific, 30, 66
  obsessional, *see* Technique, obsessional
  of non-participation, 85, 87
  of repression, *see* Repression
  paranoid, *see* Technique, paranoid
  phobic, *see* Technique, phobic
  psychoneurotic, 291

Index

Ego-structures—
  differentiation of, 101, 171, 172
  dynamic nature of, 88, 160, 167, 177
  in dreams, 8, 99, 170
  internal object-relations of, 102–5,
    133–4, 167, 170, 178
  personifications of, 216–20, 221–2
  repression of, 89–90, 108, 112, 114,
    115–16, 118–19, 135, 147, 158, 159,
    168, 170–1, 172, 173
Elation, 202, 209, 216, 219, 221
Emptiness, state of, 11
Emptying of the object, 23
Endopsychic structure(s), 85, 88, 99,
    117, 120, 148–9, 170
  differentiation of, 109, 174
  dynamic nature of, 157, 170
  internalized objects as, 82, 89, 95, 99,
    132, 154, 168, 177
  psychical energy inseparable from,
    126, 176
Enuresis, nocturnal, 268
Epistemology, Stephen's, 139
Epistle of St. Paul to Titus, 251
Erotogenic zones, 29–34, 72, 138–43,
    155, 162
  and specificity of instinctive object-
    seeking, 141–3
  and the reality principle, 139–41
  as channels of object-seeking libido,
    31–4, 72, 138
  atomistic conception of, 138–9
Exciting object (internal), 104, 105, 108,
    111–12, 114–18, 121–5, 128, 130,
    133–6, 147, 149, 159, 170–5, 178–9
Exhibitionism, 40
  unconscious, 211
Exhibitionistic—
  anxiety, 16
  technique, 16–17
Exogamy, 236–7
Experience—
  and reality sense, 140, 157
Expulsion—
  and retention, 44–5
  and separation, 43–4
Exteriorization *or* Externalization, *see*
  Internal object(s), externalization of

Extravert, 56, 164

Faeces as symbolic object, 31, 40
Family group, the, 153, 235–42, 244–5,
    259, 284
Fascist Italy, 241, 243
Father—
  ambivalence towards, 121
  as natural object, 40
  as parent without a breast, 122, 174
  in Œdipus situation, 121–4, 174–5
Father substitutes, 191
Female castration complex, 199, 220–1
Fixation, 29, 30, 40
  anal, 207
  on breast, 86
  on grandfather, 206
  on mother, 23
  oral, 11–12, 18, 24–5, 29, 33, 56, 58,
    207
Free association method, 248
Freud, 10, 29, 42, 59, 60–2, 64, 70, 73,
    76, 81–2, 88–90, 92, 94, 99, 103,
    106–9, 116, 118–19, 124, 126, 128,
    130–1, 138, 148–9, 152–60, 162,
    164–71, 174, 176–7, 217–20, 222,
    233, 235, 241, 280, 291
Frigidity, 95–6, 107
Frustration, 140, 162
  emotional, 17–18, 39–40
  libidinal, 109–14, 121–2, 143, 171–2
  oral, 18
Fugue, 271
Fullness, state of, 11
Fusion of internal objects, 123, 175
Futility, schizoid affect of, 51, 91, 114,
    131, 163, 173

Genital attitude, 32
  contrasted with anal and oral atti-
    tudes, 86
Genital defect, 197–200, 220, 226
Genitals—
  as libidinal channels, 32, 142
  as natural (biological) objects, 31, 144
  as symbolic (phallic) objects, 40
  hysterical rejection of the, 38
  identified with breast, 33, 38, 41

Index

Index

Identification—
　of ego with super-ego, 61, 164
　of external object with internal object, 51
　of objects, 33, 35, 38, 45, 62, 86
　primary, 34-5, 42, 145, 275-8, 279
　relationships based on, 277-8
　secondary, 34-5, 145
Ideologies, 253
Impulse—
　as the dynamic aspect of structure, 88, 119, 150, 157, 167
　inseparable from structure, 85, 88, 90, 119, 126
Impulse psychology, 59, 157, 158
　limitations of, 84-8, 150, 167
Incest, 236, 242
Incestuous wish, 37
Incorporated object(s), 34, 38, 40, 42, 53, 56. *See also* Internal *or* Internalized object(s), *and* Introjected object(s)
Incorporation, 11, 14-15, 17-18, 24, 34, 35, 39, 49, 56, 138, 145-6, 154, 156, 223. *See also* Internalization, *and* Introjection
　and identification, 42-3, 48, 145
　and splitting of the ego, 10
　mental or psychological, 18, 41, 146
　of objects and libidinal development, 34
Infantile dependence, *see* Dependence, infantile
Infatuations, 21, 42
Inner reality—
　dramas in, 85
　dreams as dramatizations of, 8, 98-9, 105, 170, 216-19
　schizoid overvaluation of, 18, 23
　schizoid preoccupation with, 6
　schizophrenic failure to discriminate outer reality from, 18
Instinctive behaviour, 140-2
Instincts, 150, 157, 218
　aggressive, 158, 248, 250
　death, 78-9, 84, 166
　ego, 83
　hypostatization of, 84-5, 139, 150

　object, 83
　sex, 248, 250
Integration, scale of, 9-10
Intellectualization—
　as a resistance, 20
　defence of, 20-3
Internal *or* Internalized object(s), 22, 40, 41, 45, 50, 51, 60, 61, 69, 74, 82-6, 89, 93-5, 99, 100-4, 106, 114, 117, 123-4, 131-2, 133, 135, 143, 146, 148-9, 153-4, 155, 156, 159-60, 162, 164, 167-77, 224, 229. *See also* Incorporated object(s), *and* Introjected object(s)
　ambivalent, 135-6, 178
　as endopsychic structure(s), 82, 89, 95, 99, 132, 154, 168, 177
　bad, 62-6, 69-70, 74-6, 78, 79, 89, 93-5, 108, 111, 114, 121, 134, 147, 157-60, 164-73, 175
　cathexis of, 20, 50, 132
　dynamic nature of, 132, 177
　exciting, *see* Exciting object (internal)
　externalization of, 36, 38, 39, 45-6, 153-4
　fusion of, 123, 175
　good, 61-2, 66, 70, 134, 159, 165
　identification of ego with, 8, 18, 22, 165, 170
　identification of external object with, 51
　in dreams, 8, 99, 132, 170
　layering of, 123, 175
　libidinal cathexis as source of dynamic nature of, 177
　over-exciting element in, 135, 170, 178
　over-frustrating element in, 135, 170, 178
　parts of the ego as, 83, 84-5
　persecuting, 93, 154, 169
　pre-ambivalent, 134-5, 178
　rejecting, *see* Rejecting object (internal)
　repressed, 73-6, 117, 135, 147, 158, 165-6, 173
　splitting of, 111, 114, 121, 122, 147, 159, 170, 172, 178

303

Index

Loss—
  of ego, 52, 113
  of libido, 52, 113, 173
  of object, 47, 51, 54–6, 113, 173
Love—
  apparent destructiveness of, 25, 50
  ' partial ', 31
  substitution of hate for, 26–7

Malingering, 282
Manic—
  defence, 30
  state, 206, 213, 220, 226
Manic-depressive psychosis, 25, 29, 57,
    202, 221, 226
Masochism, 40, 79
  phobic, 44
Masserman, J. H., 4
Masturbation, 33, 40, 184, 194–6
  hysteria and infantile, 143
Mature dependence, see Dependence,
    mature
Melancholia, 90–2, 158–9, 168, 220.
    See also Depression
  involutional, 54–5
Memories—
  revival of repressed, 77, 204–5
  traumatic, 63, 78
Menstruation, vicarious, 199, 207
Mental apparatus, Freud's theory of the,
    88, 106–7, 119, 128–9, 131, 148–9,
    157, 167–8, 171, 217–18, 222
Mill, J. S., 152
Moral defence, see Defence, moral
Moral values, 68, 160, 169
Morale, 81, 167, 279, 281–7, 290, 295
  super-ego as source of, 81, 167
Mother—
  as ambivalent object, 110
  as bad object, 17, 110
  as exciting object, 115
  as original whole object, 11, 40–1, 48,
    109–10, 144, 174
  as rejecting object, 112–13, 172
  as sexual object, 224
  fixation on, 23
  identification with, 276
  in Œdipus situation, 119–25, 174–5

the indifferent, 13, 23
the internalized, 224
the possessive, 13, 19, 23
Mouth—
  as breast-seeking organ, 138, 142
  as libidinal channel, 10–11, 32, 142
  diversion of libido from genitals to,
    142–3'
  diversion of libido to genitals from,
    142–3
  genitals identified with, 33, 41
Multiple personality, 5, 90, 159, 168,
    218–20, 221

Narcissism, 50, 83, 201, 215
  primary, 48
  secondary, 22, 48, 54
Narcissistic choice, 42
Nation, the, 237–41, 243
Nausea, 38, 86
Nazi Germany, 235, 241, 243, 252, 284
Negative therapeutic reaction, 69, 73,
    117, 165
Neurasthenic state, 194
Nightmares, 42, 77, 276. See also
    Dreams

Object(s), 32, 34, 39–56, 60–81, 82–3,
    86–8, 95–8, 100, 102–4, 106, 109–
    117, 121, 123–4, 130, 132–5, 138–47,
    153–6, 159–60, 162–79, 224, 228–9,
    259
  acceptance of, see Acceptance
  accepted, 35, 37, 39, 45–6, 53, 133–6,
    177, 179
  ambivalent, 110, 121, 124, 172
  anxiety over emptying, 23
  anxiety over loss of, 113
  appropriate biological, 144–5, 155
  as libidinal goal, 31
  bad, 17, 36, 62–81, 84, 93, 110–11,
    113–14, 121, 134, 139, 146, 154,
    156, 165–6, 172, 178
  breast as, see Breast
  conditionally bad, 66
  depersonalization of, 14
  dichotomy of the, 35, 37, 39, 53
  differentiated, 42, 145–6

305

Index

Oral—
  contrasted with anal and genital attitudes, 86
  incorporation, *see* Incorporation
  phase(s), *see* Phase(s), oral
  stage, *see* Stage, oral
Oral sadism, 213–15, 221, 223–9
  towards penis, 207–12

Paranoia, 36, 38, 132
Paranoid—
  attitude, 130, 270
  features, 94, 130, 169
  features in hysteria, 130
  state, 30, 45, 213–15, 221
  symptoms, 30, 226–7
  technique, *see* Technique, paranoid
Parents, relationships between, 122, 175
Passivity—
  in hysterical state, 104
  in phobic state, 44
Patricide, 228, 236, 242
Penis—
  as breast, 41
Penis-envy, 206–7, 220–1
Persecution—
  delusions of, 215
  dreams of, 214–15
Personality—
  and object-relations, 84–5, 88, 153–4, 164, 167
Personifications—
  in dreams, 216–19
  of bodily organs, 79
  of ego-structures, 216–20, 221–2
Perversion, 40, 123, 175, 290–3
  contrasted with psychoneurosis, 291–2
Phallic—
  attitude, 33
  phase, *see* Phase(s), phallic
  technique, 33
Phantasies—
  erotic, 191, 192
  religious, 183–93
Phantasy—
  author's views on, 98–9, 170
Phase(s)—
  anal, 29–31, 34, 35–6

early oral, 10–15, 17–18, 23–5, 29, 35, 39, 41, 48–50, 55–6, 58, 147, 178
genital, 31, 32, 35
late oral, 24, 29, 31, 35, 39, 41, 48–9, 53–4, 55–6, 58, 147
phallic, 29, 30, 32–3, 34, 35, 36, 124
Phobic—
  anxiety, 43
  conflict, 44, 45
  masochism, 44
  state, 30, 38, 43, 45
  symptoms, 257, 272
  symptoms with schizoid basis, 4, 30
  technique, *see* Technique, phobic
Pleasure principle, 83–4, 139
  deteriorative nature of the, 139–40, 157, 168
  secondary nature of the, 89, 157, 168
Pre-ambivalence of early oral phase, 24–5, 39, 48
Pre-ambivalent object, 134–5, 178
Primal scene, 122, 175
Prince, Morton, 5
Process theory, Brierley's, 139
Projection, 75, 153–4, 166, 214–15, 227
Pseudo-independence, 267, 270–1
Psychical energy—
  inseparable from structure, 126, 176
Psychoanalysis, 60, 87, 94, 150, 177, 247–55
  hysterical phenomena as basis of, 92, 130, 168, 177
Psychoanalytical—
  research, 33, 83, 84, 250
  technique, and its aims, 73
  theory, 59–60, 72, 82, 90, 92, 130, 149, 150, 154, 156, 162, 168, 176, 188–9, 233–4, 247–52, 254–5
  treatment, 3, 22, 84–5, 87, 165–6, 197, 248–9, 254–5
Psychological types—
  author's theory of, 56–8, 164
  Jung's theory of, 56–7
  Kretschmer's theory of, 57
Psychology—
  as study of individual's relationships with objects, 60
  of religion, 188–9

307

Index

Psychology—
social, *see* Social psychology, *and* Group psychology
Psychopathic personality, 4, 118, 267, 270–1, 282, 291–2
Psychopathology—
as study of relationships of ego with internalized objects, 60
Psychosexual attitude, 123, 175
Psychotherapy, 68–70, 85, 87, 289–90, 293–6
and war neuroses, 81, 287, 295–7
group, 296

Quakerism, 191
Quasi-independence, 260
stage of, *see* Stage of transition

Rationalization, technique of, 215
Reality principle, 139
and erotogenic zones, 139–41
primary nature of the, 89, 140–1, 157, 167–8
Reality sense, disturbances of, 5
Reference, ideas of, 213
Regression, 13, 17, 23, 55, 58
Rehabilitation—
as contrasted with treatment, 289, 292, 294–6
Rejected object, *see* Object, rejected
Rejecting object (internal), 104–5, 111, 114, 115–16, 121, 122–4, 128, 130, 133–6, 147, 149, 159, 170–5, 178–9
Rejection by the object, 93, 113–14, 121, 124
Rejection of the object, 35–6, 39, 47–8, 50, 67, 86, 115–16, 135
defaecation as symbolic, 35, 138
hysterical, 36, 38, 44–6
obsessional, 36, 38, 46
paranoid, 36, 38, 46
phobic, 45–6
simple non-aggressive, 48–9
urination as symbolic, 36, 138
vomiting as, 138
Relationship(s), 60, 162, 277
based on identification, 277–8
between ego and bad internalized object, 62

between ego and good internalized object, 61–2
between ego and internalized objects, 60, 61, 84, 164
between ego and objects, 88, 153, 167
between ego and super-ego, 61, 66, 93, 149, 156, 164–5
between ego-structures and internalized objects, 167, 170
between endopsychic structures, 99
between parents, 122, 175
between parts of the ego, 83, 85, 160, 170
between structures, 150, 176
by default, 40
capacity for, 145
emotional and physical, 121–2
establishment of, 146
renunciation of, 146
social, 279, 294–6
structural, 150, 176
with bad objects, 63–4, 71, 76
with father, 121–2, 174–5
with internalized bad objects, 64–5, 79
with internalized objects, 40, 60, 74, 160, 162, 164
with military group, 278, 281
with mother, 120, 122, 174–5
within the personality, 84–5, 153–4, 164, 167
Religion, psychology of, 188–9
Repetition compulsion, 78, 84, 166
daemonic character of, 78
Repressed, the, 60–2, 73, 76, 94–5, 117, 158, 165, 168, 170, 221
return of, 75–7, 81, 165–7, 210, 214
Repressed libido—
manifestations of, 72
release of, 205–6, 210, 214
Repressed memories—
revival of, 77, 204–5
Repression, 24, 52, 60, 65, 73, 92–3, 109, 111–12, 135, 139, 147, 157, 164–5, 169, 196, 249, 291
agency of, 73, 92, 158
aggression as the dynamic of, 108, 112, 116, 147, 171

Index

Repression—
and splitting of the ego, 21, 90, 108,
112, 114, 116, 118, 135, 147, 158-9,
168, 170-1, 172, 173
as a defence, 62
as a schizoid process, 131, 158
as an ego-function, 61, 89, 164
author's theory of, 89-90, 115-20,
158-60, 174
direct, 118, 147, 173
distinct from the defence of guilt or
super-ego, 66, 69-70, 92-3, 165,
169
exercised more over libidinal than
over aggressive components, 118-
119, 173-4
Freud's theory of, 61-2, 72, 89, 90,
92, 94, 116, 119, 129, 156, 158-60,
164, 168-70, 173, 174
indirect, 118-19, 147, 160, 173
libidinal resistance as a resultant of,
117
of affect, 15, 20-1, 131
of ego-structures, 89-90, 108, 112,
114, 115-16, 118-19, 135, 147,
158, 159, 168, 170-1, 172, 173
of guilt more drastic than repression
of guilty wishes, 213, 221
of internalized bad objects, 62-4, 65,
70, 74, 76, 78, 89, 93, 95, 108, 111,
114, 147, 156, 158, 159, 164-5,
168-73
of libidinal part of ego, 21
of over-exciting and over-frustrating
elements in the internal object, 135,
178
of super-ego, 94-5, 159, 170, 221
primary, 115-16, 173
principle of, 119, 174
secondary, 115, 173
super-ego as instigator of, 61, 90, 94,
153, 156, 158, 168
Resistance, 22, 67, 69, 73, 117, 165, 215,
221, 249, 251, 287
cathexis of repressed objects as a,
72-4, 116-17, 165-6, 173
fear of return of repressed objects as
a, 69

guilt as a, 69
intellectualization as a, 20
libidinal, 72-4, 116-17, 165-6, 173
social, 251
Restitution of the object, 226
Retention—
anxiety over, 44
expulsion and, 44-5
Return of repressed objects, 67, 69, 73
psychopathological, 75-8, 166-7
therapeutic, 69-70, 74-5, 165
Role-playing, technique of, 16-17

Sadism, 40, 79
anal, 227
of obsessional technique, 44
oral, see Oral sadism
urinary, 226
St. Paul, 251
Saudek, R., 183
Schizoid—
affect of futility, 51, 91, 114, 131, 163,
173
and depressive positions, 91
and depressive states contrasted, 49,
55-6
and depressive types, 56-8, 164
and introvert, 7, 29
appeal of art, 19
appeal of science and intellectual
pursuits, 6
attitude and oral incorporation, 10
background of psychoneurotic symptoms, 4, 28, 30, 91-2, 223-4
basis of dissociation, 5-6, 92, 159
character, 4, 9
compulsiveness towards object, 47
concept of, 7-8, 29
conditions, 3, 29
conflict, 49-53
detachment, 6, 8, 131
factor in hysteria, 4, 6, 108, 131, 183
features, 5-6, 28, 51
features in psychoneurotic cases, 4
group, 6-7, 28-9
individuals, 3, 42, 89, 168
infatuations, 21, 42
intellectualization, 20-3

309

Index

Schizoid—
nature of dreams, 8–9
nature of earliest psychopathological process, 131
nature of repression, 131, 158
omnipotence, 6
orientation towards partial objects, 12–14
over-valuation of inner reality, 18, 23
over-valuation of mental contents, 15, 22
personality, 4, 9, 12, 98
phenomena, 5, 8, 99
position, 8–9, 25–7, 91, 101, 107–9, 147, 158, 169
position in hysteria, 91–2, 109, 158
preoccupation with inner reality, 6
repression of affect, 15, 20–1, 131
reversal of values, 27
secrecy, 22
state, 4, 12, 30, 55, 77, 114, 131, 265
superiority, 22, 50–1
techniques, 22, 19
tragedies, 25–6
withdrawal of libido, 50–2
Schizophrenia, 4, 7, 10, 57, 109, 155–156, 158–9, 163
catatonic outbursts in, 20
incongruity of affect in, 20–1
omnipotence in, 213
Schizophrenic handwriting, 183
Schizophrenics, 9, 12, 23, 92
absence of amnesia for childhood in, 64, 77
distinction between inner and outer reality obscured in, 18
substitution of ideas for feelings in, 20
Science, 218, 250
schizoid and obsessional appeals of, 6
Scientific background—
contemporary, 127–8, 150, 176
Freud's, 126–7, 150, 176
Secrecy, schizoid, 22
Self-consciousness, 51, 211–13, 261
Self-reference, 211, 213–14, 226
Self-reproach, 116, 286
Separation, 43–4, 46, 109–10, 145, 166, 172, 260–1, 271, 273, 275, 278, 281

and excretory expulsion, 43–4
Separation-anxiety, 39, 43–4, 80, 110, 145, 167, 223, 263, 265–7, 271–3, 275–8, 280–1, 285
Sin—
Christian and Hebraic conceptions of, 74
Social group—
attitude of perverts towards the, 292–3
Social groups, evolution of, 235–40, 243, 246
Social institutions, 129
Social psychology, 129. See also Group psychology
Socrates, 249
Soviet Russia, 234, 238, 241, 243
Splitting of the ego, 8–10, 20–1, 29, 51, 83, 101, 107–8, 115–16, 131, 147, 158–9, 160, 162. See also 218–20, 221–2
aggression as dynamic of, 108, 114
and hysterical dissociation, 92, 159
and incorporation, 10
and repression of ego-structures, 21, 89–90, 108, 112, 114, 115–16, 118, 135, 147, 158–9, 168, 170–1, 172, 173
in dreams, 8–9
in hysteria, 92, 158–9
Splitting of the object—
(external), 110, 114, 121, 135
(internal), 111, 114, 121, 122, 147, 159, 170, 172, 178
Stage(s) (developmental), 30, 145, 155, 221
alloerotic, 31
anal, 146
autoerotic, 31
genital, 32
narcissistic, 31
of infantile dependence, 35, 39, 41, 46–9, 145, 163, 267
of mature dependence, 35, 39, 41, 145, 163
of partial love, 31
of transition or quasi-independence, 35, 39, 41–6, 145–6, 155, 163
oral, 32, 221

Index

Stalin, J. V., 239

State, the, 238, 284–5

Stephen, A., 139

Sublimation, 90, 168, 188, 213, 221

Substitutive satisfactions, 40

Sucking, 39, 48, 138, 147

Suffering, psychoneurotic, 103, 125, 291, 293

Suicidal tendency, 203, 226, 266, 271, 274

Super-ego, 200, 203, 204, 209, 210, 212–13, 214, 217

  and splitting of ego, 9

  as agent of the moral defence, 66, 93, 165, 169

  as ego-ideal, 81, 136, 153–4, 156, 159, 179, 233, 286–7

  as endopsychic structure, 82, 90

  as good object to ego, 61, 66, 93, 149, 156, 165

  as instigator of repression, 61, 90, 94, 153, 156, 158, 168

  as internalized object, 61, 66, 82, 93, 94, 131, 148–9, 153–4, 156, 164, 165, 171

  as product of object-relationships, 153

  as source of morale, 81, 167

  author's views regarding the, 93, 101, 107, 108, 136, 149, 156, 171, 179

  concept of internal saboteur compared with concept of, 106–7, 159–160

  disintegration of the, 286–7

  Freud's conception of the, 62, 88, 90, 106–7, 116, 128–9, 131, 148–9, 153–4, 156, 157, 158, 160, 164, 167, 168, 171, 217–20

  guilt generated by the, 68–70, 94, 107

  inconsistencies and weaknesses in Freud's theory of, 92, 94, 129, 131–132, 169–70, 217–20

  level of the, 68–70, 93–4, 99–100, 101, 107, 169, 171

  omnipotence involving, 213

  question of repression of the, 94–5, 159, 170, 221

repression distinct from the defence of the, 66, 69–70, 92–3, 165, 169

strata (genital and oral) of, 210, 221

Superiority, schizoid, 22, 50–1

Supra-national group, 239, 243–4

Symbolic object—

  faeces as, 31, 40

  genitals as, 40

Taboo, 251, 252

  on incest, 236, 242

  on patricide, 236, 242

Taking—

  obsessional compromise between giving and, 36

  predominance of attitude of, 11, 14, 39

Technique(s), 143, 155–6, 162–3, 213

  anal, 33, 43

  autoerotic, 34

  defaecation as basis of rejective, 35

  exhibitionistic, 16–17

  hysterical, 30, 36, 38, 39, 44, 45–6, 56, 66, 136, 146, 163, 179, 265

  manic, 30

  obsessional, 30, 36, 38, 39, 44, 45–6, 56, 66, 94, 136, 146, 163, 179, 265

  of delusion-formation, 215

  of 'divide et impera', 114–15, 116, 125, 173

  of intellectualization, 20–3

  of internalizing bad objects, see Internalization of bad objects

  of internalizing good objects, see Internalization of good objects

  of internalizing the pre-ambivalent object, 134–5, 178

  of non-participation, 85, 87

  of rationalization, 215

  of repression, see Repression

  of role-playing, 16

  of splitting the internal ambivalent object, 135, 178

  of splitting the internal bad object, 111, 114, 121, 122, 147, 159, 170, 172

  of splitting the object (external), 110, 111, 114, 121

311